THY WORD
IS TRUTH

Some Thoughts on the
Biblical Doctrine of Inspiration

EDWARD J. YOUNG
Professor of Old Testament
Westminster Theological Seminary
Philadelphia, Pennsylvania

Wm. B. Eerdmans Publishing Co.
Grand Rapids, Michigan

THY WORD IS TRUTH
by
EDWARD J. YOUNG

Ninth printing, September 1976

LIBRARY OF CONGRESS
CATALOG CARD NUMBER: 57-11585

ISBN: 0-8028-1244-9

PHOTOLITHOPRINTED BY EERDMANS PRINTING COMPANY
GRAND RAPIDS, MICHIGAN, UNITED STATES OF AMERICA

To
MRS. FRANK H. STEVENSON

in gratitude
for her many kindnesses

PREFACE

The present work is not a technical theological treatise. It is simply a popular book, designed to acquaint the intelligent layman with the Biblical doctrine of inspiration and to convince him of its importance. It would specifically appeal to the modern evangelical not to cast aside the time-honored Biblical view of inspiration.

Despite all that is being said and has been said to the contrary, the doctrine of inspiration is of the utmost significance and importance. If the Bible is not infallible, then we can be sure of nothing. The other doctrines of Christianity will then one by one go by the board. The fortunes of Christianity stand or fall with an infallible Bible. Attempts to evade this conclusion can only lead to self-deception.

There is today a tendency among evangelicals to yield to some of the demands of modern unbelief. This is seen both in a general depreciation of doctrine and a lack of clarity and positiveness in stating it, and also in acceptance of some of the tenets of "higher" criticism. Sometimes it is also seen in an unwillingness to come out resolutely in opposition to the trends of the times and to bear the reproach of Christ. It is to those who may have yielded somewhat to the prevailing trend that this work is directed.

Many scholars are concerned only with, what they call, the human side of the Bible. If this meant that they merely wished to study the languages, geographical and historical background, and questions of special introduction, always paying due heed to the supernatural character of the Bible, there could be no objection. Such is, however, not the case. Rather, that which engages their attention is a study of the above-mentioned and kindred subjects in complete disregard of the Bible's attestation to its own divinity. One receives the impression from reading many modern books on the Bible that there is no real coming to grips with the doctrine of special revelation and all that it involves. The issue, however, lies even deeper. Modern thought to a large extent rests upon a philosophical foundation which in its very

5

nature is hostile to supernatural, revealed Christianity. It has no room for God (*i. e.*, the Almighty Creator of heaven and earth); it has plenty of room for a god who is somehow bound up with man in the universe and whom man in the last analysis can control. The issue at stake is basically that of Biblical theism.

It is sometimes maintained that the latest theology has rescued us from modernism and has brought us back to the Bible! But to what Bible has it brought us back? Not to the infallible Book which was accepted by Christ and His apostles and which was defended against the assaults of modernism by men like Warfield, Hodge, Green, and Machen. No, not to this blessed Book which tells of a Savior's love, but to a Bible filled with error and characterized by fallibility, a Bible that is only a witness to the Word of God. Such a Bible can be of little help to the one who is in the throes of conviction of sin. The sinner does not need a book whose fallible words are only witnesses to some nebulous "Word" of God. He needs a Book whose very words are the Word of God. One thing is surely clear. The view that the words of the Bible are only witnesses to revelation and are not themselves revelation is not taught in the Bible. It is not a Biblical concept.

If it be asked why so many learned and good men do not accept the Scriptural witness to itself, I think that Thomas Boston has given the answer: "And this is the reason why great scholars may be less persuaded of this truth than the most unlearned peasants, because though the sun discovereth itself sufficiently, yet blind men cannot see it."

In the first chapter I have followed Warfield rather closely, for he, in my opinion, more than anyone else, has shown the importance of the correct interpretation of 2 Timothy 3:16. This passage is not an isolated peg upon which to hang the doctrine of inspiration, but is simply an expression of the teaching, so common in the Old Testament, that God has indeed spoken.

It may be thought that too much prominence has been given to the first chapter of the Westminster Confession. But no creed has so accurately stated the Scriptural doctrine of inspiration. One of the greatest blessings that could come to the modern Church would be a careful study of this confession of faith.

There is no discussion in the following pages of the canon of Scripture. My principal concern is with the Bible as authoritative, and the question of the extent of the Bible is therefore somewhat subsidiary. Likewise, there are several aspects of the doctrine of inspiration which, because they are not immediately germane to the principal purpose of the book, have not been discussed. Although I reject most heartily the modern views of the Bible, I have the greatest respect for some of the men who hold these views. The frequent reference to the writings of Otto A. Piper and Alan Richardson, even though so often by way of disagreement, will, I trust, be regarded as an evidence of the respect in which these writers are held. In his work, *God in History*, Professor Piper has given, in my opinion, one of the clearest and best statements of the view which is commonly called *Heilsgeschichte* or "Holy History."

I wish to express my gratitude to the following for permission to quote from the writings which follow their names. The Johns Hopkins Press, *From the Stone Age to Christianity*, by William F. Albright; the Fleming H. Revell Company, *Inspiration*, by Nolan R. Best; Macmillan, *God in History*, by Professor Otto A. Piper, and The Presbyterian and Reformed Publishing Company for permission to quote from the writings of the late Benjamin B. Warfield.

It is a pleasure to express my thanks to those who in one way or another have given of their help in the preparation of the work. I wish to thank the Revs. John Murray, Paul Woolley, and Cornelius Van Til for help given on particular points. The Revs. Arthur W. Kuschke and John H. Skilton have each read portions of the manuscript and have made valuable suggestions. My wife has also read a portion of the work and has made useful comments. To my former student, Mr. George W. Knight III, who has prepared the major part of the index, I am most grateful. Mrs. Donald M. Long has read a part of the manuscript in a different form. Her suggestions have been most useful and I am grateful for them. As always, the Wm. B. Eerdmans Company has been most cooperative. It is a pleasure to work with them. Lastly, I am deeply indebted to Miss Lois Jane Mayson for the careful manner in which she prepared the typescript.

— EDWARD J. YOUNG.

Philadelphia, Pennsylvania

Table of Contents

Preface   5

1. THE ISSUE BEFORE THE CHURCH   13

2. THE EXTENT OF INSPIRATION   39

3. THE HUMAN WRITERS OF THE SCRIPTURES   65

4. SOME REFLECTIONS UPON INSPIRATION   85

5. WHAT IS INERRANCY? (I)   113

6. WHAT IS INERRANCY? (II)   143

7. ARE THERE ERRORS IN THE BIBLE?   165

8. DOES IT MATTER HOW WE APPROACH THE BIBLE?   189

9. SOME MODERN VIEWS OF THE BIBLE (I)   211

10. SOME MODERN VIEWS OF THE BIBLE (II)   239

11. THE BIBLE AND SALVATION   267

Appendix   277

Indexes   283

The Issue Before the Church

" . . . *that we must not suppose that the language proceeds from the men who are inspired, but from the Divine Word which moves them."* JUSTIN MARTYR

"Whatsoever the Divine Scripture says is the voice of the Holy Spirit." GREGORY OF NYSSA

"Therefore we yield to and agree to the authority of the Holy Scripture which can neither be deceived nor deceive." AUGUSTINE

1

The Issue Before the Church

To SAY THAT Christianity is now at the crossroads is to engage in the trite and the commonplace. Without any doubt, Christianity is at the crossroads. From the beginning she has been compelled to choose the road upon which she would travel. Our Lord did indeed say that the gates of hell would not prevail against His Church, but He did not deny that they would try to prevail. Ever since her founding, the Church of God has been engaged in a spiritual battle. Against her, powerful foes have fought, foes which at every turn of the road have sought to deflect her from the true course and, if possible, to destroy her. The apostle knew whereof he spoke when he said that ". . . we wrestle not against flesh and blood, but against principalities, against powers, against the rulers of the darkness of this world, against spiritual wickedness in high places."[1] Throughout the whole course of her life the Church has been faced with the choice "for Christ" or "against Him." She has always been at the crossroads. Some crossroads are clearly marked so that there is no excuse for getting lost. Others, however, are poorly marked, and one comes upon those that seem not to be marked at all. What makes the present situation difficult and fraught with such dire consequences for the well-being of the Church, is that the signposts have been tampered with, so that they intentionally lead one astray. The guidebook and map, it is true, remain the same, and to those who will read and understand, their message is clear, for they were given by the Lord of the Church who is Truth itself and cannot lie. In fact, so accurate are they that he who follows and obeys their directions need not go astray. If, therefore, the Church today takes the wrong turning and finds herself in the land of despair and doubt, she has not harkened to the Guidebook, but has allowed

1. Ephesians 6:12.

13

herself to be deceived by signposts with which her enemy has tampered.

What is the particular choice of route which faces the Church at the present time? It is, we confidently assert, the old one between supernatural and man-made religion. Shall the Church follow God, or shall it follow man? This is today, and has ever been, the alternative which lies before the Church and before all those who name the Name of the Lord. It was so at the time of Athanasius, for example, when the Church had to decide whether she would listen to the voice of man, or hear her Divine Lord. At that time of decision, God was good to His Church, and in His gracious providence brought it about that she should listen to Him and reject the enticing voice of man. The issue in those days also was that of supernatural religion versus a religion which flowed from the human heart. It came to particular expression in the question whether Jesus Christ was true God, or merely like God. To be merely like God, however, and hence something lower than God, is to be infinitely lower than God. One who is infinitely lower than God must be a creature, and cannot save those who put their trust in Him. The Church decided, following the voice of God speaking in the Scripture, for the side of supernaturalism. She valiantly declared that Jesus Christ is true God, indeed very God of very God.

Today also there are many points at which the battle between supernaturalism and naturalism expresses itself. There is, however, one battleground in particular where the fighting is raging and the battle must be fought to a finish. It has to do with the relationship between the Bible and the Church. More properly, it has to do with the very nature of the Bible itself. What is the Bible? That is the great question, and closely bound up with it is another: What is to be our attitude and the attitude of the Church toward the Bible? This issue is constantly being raised. One has but to pick up a modern book, that is, one written since the close of the second decade of this century, and he is likely to find thoughts such as the following. There was a time, he will be told, when a static conception of the inspiration of the Bible prevailed. Then came the new scientific approach to the Bible, and with this new approach an evolutionary philosophy of history. For a time it seemed as though whatever religious and spiritual value the Bible had was to be discarded altogether. However, the studies of the nineteenth century revealed that they had been too one-sided. The two world wars of this century and the discoveries of archaeology have shown that there is after all an abiding religious value in the Bible. Our great task today, therefore, is to conserve the mighty gains of the scientific study of the Bible and at the same time to point out the positive message which the Bible itself contains, indicating thereby its relevance for today and calling attention to its abiding value. There is one thing, however, we are told, that we cannot do (and on this point almost all modern men seem to be agreed), we cannot, whatever else we may do, return to the old orthodox view of a mechanically dictated Scripture. We want no static conception of inspiration.

The Bible, therefore, whether we will or no, is constantly being thrust into the forefront of discussion and one can only be amazed, to say nothing of being saddened, at the glibness with which many speak of the old-fashioned view of inspiration as being out of date and not relevant for the present age. That most modern writers have not taken the trouble to state this doctrine correctly and consequently are erecting a man of straw to attack is a fact, sad but true. The real issue, however, goes far deeper. It does not lie in the fact that the Biblical and Church doctrine of the Bible is constantly being misunderstood and misrepresented. The real issue, as the present book will seek to make clear, is that modern man no longer is ready to listen to the voice of the one living and eternal God, but prefers rather the changing sands of human opinion for the foundation upon which to build his religious life.

To understand the present demand for a new doctrine of inspiration and a new attitude toward the Bible one must know something about the background and soil from which much of our modern religious life and thought has sprung. Fortunately it does not take an expert in Church History or Philosophy (the present writer is certainly neither of these) to discern the true nature of present-day religious movements and attitudes. It is, of course, impossible to keep up with the great output of literature in which the modern view of the Bible is being expounded. The present writer, for example, has been compelled to confine his own reading and study almost exclusively to the field of the Old Testament. Nevertheless, even this limitation is not too serious a handicap, for in whatever field it may come to expression, the modern movement is essentially the same, and it may probably be as well evaluated from the field of Old Testament studies as from any other.

In the providence of God the Reformation gave to the world an open Bible. During the eighteenth century, however, men refused to take the Bible at face value, and rationalism came to the fore. In the nineteenth century, thinkers were greatly under the influence of Hegel and Darwin, and evolution undergirded the outlook in Biblical studies. From this background arose that phenomenon which has commonly been known as modernism, a phenomenon which, although it does not occupy the forefront of thought and opinion as was once the case, is by no means dead today. In its place there is now great stress upon a theology of the "Word" coupled with much usage of the traditional terms of historic Christianity. In reality, however, this modern substitute is anti-intellectual in nature and, if anything, a deeper foe of true Christianity than was the modernism which it is replacing.

Adherents of the modern movement are ofttimes very critical of the older modernism, and of the "scientific" study of the Bible which was carried on during the nineteenth century. This study, they are wont to tell us, neglected the spiritual values of the Bible and also lost sight of its abiding worth. Before us now there lies a new task. We are to conserve all the great gains of "scientific" Biblical scholarship, and at the same time do justice to the permanent aspects of the Bible. To accomplish this task we must, of course, abandon the old-fashioned view of an infallible Scripture, and adopt in its place one which will be acceptable to the modern mind. This, we are being told over and over again, is the great question which faces the Church today.

In the face of this constant demand for a new doctrine of inspiration, what attitude is the Christian man to adopt? It is this question precisely which shall occupy our thought in this study. Can we, as those who believe in the Triune God and trust the Lord Jesus Christ as our Savior from sin, fall in line with the modern insistence upon a new doctrine of inspiration? Must we, too, agree that one can no longer hold to the old Church teaching? Must we abandon this view and adopt something else in its stead? Have the findings of "scientific" Biblical study actually demonstrated the untenability of the traditional attitude toward inspiration? There are some evangelical Christians who apparently think that such is the case. There are some who seem all too willing to give up the time-honored Biblical doctrine and to substitute in its place the shibboleths of some of the forms of modern theology. Shall we, too, join them? Must the battle at this particular point be given up?

For our part, we believe that these questions should be answered with a resolute negative. We do not believe for a moment that this precious heritage must be cast aside. We do not believe that the "facts" which the modern "scientific" study of the Bible has brought to light compel us to change or modify or abandon the historic doctrine of inspiration which finds such a classic expression, for example, in the first chapter of the Westminster Confession of Faith. We are, rather, somewhat concerned over the attitude of those evangelicals who seem ready to abandon this teaching and over the widespread ignorance of the true doctrine which is found even in evangelical circles. The present work would serve as a warning to evangelicals not to cast overboard the historic faith as to inspiration, and would also stress the true importance of this doctrine for the welfare of Christianity today.

In the first place, therefore, it is necessary to insist that the doctrine of inspiration which we adopt must be that which the Bible itself teaches. This point would seem to be obvious, and one would hardly think of dwelling upon it were it not for the fact that it is almost constantly overlooked and disregarded. Men have no hesitancy in telling us what we may and we may not believe concerning inspiration. They are quite concerned to offer a view which will satisfy the demands of the modern twentieth-century individual, and, indeed, they sometimes give the impression that the determining factor as to what we may accept is its acceptableness upon the part of modern man. It hardly ever seems to occur to some modern writers that the Bible itself should be permitted to tell us what kind of a book it is.

With such an attitude the true Christian can have no part whatever. Suffice it, however, for the present, to insist that the doctrine of inspiration which we are to embrace must be derived from the Scriptures themselves. It is strange that men do not recognize this fact. It is strange that men will give to other considerations a place of priority over the testimony of Scripture. It is as though a foreigner should come to our shores and we should desire to know his nationality and something about his background and history. There are many ways in which we might proceed to obtain information. We might call in a number of people and engage in guessing-games on a large scale. We might ask different individuals to make a thorough study of the man's appearance and clothes and then give us their "unbiased" judgment as a result of such "scientific" study. There is also another way in which we might proceed. We might ask the man himself to tell us the answers to our questions.

So it is with the Scriptures. We might judge the Bible by the standard of whether modern man thinks it relevant to his day. We might judge the Bible upon the basis of what certain scholars are ready to say concerning it. We might submit it to the testimony of the "experts" and then abide by that testimony. There are those who seem to be willing to do just that. If, however, we are to know what the Bible really is, it is to the Bible itself that we must go and its teaching concerning itself we must heed. The reason why this is so will become clear as we proceed.

To discover what the Bible has to say about itself is not a particularly difficult task, and to accomplish it we need not be skilled linguists with a mastery of Greek and Hebrew. We do not have to search long and tediously for a stray hint here and there, for the Bible bears within itself the marks of its Divine origin, so that wherever we read we are confronted with the evidences of its divinity. There are, however, certain very express statements which tell us in clear-cut terms what kind of a book the Bible is, and just what is meant by its inspiration. In considering these verses we are not engaging in any very new task, for there are extant several profitable and valuable treatises on the subject. We do not wish nor are we able to duplicate these treatises. Our purpose is simply to examine a few of the principal statements which the Holy Scriptures make concerning themselves.

In the first place, then, we shall do well to consider the well-known passage 2 Timothy 3:16. In the King James translation the verse reads as follows: "All scripture is given by inspiration of God, and is profitable for doctrine, for reproof, for correction, for instruction in righteousness: that the man of God may be perfect, throughly furnished unto every good work." As is the case with so many of the great doctrinal passages of the Bible, the present text is found in a setting that is practical throughout. Paul is acting as a minister of human souls, and in writing to the youthful Timothy is encouraging him to abide steadfast in those things which he has learned. He reminds Timothy that from the time of his childhood he has known the Holy Scriptures which are able to make him wise unto salvation through faith which is in Christ Jesus. It is a glorious reminder and must have produced within Timothy's heart great rejoicing. From childhood Timothy has known the Holy Scriptures. As the late Benjamin B. Warfield so aptly put it, Timothy has had before him an "open Bible." It is after this tender reminder that the Apostle utters the words with which we are now directly concerned.

If we were to examine the verse under consideration as it appears in the English Revised Version, we should notice quite a difference in the translation. In the place of the familiar "All scripture is given by inspiration of God," of the King James, we meet, "Every scripture inspired of God is also profitable." If we set these two translations side by side we may more readily note their difference.

King James	*English Revised*
All scripture is given by inspiration of God . . .	Every scripture inspired of God . . .

One translation speaks of "all scripture"; whereas the other speaks of "every scripture." What is the difference between the two, and is that difference an important one? Well, a little close examination will make it clear to us that the difference between the two is not, for our present purpose, of great moment. If Paul means "every scripture," he is looking at the various parts of the Bible, that is, he is considering Scripture distributively. He is then saying that whatever Scripture we consider, it is inspired of God. On the other hand, if he means "all scripture," it is clear that his reference is to the Scripture in its entirety. In either case he is saying that whatever may be called "scripture" is inspired of God.

At the same time, despite the fact that for our present purpose it does not matter essentially which of the two above-mentioned translations be adopted, we believe that the King James rendering has more in its favor than does that of the Revised Version. The evidence tends to support the view that Paul is here speaking of "all scripture" rather than "every scripture." Furthermore, the word "inspired" is, we believe, not to be considered as belonging to the subject of the sentence.

There is further a misconception which on the basis of the translation, "Every scripture inspired of God . . ." may easily arise. This rendering seems to leave open the possibility that Paul considered some Scriptures inspired and others not inspired. Those which are inspired, Paul on this viewpoint might be represented as saying, are profitable, but possibly there are Scriptures which are not inspired. A translation which leaves open the possibility of this idea, an idea that is so far removed from what the Apostle actually believed, must be considered unfortunate indeed. Whatever modern men may think about the matter, one is certainly safe in asserting that the Apostle Paul firmly regarded all Scripture, all that to which the name Scripture could be given, as inspired of God. There is not a particle of evidence to support the position that Paul thought some Scripture uninspired. All things considered, we believe that the thought of the Apostle is most accurately set forth in the words "All scripture is inspired of God."

The word which for our purpose is of supreme importance is the word *theopneustos,* translated in the English Bible, "inspired of God." It is a compound, consisting of the elements *theo* (God) and *pneustos* (breathed). Now, it is well to note that the word ends in the three letters -*tos*. In the Greek language, words which 1) end in -*tos* and 2) are compound with *theo* (God) are generally passive in meaning. An example will make this clear. There is a Greek word *theodidaktos,* (many others might also be brought forth) which means "taught of God." As may be clearly seen, it ends in -*tos* and also contains the element *theo* (God). Precisely similar is the important word which we are now engaged in considering, namely, *theopneustos.* It likewise is passive in usage, and we should properly translate, "breathed of God." This point is often overlooked, and there have been those who have somewhat vigorously insisted that the meaning is active. They would therefore translate by the phrase "breathing out God," in the sense that the Scriptures breathed forth or were imbued with the Spirit of God. Such, however, as has been noted above, is not the true meaning. The true meaning is passive, "that which is breathed out by God," and it is this strange designation that the Apostle here applies to the Old Testament Scriptures.

What, however, can such a strange designation mean? Why did Paul thus speak of the Scriptures? He thus spoke, we believe, because he wished to make as clear as possible the fact that the Scriptures did not find their origin in man but in God. It was God the Holy Ghost who breathed them forth; they owed their origin to Him; they were the product of the creative breath of God Himself. It is a strong figure, this expression "breathed out by God." A strong figure, however, is needed, in order that Timothy may realize that he is being asked to place his confidence not in writings which merely express the hopes and aspirations of the best of men, but rather in writings which are themselves actually breathed out by God, and consequently of absolute authority.

A strange expression indeed, but the idea set forth by it is not without former Biblical precedent. In the Old Testament the "mouth" of God was regarded as the source from which the Divine message came. "The word is gone out of my mouth," said the Lord, when asserting the steadfastness of His promises of salvation. Likewise, when the tempter came to Him our Lord rebuked him with the words of the Scripture, "Man shall not live by bread alone, but by every word that proceedeth out of the mouth of God." It is not a new idea that Paul here sets forth, even though the particular Greek word which he employs has not yet been attested earlier than his time. Paul is in line with what both the Old Testament and our Lord had said, namely, that God had spoken, and that words had come from His mouth. Paul, be it noted, goes a step further, and says not merely that one word or more words had come from the mouth of God, but indeed that the Scriptures — all, in fact, that might be designated as Scripture — had come from the mouth of God, had been breathed out by God.

The Scriptures therefore are writings which found their origin in God; they are the very product of His creative breath. It is this, then, that we mean when we speak of the inspiration of the Bible. Now the term *inspiration* is, in the humble opinion of the present writer, not a happy one. The word inspiration means that which is breathed in. It comes to us from the Latin, and in the Latin translation of the Bible, commonly known as the Vulgate, is used as a rendering of the Greek *theopneustos* (God-breathed). We are not satisfied with this translation, for the English word inspiration, as has just been remarked, means a "breathing in," and, as we have seen, that is not at all what Paul intends to say. We must be very explicit on this point. In writing to

Timothy, Paul does not wish Timothy to understand that the Scriptures are a body of human writings into which something Divine has been breathed. That is precisely what he does not wish Timothy to understand. According to Paul, the Scriptures are not writings into which something Divine has been breathed; they are not even writings which are imbued with the Divine Spirit (at least, that is not his emphasis in this passage). The Scriptures, Paul vigorously asserts, are writings which came into being because they were breathed out by God Himself. And that is something quite different from what is commonly suggested by the word "inspiration."

In daily life we often employ the word inspiration. For example, we speak of a poet or musician as inspired. When we listen to the indescribable beauty of the fourth movement of Brahms' first symphony, to take an example, we say that Brahms was inspired. What we mean is that Brahms was so overcome by and filled with the gift of music that he breathed into what he wrote the best of his genius and talent and so produced an unutterably great work. We may also speak of the music itself as inspired since it is a composition into which the genius of the composer has been breathed. True enough, when we thus speak, we are not doing full justice to the situation. Such music is a gift of God, and when we listen to it we should utter thanks to Him who has placed it in the heart of man. At the same time it is certainly legitimate to speak of the inspiration of a musician or poet or painter.

Upon reading a bit of great poetry, we find that we are stimulated and excited. We are enthusiastic about what we have read. The poetry, we remark, has inspired us. Such a usage is not what the Apostle has in mind when he writes to Timothy that the Scriptures are God-breathed. That the Scriptures are God-breathed is, it would seem, a fact, whether they inspire the reader or not. The reader may think them very dull, may disagree entirely with them, may not understand them, and may dislike them intensely, nevertheless they are God-breathed.

It is, of course, true that the Bible is an inspiring book. Like no other writing it lifts the soul to the heights. Dull and prosaic must that heart be that is not stirred to its very depths by the account of Paul's farewell with the elders of Ephesus. How tender and restrained are the words that Luke has used to tell the birth of the Lord! With incomparable nobility of style

Isaiah, by the sheer beauty of his language, brings rapture to the soul as with matchless diction he tells of Him who will feed His flock like a shepherd. Truly, the Bible is an inspiring Book. One need but think of the great music, poetry, art, and architecture that has come into being as a result of inspiration derived from the Bible. Here, if ever, we may truthfully say, is an inspiring Book.

That the Bible has been and still is a source of inspiration is something that cannot be denied. In writing to Timothy, however, Paul expresses a truth far more profound than that. What Paul wishes to assure Timothy is that the Bible is the product of the Divine breath, and it is this fact of being breathed out by God that constitutes the very heart and core of the Biblical doctrine of inspiration.

If then the Scriptures are breathed out by God, it is clear that they find their origin in Him. Indeed, the language of the Apostle is but a vigorous way of stating and asserting the Divine origin of these Scriptures. They did not come into existence because men of genius in moments of inspiration composed them. They did not arise because God chose the best that men had written and then imparted to this best somewhat of the Divine. They did not come into being because the ideas which they contained were somehow ideas of which God approved. Not in any of the above-mentioned ways did the Bible have its origin. The Scriptures came into existence in an utterly unique way. They, and they alone of all writings, were breathed out of the mouth of God. Could words be found to make clearer the Divine origin of the Bible?

What Paul has written to Timothy must be set in sharp contrast with what is often said today about the origin of the Scripture. Modern theories of inspiration wish more and more to give a larger place to the activity of man and a lesser place to that of God. In many modern theories, the role which God plays is comparatively minor. One sometimes receives the impression that God is really not at all necessary to inspiration. How different is the language of Paul! And if Paul is correct, how different are the Scriptures! First and foremost in our study of the Scriptural doctrine of inspiration we must vigorously assert the fact that Scripture regards itself as God-breathed.

Likewise very instructive for our purpose is a consideration of 2 Peter 1:21; "For the prophecy came not in old time by the will of man: but holy men of God spake *as they were* moved by the Holy Ghost." A mere reading of these words makes it clear that here is a strong support and reinforcement of what we have already learned from the Pauline passage. In exhorting his readers Peter tells them that we have a more sure prophetic word, and to this prophetic word we are to give heed. This prophetic word he sets over against the testimony of those who had been eyewitnesses of the majesty of Christ. It is, of course, the Scriptures of which he speaks and to which the readers are urged to take heed.

Peter then proceeds to set forth the reason for his exhortation. "No prophecy of the Scripture," he says, "is of any private interpretation." There is question as to what precisely Peter has in mind by these words. In mentioning the prophecies of Scripture, does he intend us to understand only those portions of the Bible which are generally regarded as prophetic, or is he rather speaking of the entirety of the Scriptures as prophetic? Possibly these questions cannot be answered with certainty, although, for various reasons, we incline toward the latter view. We incline toward the position that Peter is here denominating Scripture in its entirety as prophetic. Which of these views we adopt does not make too great a difference, for in either case he is asserting that the origin of the Scriptures — in the one case, of the entire body of Scriptures, in the other, of the prophetic portions — is not to be found in man. It is not, he says, a private interpretation, and by this phrase he means that the Scripture did not come into being as the result of individuals investigating into matters and then writing down their findings. The Scriptures are not the product of human investigation and reason. That there may be no misunderstanding on this point, the Apostle goes on to say that the "prophecy came not in old time by the will of man." These words are negative; they tell us how the prophecy did not come. It is of the utmost importance that we grasp this fact. In order that we may the more clearly understand how the prophecy did come, we must know how it did not come. It did not come, says Peter, by the will of man. That is, it was not of human origin. With this negative statement serving as a background, we are prepared for the positive declaration as to how prophecy did actually come.

With great force and clearness Peter writes, "Being borne by the Holy Spirit, men spake from God" (*translation by the author*), and in this declaration gives us the heart of the matter. In language as unmistakable and direct as that of Paul, he maintains that the Scriptures have their origin in God. Men spake from God, he asserts, and then further remarks that these men were borne by the Holy Spirit. There is here no conflict with Paul. Paul stresses the Divine origin of the Scriptures, and Peter does the same thing. Whereas, however, there is no con-- flict, it is true that Peter does say more about the Scriptures than did Paul in his epistle to Timothy. Peter insists that the Scriptures are from God, but he goes on to say that men, being borne by the Holy Spirit, spake, and in this utterance tells us quite a bit as to how God breathed forth or produced the Scriptures. The Scriptures, according to Peter, are not a magical book dropped down from heaven but, rather, God gave them to us by means of men who spake from Him.

The language is quite striking. The men who spake from God are said to have been borne by the Holy Spirit. That is, the Spirit actually lifted them up and carried them along, and thus they spake. They were borne or carried along under the power of the Spirit and not by their own power. If a person picks up something and bears it, he does it by his own power. That which is picked up and borne, however, is absolutely passive. So the writers of Scripture who spake from God were passive. It was the Spirit of God who bore them. It was He who was active, and they who were passive.[2] Thus He bore them to the goal of His own desiring.

If we examine closely the language of Peter, we shall note that it was while they were in this condition of being borne by the Spirit that men spake from God. The source of their words is said to be God, and they spake these words while they were being borne of the Holy Spirit. While they spoke they were passive, and God was active. It was He who bore them, and as He bore them, they spoke. It was, therefore, not in the void, but rather through the instrumentality and medium of men who were borne by the Spirit, that God spake.

Peter thus makes it clear that human beings actually spoke from God. That is, there were human writers of the Scriptures. The things which they uttered were not their own, but, since they had been borne by Him, were of God Himself. Since God gave His word through human writers, we may truly speak of a human side to the Bible. The message of God was communi-

2. In being borne by the Spirit the writers were passive; in speaking and writing they were active. This might seem to be a contradiction, but it is not. It is simply an expression of the mystery involved in the truth that the words of Scripture are divine words and yet are also the words of human writers.

cated by means of the instrumentality of men who were under the influence of His Spirit.

At this point it is necessary to avoid a serious misunderstanding. Since the writers of the Scriptures were under the influence of the Holy Spirit, it might be argued that they were nothing more than mere passive instruments through whom He spake. In speaking from God they were utterly passive, mere automata, who simply repeated the message that had been given to them. Their human characteristics were in a state of suspended animation, and they, in reality, amounted to no more than dictaphones. Hence the cry is constantly raised: "We want no mechanical dictation theory of inspiration."

It is true that the present passage does place its emphasis upon the fact that the writers of Scripture were borne by the Holy Spirit. It also says of them that they spake. When we examine the other phenomena which the Scripture presents, we shall note that the human writers were in no sense mere automata but, rather, men whose own gifts and talents were brought into usage in the composition of Scripture. For the time being we need do nothing more than register our protest against this all too common caricature of the Scripture doctrine of inspiration. Peter does call attention to the human side of Scripture, and those who have sought to embrace the Scriptural doctrine of inspiration have, following in the footsteps of Scripture, attempted to do the same thing.

Jesus Christ Himself also had something to say about the authority of the Scriptures. There was a time when the Jews, charging Him with blasphemy because He had made Himself equal with God, took up stones to stone Him. In defense He appealed to the Scriptures, and of these He said, "And the scripture cannot be broken" (John 10:35). We need not trace in detail the development of His argument, but there are certain points which must be noted. Christ appeals to the Jews with the words, "Is it not written in your law?" This might lead us to think that He had reference to a passage in the Law of Moses. Such, however, is not the case. The words which Christ employs are not found in the Pentateuch but in Psalm 82:6. It would seem that His purpose was to attribute to the Scriptures a legal or authoritative character, and thereby to establish them as writings to which appeal such as He was then making might legitimately be directed. By His question our Lord brings to the minds of His hearers that body of writings which they would also recognize as the final court of appeal. He does more than that, however; He stops the mouths of all opponents once and for all by His added observation, "The scripture cannot be broken."

The concept of breaking a law is one that is clearly comprehended. If a man breaks a law, he is guilty and so liable to punishment. When he breaks the law, the lawbreaker treats the law as nonexistent, and in effect annuls it. The Scriptures, however, possess an authority so great that they cannot be broken. What they say will stand and cannot be annulled or set aside. If the Scripture speaks, the issue is settled once and for all; it cannot be broken. Since the Scriptures cannot be broken, so our Lord's argument runs, these particular words, which form a part of the Scriptures, likewise cannot be broken.

It is with some surprise that we note what these particular words are. In Psalm 82 we read, "I have said, Ye *are* gods; and all of you *are* children of the most High." The Psalmist is speaking of the judges of Israel and of them he says, "Ye *are* gods." Our Lord quotes the first part of the verse, "I said, ye are gods," and it is this which He refers to as law and Scripture, indeed as irrefragable, indefectible Scripture. How casually these words are introduced in the Psalm! It is, however, of this clause that our Lord says "the scripture cannot be broken." He might have said "this scripture is true," or "this particular scripture cannot be broken." Instead, He makes an assertion about the Scriptures as a whole: The scripture as a whole cannot be broken. This one example makes it clear that every part of Scripture, even to minute details and particulars, is of such authority that it cannot be broken.

The three passages which we have just considered, even though our examination has been brief, set forth clearly the essential elements in the Biblical doctrine of inspiration. If we are to gather from them what they have to teach about the inspiration of the Bible, we might formulate that teaching somewhat as follows. According to the Bible, inspiration is a superintendence of God the Holy Spirit over the writers of the Scriptures, as a result of which these Scriptures possess Divine authority and trustworthiness and, possessing such Divine authority and trustworthiness, are free from error.

It is, of course, incumbent upon us, as we proceed with our argument, to develop in some detail the implications of this definition. What we are immediately concerned with, however, is to make clear that this conception of inspiration is one which is based upon the teaching of the Bible. We ourselves may agree with the definition or we may disagree with it. What matters is that we recognize it as setting forth the teaching of the Scriptures themselves. It is what the Bible has to tell us about itself. To understand this fact clearly is of utmost importance.

When we have once grasped the idea that we must derive our doctrine of inspiration from the Bible, we may begin to understand what the real issue before the Church is. The real issue is not whether we are to substitute one doctrine of inspiration for another. That is at the most a somewhat secondary question. The real issue before the Church today, and for that matter before every individual Christian, is whether the Bible is any longer to be regarded and accepted as a trustworthy teacher of doctrine. In other words, when the Bible testifies as to its own nature, are we to pay heed to what it has to say? When the Bible tells us clearly what kind of a Book it is, are we to reject its testimony as unworthy of belief? That is the real issue which faces us today.

It is necessary to give due heed to the seriousness of this issue. Hitherto the Church has derived all her doctrines from the Scriptures. Whenever in the course of her long history the question arose, What is to be believed? it was to the Bible that the Church turned. To frame an answer to the question, What is God? the Church did not turn to her greatest minds, but to the Bible. Again, to settle the question of how many persons there are in the Godhead, the Church went to the Bible to find an answer. Who is Jesus Christ? What must I do to be saved? Who is the Holy Spirit? Is Jesus Christ the only Savior and Redeemer? For the answers to these and to a thousand other questions, answers which have found formulation in her great creeds, the Church has listened to the words of the Bible. In fact, the creeds are nothing more than attempts upon the part of man to formulate accurately what it was believed the Bible taught. How much loving and devoted labor has gone into the writing of these creeds! How much care and precision has been exercised in their composition! The reason for such loving devotion is to be found simply in the fact that the authors of the creeds were striving to the best of their ability to set forth what they believed the teaching of the Bible to be. Until the present day the Church has exercised great toil and care in an endeavor to present to the world her message, a message which she firmly believed was derived from the sacred Scriptures themselves.

Now, it would seem, all this is to be reversed. When we talk about what kind of a Book it is the Church has been listening to ever since her earliest history, we want to close our ears to anything this Book itself has to say. When, for example, the Church was ready to formulate the Nicene Creed, it listened to the Bible; but now we think that we can abandon this attitude. We are not going to ask the Scriptures what they have to say about themselves. We are going to learn our doctrine of inspiration in some other way.

This reversal of the Church's practice of appealing to the Bible is a strange procedure indeed, but perhaps not unexpected. When we consider the utilitarian character of the age in which we live, and the constant exaltation of man and his powers, it is not so surprising. A generation which has as its background the rationalism of the eighteenth century, the evolutionism and "higher" criticism of the nineteenth century, and the "neo-orthodoxy" and dialectical theology of the early-twentieth century, may perhaps be expected to set itself up as a better judge of the Bible than the Bible itself.

And herein lies a disturbing question which must be raised. If we are not to regard the Bible as a trustworthy witness when it tells us what kind of a Book it is, and if we should listen to modern scholars rather than to the Bible, how do we know that the Bible is a trustworthy witness when it speaks to us about other matters also? Let us state this question as clearly as possible. The Bible, we say, is not to be relied upon when it tells us what kind of Book it is. But if it is not to be depended upon when it speaks of itself, how do we know that it is to be trusted when it speaks about anything else? If it is so unreliable that we cannot accept its witness to itself, might it not be wise to reject all that it has told us about other matters as well?

We listened to the Bible when it told us of the existence of the one living and true God. The Bible, however, we now learn, is not a trustworthy character witness. It has deceived us when it told us about its own inspiration. Possibly, after all, it was also wrong when it spoke about God! Possibly God, if there be a God, is quite different from the God we have learned to know from the pages of what we in our naiveté thought was a Holy Book. Futhermore, what about Jesus Christ and that wondrous work of redemption He wrought for us upon the Cross of Calvary? Is it a reliable account that we have in the Bible? Has the great burden of our guilt really been removed, and are we living in a right relation with the Holy God, or have we been relying upon an account that is not trustworthy? If this Book is not reliable when it tells us what kind of a Book it is, how then can we possibly trust it when it speaks to us of other matters? If the Bible is not a trustworthy witness of its own character, we have no assurance that our Christian faith is founded upon the truth. We are left in the darkness of ignorance and despair.

If, therefore, we are going to reject the trustworthiness of the Scriptures when they speak of themselves, let us by all means note the consequences of what we are doing. Let us not merely say that the great issue before the Church is to adopt some doctrine of inspiration which will appeal to the thinking man of today. Let us, rather, state the issue clearly, and say that we no longer wish to regard the Bible as a trustworthy teacher of doctrine. Let us bravely — if we must adopt this position — accept the consequences. To do this will, of course, be a hard thing. It will be unpleasant. There is one advantage, however, which it will have, and that is the advantage of honesty. It sets before us clearly what the issue actually is, and the real issue, we may repeat, is whether we are any longer to listen to the Bible as a trustworthy teacher.

One sometimes hears it said that there is no necessity to stress this high doctrine of inspiration. Even if there are errors in the Bible, it is objected, cannot men be saved from their sins? Cannot they be blessed of God and grow in the grace of Jesus Christ? Why, then, such an insistence upon an infallible Scripture? In answer, we would, of course, maintain that God could have revealed His will to us in some other way. As a matter of fact, however, He chose to reveal it to us in the Bible, and this Bible claims to be His very Word. It is therefore of the utmost importance that we do full justice to what the Bible teaches. We hold to a high view of inspiration for the simple reason that the Bible teaches a high view.

It is, of course, true that, even if there had been no inspired Bible, Jesus Christ could have come to this earth and lived upon it a sinless life and died for His own upon the Cross of Calvary. All this might have been true, even if there had been no inspired Bible or any Bible at all. As a matter of fact, however, God did give us an infallible Bible. Consequently, there is not much point in talking about what might have been, had there been no Scripture.

The Bible is of the utmost importance, for as much as men of the twentieth century seem to dislike the fact, the Bible has been, all along, their teacher. The Bible teaches what we are to believe about God and our relation to Him, and it also reveals what is His will. Throughout the centuries the Triune God has watched over His Church. The words of the risen Redeemer, "Lo, I am with you alway, even unto the end of the world," have been shown to be true. Christ has indeed been with His Church, and His Spirit has been her Teacher. The Holy Trinity has kept the Church dependent upon His Word, so that she might learn therefrom. In so far as she has learned from that Word, she has been blessed, and men and women, wearied with the burden and guilt of their sins, have learned of Him who bore their griefs and carried their sorrows, and have found Him to be "a covert from the tempest; as rivers of water in a dry place, as the shadow of a great rock in a weary land."[3] We believe the Scriptures to be of the utmost importance, and we also regard as of the utmost importance what doctrine of inspiration a man embraces. It is for this reason that we are concerned that the issue before the Church be clearly grasped and squarely faced.

The issue before the Church then, as we have said, is simply, whether we are any longer to accept the Bible as a trustworthy teacher. When we put the matter in this way, there will doubtless be those who will say, even though they have come this far with us, "It is true that the question before us is whether we are willing any longer to receive the Bible as a trustworthy teacher or witness, and we are willing to answer that question in the negative." Not all, of course, will give such a forthright state-

3. Isaiah 32:2.

ment of the case, and because the question is often beclouded, the issues which are involved are not always clearly seen and grasped. We must therefore note what the consequences are of rejecting the Bible as a trustworthy witness.

It is in reality the age-old question that faces us, Shall we listen to God or to man? Is God to tell His Church what it is to believe, or is the Church to learn her doctrine from man? This is the question with which we are now confronted, and it is a question which we cannot escape. If the Bible is the Word of God, it follows that we are listening to God when we harken to its teaching. If the Bible is the Word of God, and we reject its teaching, it certainly follows that we are listening to the voice of man rather than of God.

At this point, it may well be, an objection will be raised. Have we not been assuming, it may be objected, that the Bible is the Word of God? Have we not been arguing that, since the Bible is the Word of God, he who will not harken to the Bible is refusing to listen to the voice of God and, instead, is listening to the voice of man? Suppose, however, that the Bible is not the Word of God, does not the entire picture then change? Does not our whole argument fall to the ground? We have been assuming that the Scriptures are from God, and in making this assumption we have furthermore been assuming the truth of theism. By what right do we do this? Would not our argument be more convincing if we were to begin with a neutral position and from that reason step by step to the conclusion that the Scriptures are from God?

In answer we would reply that we have indeed begun our discussion upon the presupposition that God is, and that the Scriptures are His Word. If God is the Creator of all things, then all things are His and must bear His impress upon them. There can be no neutral position. We believe that either God is our Creator and the One who alone gives meaning to all aspects of life, or that we are faced with the dismal gloom of relying upon the human mind as the ultimate point of reference and predication. For our part, we do indeed look to God, Creator of the heavens and the earth, as the Author and Source of all wisdom, and we believe most sincerely that He has spoken to man, and, in a sense which is true of no other writings, that the Bible is His Word.

Is our faith in the Bible justified? Are we following cunningly devised fables, or has God actually spoken in a unique manner in the Bible? Well, to this question the Christian has a ready answer. He believes that the Bible is God's Word, for he sees the marks of divinity which God placed therein. They make it clear that the Bible is of Divine origin. The Christian sees in this Book the impress of Deity. The evidences for the Divine origin of Scripture are unmistakable, so that he who beholds them not is without excuse.

For example, we may remind ourselves of the Divine doctrine taught in the Bible. When compared with other literature from the ancient Near East, the Bible stands out like a fair flower in a dreary, barren desert. We read the crude polytheism of the Babylonian documents, and then open the pages of Holy Scripture and learn of Him who is good and true and holy. We read the pseudo-creation accounts of the ancient world and then listen to the majestic account of true creation given in the Bible. We read of the struggles and strivings of men to atone in one way or another for their sins. How dark was the light of ancient religion! Then we learn from the Bible that man cannot save himself, but that God has provided the one Lamb that taketh away the sin of the world. How unspeakably grand is the doctrine of salvation by grace! When we read of the saving love of Jesus Christ we know that here is a message of heavenly origin, and that nothing from that dark world of old can compare with it. When we turn to the philosophies of modern men, it is as though we had stepped out of the light of God's sunshine into a dimly lit cavern. Gloomy indeed are the thoughts of the modern man! How superficial is his attitude toward sin and its removal! In contrast, how the heart rejoices when it first learns from the Bible the true meaning of that wondrous thing that was done in Palestine outside the city wall of Jerusalem.

Many and convincing are these evidences whereby the Scriptures reveal their Divine origin. Yet, despite their clarity, not all men are willing to accept these evidences, and the reason for this unwillingness is not far to seek. Is it because there is some defect in the evidences themselves? Are not they of sufficient clarity and cogency to convince all men? The answer is that the evidences are clear enough; indeed so clear are they that he who is not convinced by them has no excuse. The reason, however, why men do not perceive the force of these evidences is that their understanding has been darkened by sin. There is not much point in talking to a blind man about the light of the sun. He may take your word for it that the sun gives light, but he himself has not seen that light. He has a desperate need. That need is not for light; it is rather for an opening of the eyes. So, too, the need of mankind today is not for heavenly light; that heavenly light is here, shining about us, a lamp unto our feet and a light unto our path. The need of mankind is rather an opening of the eyes of the understanding. As long as men remain spiritually blind they will not see the truth, even though the truth be blazoned before them with the brightness of full noon.

The Christian believes that his own eyes have been opened. He believes that the eyes of his understanding have been opened, not by man but by God. He is convinced, in other words, that the Bible is the Word of God, because God has told him so. Thus we come to the blessed doctrine of the internal testimony of the Holy Spirit. The Christian is persuaded and assured of both the infallible truth and the divine authority of the Bible by this inward work of the Spirit within his heart, who opens his mind to perceive the true nature of Scripture and who applies the Word with force and conviction that man may experience the truth that the Bible is from God. It is God, the Christian gladly declares, who testifies to His own Word. It is God who identifies what He Himself has spoken; and we may ever be grateful to Him that He has thus testified to His Word for us.

What, precisely, is this work of God's Spirit? Well, of one point we may be sure. It is not the communication to us of information beyond what is contained in the Bible. It is not the impartation of new knowledge. It is not a new revelation from God to man. It is rather that aspect of the supernatural work of the new birth in which the eyes of our understanding have been opened so that we, who once were in the darkness and bondage of sin, now see that to which formerly we had been blind. The new birth is the work of the Spirit of God alone, and one of the blessed consequences of this new birth is that the eyes of the blind are opened. As a result, the mind has understanding; it sees clearly, whereas formerly it had been in the darkness of spiritual blindness. Now, at last, the sinner is convinced that this Book is different from all other books. He beholds that it is from God in a sense that is true of no other writing. The divinity of the Scriptures is for the first time clearly perceived, and the voice of the heavenly Father distinctly heard.

It is then from God Himself that we learn the true character of the Scriptures. In the very nature of the case, it must be so. Only God can identify what He Himself has spoken. If man, unaided, could identify God's Word, man would have powers which are God's alone. And if man really has these powers, God, whatever else He might be, would not be the One of whom the Bible speaks. We are in reality face to face with the question of theism. Unless we first think rightly of God, we shall be in error upon everything else. Unless we first think rightly of God, we shall indeed be in error when we come to consider His Word. We Christians need not be ashamed to proclaim boldly that our final persuasion of the Divinity of the Bible is from God Himself. God, in His gentle grace, has identified His Word for us; He has told us that the Bible is from Himself. Those who know Him not may depreciate this doctrine of the internal testimony of the Spirit; those who are His know that God has truly brought them out of darkness into light.

The Church is indeed at the crossroads. Shall she listen to God or to man? Will she receive what the Spirit says concerning inspiration, or, turning her back upon Him, will she cleave unto man? This is the choice to be made. Sad is it, however, that many do not realize the necessity for making a choice. Having their vision obscured by the dense fog that modern theology is casting over the way, many do not realize that there is a crossroad. They are not aware that they must decide which road they will follow. Unless something is done, they will travel on, taking the wrong turning, until the road leads them at last into the valley of lost hope and eternal death.

Pray God that He will awaken His people from their slumber. Pray that He will warn them of the dangers that lie ahead in the forsaking of His Word. May He raise up even in our day those who will call the Church back to Him, so that there may be a deep revulsion from the shallowness of our present religious life and a mighty return unto the one eternal God. Then "out of Zion shall go forth the law, and the word of the Lord from Jerusalem."[4] Then men and women, burdened with the toils

4. Isaiah 2:3.

of life and weighted down by their sins, will find refreshment for their souls and strength for their needs in the grace of Him whose Word cannot be broken.

The Extent of Inspiration

"We cannot say of the writings of the Holy Spirit that anything in them is useless or superfluous, even if they seem to some obscure."   ORIGEN

"There is no discord between the Law and the Gospel, but harmony, for they both proceed from the same Author."   CLEMENT OF ALEXANDRIA

"All Scripture, as it has been given to us by God, will be found to be harmonious."   IRENAEUS

2

The Extent of Inspiration

ONE WHO DESIRES to be able to identify counterfeit money should make himself thoroughly familiar with the genuine article. If he knows the genuine thoroughly, he will not have much difficulty in detecting the counterfeit. On the other hand, if he knows only what is false, he will have great difficulty in distinguishing genuine from counterfeit. It is for this reason that we intend to spend some time in a study of what we believe to be the true and genuine doctrine of inspiration. If we have a clear picture of what the Bible itself teaches about inspiration, we shall be in a far better position to deal with views and opinions which, although quite prevalent, are nevertheless to be placed in the category of counterfeit.

One reason, it may be observed in passing, why many today are willing to embrace new views of inspiration is possibly to be found in the fact that the Scriptural teaching is not well known. The American Protestant Church of the first half of this century can hardly be characterized as one in which doctrinal preaching and catechetical instruction have held a very large place. As a result the membership of the Protestant Church is quite ignorant of doctrine and even of the simple contents of the Bible. It is an easy prey to whatever happens to come along, and modern theology, because of its usage of orthodox terminology, is readily misunderstood by many. Very few seem able to distinguish between what is Scriptural and what is not.

If the Scriptural doctrine of inspiration were better known, the newer views would have more difficulty lodging themselves in the modern Church. It will be necessary therefore to examine in more detail what the Bible itself teaches concerning inspiration. If what we have been saying in the preceding chapter is true, the great issue before the Church today is whether to listen to the voice of God or of man. That expresses itself, we have seen, in the question whether one may any longer regard the Bible as a trustworthy teacher of doctrine. Throughout the course of Church History the Church has derived her doctrines from the Bible. Is she now, at long last, when so many alternatives and substitutes are being proposed, to reject the testimony which the Bible gives concerning itself? Since the Bible is God's Word, to reject what the Bible has to say about itself is to reject the voice of God Himself. What lies before the Church at the present time is the old issue of supernatural versus man-made religion.

In turning to the Bible to discover what it has to say of itself we learn that the Scriptures are said to be God-breathed; that holy men spake from God as they were borne by the Holy Spirit; and that, in the words of the Lord Himself, the Scripture cannot be broken. Before we devote any attention to alternative views, it is first necessary to examine more closely this teaching of the Bible and to notice certain of its implications.

The passages of Scripture to which we have given consideration teach that the Bible is the Word of God, actually spoken from His mouth. The expression "Word of God" will be more readily understood if we state clearly what a word itself is. A word is simply the vehicle by means of which thought is communicated from one mind to another. And when we then speak of the Word of God, we are employing an expression to designate the means which God uses to convey to us the thoughts of His heart. God has spoken to us in order that we may know what He would have us do: through the medium of words He has revealed His will.

Whatever Word He has uttered, since it has come from His mouth, is true and trustworthy. "The words of the Lord *are* pure words," the Psalmist declares, *"as* silver tried in a furnace of earth, purified seven times."[1] What has been spoken by God, who cannot lie, must be pure and true altogether. Every word which proceedeth from the mouth of the heavenly Father must in the very nature of the case be absolutely free from error. If this is not so, God Himself is not trustworthy.

If, therefore, the Scriptures are the Word of God, breathed out by Him, it follows that they, too, are absolutely true and infallible. The passage in 2 Timothy to which we have already given attention certainly teaches that the Scriptures are the Word of God. Is it, however, an isolated passage? Is there no other line of evidence

1. Psalm 12:6.

that we can follow? Does this one verse stand by itself, a lonely signpost pointing to the Divine origin of the Scriptures? Happily, such is not the case. The testimony of the Bible to itself is abundant and compelling.

The word which God in sundry times and in divers manners spake in time past unto the fathers by the prophets was a God-breathed word. It was inspired. Those whom God raised up to declare unto the nation His truth were inspired of Him. "I will place my words in his mouth," said the Lord of Moses, "and he shall speak all that which I command Him." From this passage (Deuteronomy 18:18) we learn in the first place that God did reveal His Word unto the prophets. Now it is very important to understand what is meant by the term "revelation." It is very important and necessary to know what we mean when we say that God revealed His word unto the prophets. Revelation, in the Bibical sense of the term, is the communication of information. When God reveals His Word unto the prophets, for example, He tells them something which beforehand they had not known. The purpose of the Lord in granting revelation is to impart knowledge. It is, of course, true that revelation need not be imparted by means of words. The entire creation, including man himself, is a revelation of the glory and power of God. In accents strong, though not of words, the created universe declares the mighty power and greatness of God the Creator. God has, however, also spoken in words, and the Bible lays great emphasis upon the fact that He has thus spoken.

What kind of a Word, however, did God reveal unto His servants the prophets? When they proclaimed their messages, were they preserved and kept from error so that the spoken word was actually what God had revealed unto them? Were the prophets, in other words, inspired teachers? According to the Bible they were. God placed His Word in their mouths, and consequently what they uttered was precisely what He wished them to utter. Inspiration is designed to secure the accuracy of what is taught and to keep the Lord's spokesman from error in his teaching. We must therefore make a distinction between revelation and inspiration. It is true that the two are very closely related, and it is true that in the broad sense inspiration is a form or mode of revelation. At the same time, it is well to keep in mind the fundamental distinction that, whereas revelation is essentially the communication of knowledge or information, inspiration is designed to secure infallibility in teaching. The prophets were the recipients of revelation. God did, in most loving and wondrous fashion, speak unto them and reveal what they themselves in their own strength and wisdom could never have learned. At the same time, the Word which He gave them was one which He placed in their mouth, one which, coming from Him, was pure and true and trustworthy. He also saw to it that they spoke precisely what He had commanded them. As a consequence they were men who in their public teaching were kept from error. They spoke, not the thoughts of their own hearts, but rather the Word which had been given them of God. They were, in other words, inspired organs to whom Divine revelation had come.

Very helpful for our present purpose is Exodus 7:1-2. "And the Lord said unto Moses, See, I have made thee a god to Pharaoh: and Aaron thy brother shall be thy prophet. Thou shalt speak all that I command thee: and Aaron thy brother shall speak unto Pharaoh, that he send the children of Israel out of his land." According to these words Moses stands in relation to Pharaoh as a god, and Aaron is the prophet. The origin of the message is from God; it is to be a Divine revelation. More than that, however, it is to be an infallible and trustworthy revelation. Aaron is to be the prophet of Moses and he is told the message which he is to declare. In an earlier passage, Exodus 4:15, we read: "And thou shalt speak unto him, and put words in his mouth: and I will be with thy mouth, and with his mouth, and will teach you what ye shall do." Here the idea of the inspiration of the prophet is clearly set forth. The same thought finds expression in Jeremiah 1:9, "Then the Lord put forth his hand, and touched my mouth. And the Lord said unto me, Behold, I have put my words in thy mouth." Jeremiah the prophet is clearly conscious of the fact that he has been inspired of God. The Lord has actually placed the words in his mouth, and he is told to speak "unto them all that I command thee" (verse 17). God sees to it that the prophet utters what has been revealed to him. Jeremiah is not permitted to develop the revealed message and present it in his own words. It does not come to him as a seed thought, to fructify in his own mind. Rather, the actual words which have been revealed are themselves of Divine origin, and it is these Divine words, these and no others, which Jeremiah is to declare.

That this is the case is further seen in the formula which the prophets so often employ, "Thus saith the Lord," a formula which means that the words to follow are the actual words which the Lord Himself has placed in the mouth of the prophet. The hearers are to understand thereby that these words are not the prophet's, a development of the seed thought planted in him by God, but are the identical words which God Himself has revealed. A strong confirmation of this fact has come from archaeology. In the Near East many letters have been unearthed which contain this precise formula, "Thus saith X." The words which follow the formula are then the very words which the composer has uttered. When the prophets give forth their messages, they are calling specific attention, not to themselves and their opinions, but rather to the precise words which the Lord Himself has spoken. Now, if it is true that the words which the prophet proclaims are the precise words which the Lord has revealed, it is evident that the prophet has been inspired of God, and is an inspired organ of revelation.

Strange indeed is the manner in which the prophets of the Old Testament, without any warning, lapse into the first person, as though it were God Himself who was speaking. In that tender parable of the vineyard, for example, Isaiah, who has shown a great devotion to his friend whose vineyard had been so carefully tended, yet which had disappointed its owner by bringing forth wild grapes, abruptly abandons speaking of the owner in the third person and, putting himself in the role of his friends, speaks in the first person, "And now, O inhabitants of Jerusalem, and men of Judah, judge, I pray you, betwixt me and my vineyard."[2] It is God who speaks. It is God who passes judgment upon the men of Judah and tells them what He will do to them because they have destroyed His vineyard. But how dare the prophet speak in such a fashion? What right has he to assume the prerogatives which belong to God alone, and to speak as though he were God? Certainly, no right at all, unless he believed that, in speaking as he did, he was uttering words which God actually placed in his mouth. Nor is Isaiah alone in this procedure. Other prophets did the same thing. So overcome were they by their message that they spoke in the first person. There was, however, no deception. The prophets did not claim to speak in their own

2. Isaiah 5:3.

right; nor is there any evidence that those who heard them were deceived. What a clear picture of inspired teaching this is! Are we to think for a moment that these words which the prophets proclaimed were mistaken words, tinged with error and faults? Did the prophets garble their messages? Did they somehow obscure the Word which God gave them? Were their messages not trustworthy? Against all such conceptions this fact stands out as a strong protest: though they speak in the first person, these bold men speak for God, and the words which they declare are precisely those which they have received from God Himself.

When we turn to the New Testament we discover the same thing. Those men who were the recipients of God's revelation were men who were taught of the Spirit and so were kept from error in their teaching. Our Lord promised to His Church the gift of the Holy Spirit who would ". . . teach you all things, and bring all things to your remembrance, whatsoever I have said unto you" (John 14:26). The Apostles were not to be left on their own. They would not need to depend upon their own fallible hearts and minds to tell them what to say. Rather, to them had been promised an infallible Teacher, even God and the Holy Ghost. It was thus that the Apostles themselves understood their own words. How amazing are the words that Paul sends to the Thessalonians, " . . . thank we God without ceasing, because, when ye received the word of God which ye heard of us, ye received *it* not *as* the word of man, but as it is in truth, the word of God, which effectually worketh also in you that believe" (I Thessalonians 2:13). What a remarkable verse this is! How mad Paul would have been to speak of his message to the Thessalonians in this way, if he were not uttering the solemn truth! If Paul were speaking the truth, then he was conscious that the Holy Ghost was with him, and that the words which he had so earnestly and sincerely proclaimed were not his own but the very Word of God. If he were not speaking the truth then he was, of course, the worst possible sort of impostor. In Paul's words, however, there rings a depth of earnestness which makes it clear he was no deceiver. He was conscious of setting forth the very truth which God had given him: and this Word, he says, worketh effectually in those that hear and receive it. Can there be any doubt that Paul is here represented as an inspired teacher, one who is setting forth precisely what God has given to him?

If what we have been saying, then, is correct, it follows that those to whom God gave His revelation were men borne of the Holy Spirit, whose messages were infallibly delivered and absolutely free from error, being precisely the words that God Himself wished to have declared. We might therefore assume that since God inspired the organs of revelation when they uttered the spoken Word, He would also have inspired them when they set forth the written Word. However, have we been justified in maintaining that these organs of inspiration were inspired when they proclaimed the spoken Word? It should be clear that the entire argument rests upon the assumption that the written Scriptures are trustworthy and accurate witnesses. If the Bible does not present a true picture of the inspiration of the prophets and apostles, then, of course, the argument is ended. We must, therefore, face squarely the question whether the Scriptures claim inspiration for themselves. In other words, Do they claim to be the Word of God?

The reader who has followed the discussion of the Scripture passages adduced in the previous chapter will have an idea of how we propose to answer this question. We are convinced that the Scriptures do indeed claim to be the Word of God, and since they are from Him and find their origin in Him, are therefore infallible and entirely free from error of any kind. Since their Author is Truth and cannot lie, so His Word, the Sacred Scriptures, is truth and cannot lie. The Biblical evidence to support this thesis is very clear and cogent. We shall not attempt to present all the evidence; rather, we shall content ourselves with some of the main thoughts which Scriptures has to offer upon the question.

When the New Testament mentions the Scriptures, it has in mind, for the most part, the Old Testament and it is most instructive to note the epithets which it applies to these Scriptures. Paul says that they are holy (Romans 1:2). They are holy for their Author is holy. To Paul there is a depth of meaning in this word "holy" which we in our daily usage often overlook. To Paul these Scriptures are holy because they partake of the character of Him who spoke their very words. In another verse, the Apostle does not hesitate to designate them as the "oracles of God" (Romans 3:2). An oracle is something that is spoken. The oracles of God, therefore, are those things which God has spoken to us. They are the very words of God. In the epistle to Timothy,

Paul gives them a definite religious quality when he speaks of the "sacred" Scriptures.

Not only are such high designations attributed to the Scriptures, but their very words are equated with the words of God. A few examples of this striking occurrence will suffice. In writing to the Romans (9:17) the Apostle quotes from the book of Exodus, "For the scripture saith unto Pharaoh, Even for this same purpose have I raised thee up, that I might shew my power in thee, and that my name might be declared throughout all the earth." In the book of Exodus, however, these words are attributed to God Himself. It is God who utters them through Moses to Pharaoh. According to Paul, therefore, the Scripture is saying the very things that God says. The actual words of the Old Testament are attributed to God Himself.

Very cogent is the reference of Paul in Galatians 3:8, "And the scripture, foreseeing that God would justify the heathen through faith, preached before the gospel unto Abraham, *saying*, In thee shall all nations be blessed." When we turn to Genesis when these words are taken (22:18), we notice that it is God Himself who speaks. What the Scripture declares is attributed to God. Paul here identifies Scripture with God. Scripture foresees that God would justify the heathen by faith and so it speaks. What it speaks is the very Word of God.

A few more references will be in place. In the tender and beautiful prayer of the Apostles, recorded in the fourth chapter of the book of Acts, we read, "Who by the mouth of thy servant David hast said, Why did the heathen rage, and the people imagine vain things?" The quotation is from the second Psalm, the human authorship of which is attributed to David, and it is through the mouth of David that God Himself is said to have spoken. Very similar is the passage in Acts 28:25: "Well spake the Holy Ghost by Esaias the prophet unto our fathers." Paul here has reference to the Old Testament Scriptures, to the sixth chapter of Isaiah. The human author of this book was Isaiah, but it was the Holy Spirit who spoke through him.

It will perhaps be well to bring to a close our brief survey of the Scriptural teaching concerning itself by a reference to the gracious remarks which the Apostle Peter made concerning the epistles of Paul. He speaks of these epistles in the category of "other Scriptures," and that means, of course, that Peter regards them as Scripture. More than that, he makes the bold statement that those who wrest these Scriptures, the epistles of our beloved brother Paul, do so to their own destruction. It is a phrase laden with terrible meaning. How all-important these Scriptures are to Peter! A man who wrests them does so to his own destruction and the eternal loss of his soul. It is impossible to conceive of a higher view of Paul's epistles. Very cogent, we may conclude, and very clear is this witness of the Bible to itself and its Divine infallible character. Modern man may deny its true nature, but it speaks with loud, compelling voice, for it is the infallible Word of the one living and true God.

It is conceivable that at this point an objection may be made. It may be objected that in the few passages adduced above not one word from the Lord Jesus Christ is considered. What view of Scripture, it may be asked did Jesus Christ entertain? The question is perfectly legitimate. Not that the recorded words of Christ are more trustworthy than other passages of Scripture, but what Christ has said concerning the authority of the Bible must itself always be regarded as having the utmost authority. We must always remember, however, that it is possible to know what Christ did and believed, only upon the assumption that the Scripture itself is a trustworthy and accurate witness to what He said and taught. What, then, did the Lord believe concerning the Scriptures?

An answer to this question is found in the quotation to which reference has already been made. "The scriptures cannot be broken," Christ had declared, and we may very well expect that all His utterances about the Bible will be in line with this one great statement. And indeed, this is exactly the case. A brief glance at only a few verses will provide a convincing answer. In referring to the Psalmist, Jesus Christ declared, "How then doth David in spirit call him Lord?" (Matthew 22:43). Very clearly and without any equivocation the Redeemer regards David as having spoken in the Holy Spirit. The passage which He has in mind is Psalm 110 and it is the words from this particular Psalm which the eternal Son of God says have been spoken by David in the Spirit.

Very, interesting and worthy of consideration are the words with which our Redeemer refuted the Tempter. "It is written," He said (and for Christ that was sufficient), "Man shall not live by bread alone, but by every word that proceedeth out of the mouth of God" (Matthew 4:4). How cogent this passage

is! The evil one would seek to deflect our Lord from His
determined course of saving His own. How can the Tempter
be silenced? There is one sure way. It is to quote the Scripture.
It is written, and therefore, since it is written, the issue is
settled. What the devil has to say is without force, for God
has already spoken. "It is written," and that ends the matter.

"Search the scriptures," our Lord commanded upon another
occasion (His reference being to the Old Testament), "for in
them ye think ye have eternal life: and they are they which
testify of me" (John 5:39). In almost the same breath He
goes on to say, "For had ye believed Moses, ye would have
believed me: for he wrote of me. But if ye believe not his writings, how shall ye believe my words?" (John 5:46, 47).

That our Lord believed the Scriptures to be trustworthy and to
possess an authority that was absolute is a fact that cannot be
gainsaid. It is acknowledged even by some who do not themselves believe in his deity. We may disagree with the Lord on
this point but, if the Scriptures have given an accurate picture
of Christ, we must acknowledge that He held that the Scriptures
were infallible — they could not be broken.

It should be clear to anyone who has carefully read the passages
of the Bible which we have adduced that the view of inspiration
which the Bible teaches is strongly opposed to the idea that only
in parts the Scriptures are infallible and trustworthy. It is not
only in specific teachings or in great doctrines that the Scriptures
cannot be broken. Rather, in all its parts, in its very entirety,
the Bible, if we are to accept its witness to itself, is utterly
infallible. It is not only that each book given the name of
Scripture is infallible but, more than that, the content of each
such book is itself Scripture, the Word of God written and, hence,
infallible, free entirely from the errors which adhere to mere
human compositions. Not alone to moral and ethical truths, but
to all statements of fact does this inspiration extend. That
inspiration which the Bible claims for itself is one that is full;
it is plenary inspiration. As our Lord said, in giving expression
to this very doctrine, "Think not that I am come to destroy
the law; or the prophets: I am not come to destroy, but to
fulfil. For verily I say unto you, Till heaven and earth pass,
one jot or one tittle shall in no wise pass from the law, till all
be fulfilled" (Matthew 5:17,18).

If, therefore, the inspiration of the Bible is plenary, it should be evident that it is one which extends to the very words. It is, to state the matter baldly, a verbal inspiration. That such is the case is manifest from the passages which we have already considered. With this representation of the Bible, however, there are many who do not agree. We are living in a day when men depreciate the idea that God has spoken in words. If there is any one point upon which modern thinkers are agreed, it is that they are heartily and cordially opposed to the doctrine of a verbal inspiration. When one picks up a modern book upon the nature of the Bible, he is almost certain to find the author asserting that the time has come for a new doctrine of inspiration and, coupled with this assertion, he will doubtless encounter a rejection of verbal inspiration.

It would, of course, be impossible to divorce the thoughts of the Bible from its words. The thoughts are indeed "God-breathed" thoughts, and to them we are to give our entire soul's obedience. The doctrines and the teachings of the Bible are to be our very rule of life and faith. In what manner, however, has God seen fit to reveal those thoughts to us? To ask the question is to answer it. He has revealed them through the media of words. It is just about impossible for us to conceive of any other satisfactory manner of communicating information. When we wish in adequate fashion to communicate our thoughts we are compelled to employ words; indeed, for this reason has God given us speech. We cannot have the blessed life-giving doctrines of Holy Writ apart from the words in which they are expressed. Our purpose at present, however, is not to defend this doctrine of verbal inspiration. For the present we are merely pointing out that, whether modern man likes the doctrine or no, the Bible teaches it. More than that, despite the dislike of modern man, it is our Lord Jesus Christ Himself who embraced this doctrine. Only one doctrine of inspiration is taught in the Bible, namely, that of a plenary and verbal inspiration to which the modern mind is so hostile.

The reader who has followed the argument to the present point, will, if he has meditated upon those passages of Scripture which have been presented, probably agree that the Bible itself does claim to be the Word of God. He will also agree, if he is consistent, that if the Bible is the Word of God, it must be pure and free from error. Can *Holy* Scripture contain error? Can the "oracles" of God be tinged with falsehood? The question which we are facing is, in reality, whether God Himself is pure and free from error. And if God Himself is truth, no word which has proceeded from His mouth can possibly be anything other than the absolute truth. When therefore the claim is sometimes made that the Bible does not attribute infallibility to itself, or that it does not profess to be free from error, we must insist that this claim disregards both the fact that the Bible is the Word of God and that it also claims to be pure and true.

In 1923 the General Assembly of the Presbyterian Church in the U.S.A. declared among other things the following: ". . . the Holy Spirit did so inspire, guide and move the writers of Holy Scripture as to keep them from error . . . ." This declaration on the part of the Assembly, a declaration which is in perfect harmony with the teaching of the Bible itself, was met by strong opposition.

A counterstatement appeared in a document which, because of the city in which it was drawn up, has come to be known as the "Auburn Affirmation." The Affirmation was an attack not only upon the particular declaration just quoted, but also upon several other cardinal doctrines of the Christian faith. With respect to the statement of the Assembly concerning the Scriptures, the Affirmation maintained that "there is no assertion in the Scriptures that their writers were kept 'from error.' " "The doctrine of inerrancy, intended to enhance the authority of the Scriptures, in fact impairs their supreme authority for faith and life, and weakens the testimony of the church to the power of God unto salvation through Jesus Christ." "We hold that the General Assembly of 1923, in asserting that 'the Holy Spirit did so inspire, guide and move the writers of Holy Scripture as to keep them from error,' spoke without warrant of the Scriptures or of the Confession of Faith" (i. e., the Westminster Confession).[3]

Whether the General Assembly spoke without warrant of the Westminster Confession, the reader may judge for himself by consulting the Appendix of this book and reading the Confession. Whether the Assembly spoke without warrant of the Scriptures is likewise a matter that can easily be decided. That the Scriptures claim to be, and that Jesus Christ believed them to be, the infallible revelation of God is a matter beyond dispute. We today may not believe them to be infallible, but it was Jesus Christ who

3. Cf. "AN AFFIRMATION designed to safeguard the unity and liberty of the Presbyterian Church in the United States of America," Section 2.

proclaimed of these Holy Scriptures that they cannot be broken. "Heaven and earth shall pass away, but my words shall not pass away." The omniscient Son of the living God would never have placed the imprimatur of His approval upon the erroneous statements of the Auburn Affirmation.

To realize that the Auburn Affirmation cannot be regarded as a serious treatment of the subject, one need but read in the Bible the sad account of the arrest and betrayal of the Lord. And indeed, we have mentioned this Affirmation, not because of any intrinsic merit which it possesses, for it certainly possesses very little, but rather because of the great influence which it has exerted. In the light of what is said about the Scriptures in the Passion narratives, however, the Affirmation's statements sound very hollow and unconvincing.

It was while they were at the table just before the Savior instituted the Last Supper that He, in looking ahead to His death, spoke, "The Son of man indeed goeth, as it is written of him." Seated about Him at this table were the twelve, they who had left all and followed Him. They were His disciples, and yet, one from their midst would now betray Him. He knew that this would be, and He knew which disciple would be the betrayer. He knew, furthermore, that this giving of Himself over to death would be in accordance with what the Scriptures had already said. He would go, and the course of His betrayal would be in accordance with what had already been written. It was a betrayal previously determined. It must be thus, and could not be otherwise, for it had been written. That which had been written must be fulfilled. Scripture not infallible? Scripture not inerrant? Scripture subject to the errors that attend everything human? Modern man with his superficial view of religion may think it so, but on that dark night, when the eternal Son of God faced death for His own, the words loomed large: *as it is written*. It could not be otherwise.

When they had gone out and come to the Mount of Olives, the Lord again spoke, "All ye shall be offended because of me this night: for it is written, I will smite the shepherd, and the sheep shall be scattered" (Mark 14:27). To imagine the tragedy of the scene is almost impossible. On the slope of the Mount, the sky filled with the brightness of the stars — and how brightly they shine in the Palestinian sky! — the Lord is again with the small band of disciples. They were His disciples, but that very night they would flee; they would be offended in Him. Could not such a tragic situation be averted? Could not they show themselves to be stronger men? Could not they abide with him through the hours of His agony? Why must this sad course of events follow? Why? Simply because it had been written in the indefectible Scripture: "for it is written." The matter was determined; Christ could not swerve from His course. The disciples could not do otherwise but what they were about to do. Scripture had spoken. Our Lord must face death without the support of these His followers. But the Auburn Affirmation would have us believe that the Scriptures are not, and do not claim to be, infallible.

At the time of His arrest the Lord simply said, "I was daily with you in the temple teaching, and ye took me not: but the scriptures must be fulfilled" (Mark 14:49). We may well ask, Why must these Scriptures be fulfilled? The answer is that they are the Word of God. What they utter, according to our Lord, must in the very nature of the case come to fulfillment. There is no possible alternative. How obedient He is to these Scriptures! After rebuking the one that had struck the servant of the high priest, Christ made it abundantly clear that He believed He could then and there have more than twelve legions of angels. What an aid that would have been! With twelve legions of angels the Lord could easily have escaped from the hands of the band of men who had come to arrest Him. Would not that have been the course of wisdom? Yet, He would not take advantage of the opportunity. "But how then shall the scriptures be fulfilled, that thus it must be?" (Matthew 26:54). The Lord is more concerned that the Scriptures be fulfilled than that He escape from the hand of the enemy. These words are strange to one who does not share the Redeemer's high estimate of the Bible. If Christ's utterance does not give evidence that He believed the Scriptures to be infallible, we are at a loss to understand its meaning. "Thus it must be," it cannot conceivably be otherwise. There is no possibility of change. Scripture must be fulfilled.

The evangelist Matthew, in describing the answer which the Lord gave to those who had come out to take Him, simply says, "But all this was done, that the scriptures of the prophets might be fulfilled." (26:56). This is remarkable language. The disgraceful arrest of Him who was "holy, harmless and undefiled" took place in order that the Scriptures of the prophets might be fulfilled. It is well to pause and ponder the thought. Here is the explanation for the whole sad tragedy. Here is the heart of the matter, the reason why that blessed One was betrayed and arrested and condemned to an unjust death. It was done that the Scriptures might be fulfilled, and in fulfilling the Scriptures, the Savior brought life and salvation to all who were given Him by the Father before the foundation of the world. Throughout the sad account of the last days of the Lord, days which lead up to the Cross, there is interwoven that strange note, "the scriptures must be fulfilled." Over Jerusalem there lay a cloud. It was the hour of the powers of darkness. Wicked men lifted their hands against the Son of God. Satan was preparing to bruise the heel of the Seed of the woman, yet Satan was facing his own defeat. "Now is the judgment of this world: now shall the prince of this world be cast out."[4] Now was the Son of God ready to be lifted up and to draw all men unto Him. And the Scriptures were being fulfilled. One who reads the Passion narratives carefully will not be impressed with the assertion that the Scriptures do not claim to be infallible.

The Auburn Affirmation, we may conclude, was no friend to the true Scriptural teaching on inspiration; sometimes, however, even those who do embrace the doctrine from the heart for one reason or another make statements which tend to confuse and to obscure what the Bible makes so plain. In his remarkable work *Fundamental Christianity,* the late Francis L. Patton has some rather unfortunate things to say about inspiration. They are unfortunate because they are out of keeping with the high supernaturalism which characterizes, and which Dr. Patton intended to characterize, his work. It is on the whole a fine book, and the present writer received much encouragement from it when he was a student in college, troubled by the many charges that were leveled against orthodox Christianity. We can indeed be thankful to God for the much good that is found in this book. "Conceding now the inspiration of the Scripture," writes Dr. Patton, "you cannot on that account assume that it is errorless" (p. 163). It would seem at first blush that the author was in agreement with the Auburn Affirmation. If, however, by the

4. John 12:31.

word "inspiration" we are to accept Paul's definition, and Dr. Patton apparently does, it must surely follow that what is "God-breathed" is the very Word of God, and since it is the Word of God, it must, as we have sought to point out, be pure and free from error. If, in making this statement, Dr. Patton had reference to the copies of the Bible which we now possess, one could readily agree that these present copies are not free of error, but it is not perfectly clear that this is what he means. For our part, we regard his discussion of inspiration as unfortunate and as not taking into account the consequences which can be drawn from it.

Dr. Patton further beclouds the issue when he says, "The real question is whether the Bible is true, not whether it is inspired" (*op. cit.,* p. 147). At first hearing this declaration sounds Scriptural, but it will soon appear that it seeks to make an unwarranted disjunction. What right have we to make a separation between the truth and the inspiration of the Bible? It should be noted that the Bible itself claims to be inspired of God. Is the claim true? If it is true, the Bible is inspired, and so we see that the inspiration of the Bible and its truth go hand in hand. Inspiration, let us never forget, is for the purpose of securing accuracy. Unless we were convinced that the Bible reports accurately, we could not at all be sure of the truthfulness of what it says. "Must a book," asks Dr. Patton, "be inspired in order to be true?" (*op. cit.,* p. 147). To this we answer, "Of course not." There are countless books which are true and which are not inspired. The question, however, is really beside the point. There are many books that are uninspired and yet are true. These books, however, are not the Bible. They are of human origin and, let us say, eyewitness accounts of an historical happening, and what they relate is in accord with the facts. But these writings are not of Divine origin, nor do they claim to be; they deal with matters susceptible of scientific check which can be correctly reported.

Very different, however, is the case with the Bible. If the Bible is not inspired, it cannot be completely true. It is quite possible, of course, that in an uninspired Bible there may be certain statements that are true. There might be in an uninspired Bible an accurate account of the discovery of the empty tomb. That is, up to a point the account might be accurate. The *meaning* of the Resurrection, however, would not be something that the unaided human mind could of itself discover. For that revelation is needed, and this revelation must be given to man in such a way that it is not garbled. If the Bible is a revelation from God, then that Bible must accurately speak to us, else we cannot be sure of the truthfulness of anything that it says. How are we to determine the truthfulness of what the Bible says about creation, the fall of man, the Trinity, the Person of the Lord, the Atonement, the Resurrection, the future life, the Second Advent? These are not subjects that the mind of man without Divine revelation can discover. How do we know that the Bible speaks the truth on these matters? We know it because the Bible is trustworthy in all that it says. And we believe that the Bible is trustworthy in all that it says for the simple reason that it is the Word of God. To maintain that we may first assume the truthfulness of the Bible, and then turn to the question of its inspiration, as Dr. Patton wishes to do, is to deceive ourselves. It is to engage in a method of apologetics which, in effect, has given up the battle at the outset. It is God the Holy Spirit who causes us to see the marks of divinity in Holy Scripture, so that we may receive the Word of God written, as did the Thessalonians the Word of God spoken, "not as the word of men, but as it is in truth, the word of God, which effectually worketh also in you that believe" (1 Thessalonians 2:13b). When once the Spirit has opened our eyes, we believe the Scriptures to be Divine and we place our confidence in their statements, for the simple reason that those statements are found in the Scriptures.

What, however, shall we say with respect to those copies of the Bible that are now in existence? Is the English Bible from which we read our devotions and which we hear read in the worship service on the Lord's Day an inspired Bible? Are the Hebrew and Greek texts which are now in our possession inspired copies of Holy Scripture? It should be obvious that on the basis of the definition of inspiration which we have been using, such is not the case. If the Scripture is "God-breathed," it naturally follows that only the original is "God-breathed." If holy men of God spoke from God as they were borne by the Holy Spirit, then only what they spoke under the Spirit's bearing is inspired. It would certainly be unwarrantable to maintain that copies of what they spoke were also inspired, since these copies were not made as men were borne of the Spirit. They were therefore not

"God-breathed" as was the original. This fact, of course, is not only taught in Scripture, but has also been recognized by the Church. The Nicene Creed, for example, states that the Holy Spirit spake by the prophets. That means that the words which the prophets uttered were Spirit-indicted words. It does not mean that copies of those words were spoken by the Spirit. To come closer to the present day, we may note that the Westminster Confession, which gives such a grand survey of the Scriptural teaching, asserts that the Bible was "immediately inspired of God." This, of course, means that the Bible was inspired "without means"; inspiration is a work of the immediate power of God Himself, and since this is so, it is clear that the Westminster Confession considered as inspired Scripture only those documents which were original.

Nevertheless, despite these testimonies, there have been those who apparently think that the idea that only the original manuscripts of Scripture are inspired is a somewhat recent invention designed to avoid the difficulty caused by the presence of errors in the copies of the Bible which we now possess. In the nature of the case, however, if the Bible is actually "God-breathed," there must have been an original, and that original must have been free from error. Can it conceivably have been otherwise?

Those who oppose the doctrine of inerrancy sometimes assert that God evidently did not regard the preservation of this original as a matter of importance. He apparently was content for us to have imperfect copies of the Scripture. It is, of course, a fact which all admit, that the original copy of the Bible is not preserved. Is the loss, however, a great one? Are the copies of the Bible which are now in our possession so poor that from them we cannot learn the true Word of God? If that were the case, if the Bible that is now before us were so far removed from the original that we could not learn from it the will of God, then the situation would be tragic indeed. Then we could probably say nothing whatever about the original. We might think that it was without error, but we could not know. We would have no trustworthy Bible and we would be left to our own imaginations. Those, for example, who wish to learn something of the death of our Lord from the Talmud will find there only seriously garbled traditions. The truth has been so corrupted that they cannot place their confidence in what the Talmud has to say. So it would be with us if the copies of the Bible which are extant were hopelessly corrupt.

Are these copies, however, hopelessly corrupt? For our part, we are convinced that they are not. We believe that the Bible which we have is accurate and that it is a remarkably close approximation to the original manuscripts.

Suppose that a schoolteacher writes a letter to the President of the United States. To her great joy she receives a personal reply. It is a treasure which she must share with her pupils and so she dictates the letter to them. They are in the early days of their schooling, and spelling is not yet one of their strong points. In his copy of the letter Johnny has misspelled a few words. Mary has forgotten to cross her t's and to dot her i's. Billy has written one or two words twice, and Peter has omitted a word now and then. Nevertheless, despite all these flaws about thirty copies of the President's letter have been made. Unfortunately, the teacher misplaces the original and cannot find it. To her great sorrow it is gone. She does not have the copy which came directly from the President's pen; she must be content with those that the children have made.

Will anyone deny that she has the words of the President? Does she not have his message, in just those words in which he wrote it to her? True enough, there are some minor mistakes in the letters, but the teacher may engage in the science of textual criticism and correct them. She may correct the misspelled words, and she may write in those words which have been omitted and cross out those which are superfluous. Without any serious difficulty she may indeed restore the original.

It should be clear that errors are bound to appear in almost anything that is copied. If the reader will copy out five pages of his English Bible he will doubtless make the discovery, on reading over his work, that he has made some mistakes. This does not mean that there are mistakes in the Bible but merely that there are some mistakes of copying (copyist's errors, as they are called) in what the reader has written out.

Such is the case with the manuscripts of the Bible which are extant. They are remarkably close approximations to the original, and by means of the careful study of textual criticism it is more and more possible to approach that original. An example will make this fact clear. The Hebrew language, in which our present manuscripts of the Old Testament are written, consists solely of consonants, and to these consonants there are added signs to indicate the different vowel sounds. These signs are written both within, above and below the consonant. Hence it will easily be apparent how difficult it is to write with Hebrew characters. Nevertheless, despite this difficulty, the Hebrew manuscripts have been transmitted with remarkable accuracy. There are in Hebrew three basic short vowels, and these three vowels are written with different signs, depending upon the kind of syllable in which they are to appear. They follow the rules with an almost mathematical precision. When Hebrew words are compared for spelling with those of the other Semitic languages, there is quite an uncanny agreement. One cannot but exclaim, after having spent much time in a study of the Hebrew text — and, of course, the same is true of the Greek manuscripts of the New Testament — that these manuscripts have been preserved by the singular care and providence of God.

What is the nature of the difficulties that are found in our extant Biblical manuscripts? Dr. Charles Hodge, that staunch defender of the doctrine of plenary and verbal inspiration, has well remarked:

As to the former of these objections [*i.e.,* that the sacred writers contradict themselves, or one the other], it would require, not a volume, but volumes to discuss all the cases of alleged discrepancies. All that can be expected here is a few general remarks: (1.) These apparent discrepancies, although numerous, are for the most part trivial; relating in most cases to numbers or dates. (2.) The great majority of them are only apparent, and yield to careful examination. (3.) Many of them may fairly be ascribed to errors of transcribers. (4.) The marvel and the miracle is that there are so few of any real importance. Considering that the different books of the Bible were written not only by different authors, but by men of all degrees of culture, living in the course of fifteen hundred or two thousand years, it is altogether unaccountable that they should agree perfectly, on any other hypothesis than that the writers were under the guidance of the Spirit of God. In this respect, as in all others, the Bible stands alone. It is enough to impress any mind with awe, when it contemplates the Sacred Scriptures filled with the highest truths, speaking with authority in the name of God, and so miraculously free from the soiling touch of human fingers. The errors in matters of fact which skeptics search out bear no proportion to the whole.[5]

At this point we must inject a note of caution. It is perfectly true, and it would be the part of folly to deny it, that there are things in the Bible which we cannot fully understand. There are difficulties which we cannot completely solve. There are apparent contradictions in the manuscripts which we now possess, and there are men who seem to make it their business to discover such difficulties and then to declare in triumph that the Bible is not free from error. Hence, if at present we mention even one of these difficulties, we shall make it clear that we also recognize their presence. In 1 Kings 15:14, to take but one example, it is said with respect to Asa: "But the high places were not removed." In the parallel passage in 2 Chronicles 14:5, on the other hand, we read: "Also he took away out of all the cities of Judah the high places and the images." Here there seems to be a contradiction. One passage says that the high places were not taken away whereas the other says that they were. What shall we do? Shall we throw overboard the Biblical doctrine of inspiration and join in the popular hue and cry that the Bible contains errors? That is what many are doing, and if we were to follow that procedure, we should be in a large company. We could then get along very well with modern thought. There would be many seeming advantages. Would we, however, be doing the right thing? For our part, we want no such easy and cavalier solution on the problem as that.[6]

The question resolves itself to this. Are we to abandon the Scriptural doctrine of Divine inspiration because of a few difficulties in the way of its acceptance? That would certainly be a foolish thing to do.[7]

In every doctrine of revealed religion, including that of the inspiration of the Bible, there are difficulties, and they exist be-

5. Charles Hodge *Systematic Theology*, Vol. I, pp. 169, 170.

6. We shall have occasion later to discuss the question of the relationship between these two passages (see p. 123). For the present we wish to make it clear that there is no real contradiction at all.

7. In the doctrine of the Trinity there are things hard to understand, for we are finite and have limited knowledge and apprehension. Should we therefore reject this blessed teaching of the Scripture? There are likewise perplexing questions which arise in connection with what the Bible says of the Person of our Lord. Shall we for that reason turn our backs on Jesus Christ? How much there is in the Christian view of God that raises problems in our minds? Are we then to disbelieve in Him?

cause we are but finite creatures, unable to plumb the depths of those things which God has revealed. One thing, however, is surely clear; if there are points of obscurity in Christianity, those involved in any proposed substitutes are far greater, even incalculable. In our doctrine of inspiration we are faced with certain perplexities, and they are real. Let us grant that freely. Nevertheless, they seem almost trifling when compared with the tremendous problems which face those who do not accept the Scriptural doctrine. Those who do not receive the Biblical witness to itself must explain the Bible. How did it come to be? Whence came the heavenly doctrine that is found within its pages? What is its origin? These are some of the baffling questions which face those who reject the Scriptural witness to itself. And the sad fact is that most of those who reject its witness do not realize the nature of the problem before them. Modern treatises on inspiration, modern attempts to explain the Bible, despite their constant usage of orthodox terminology, often do not even begin to come to grips with the real matters involved.

There are, then, difficulties in the doctrines which the Scripture teaches. There is this point, however, which must be kept in mind: it is that we are not omniscient, and since we are but creatures, we have no warrant for thinking that we shall ever be omniscient. It should not surprise us, therefore, if there are matters in the Bible which we cannot understand.

As knowledge increases, many things in the Bible which once were considered obscure, have been clarified. A scholar of the last century, Hartmann, thought it questionable whether writing was known in Moses' day. Not until the period of the Judges, he believed, which was some time after Moses, did writing appear among the Hebrews. Consequently, Hartmann denied the Mosaic authorship of the first five books of Scripture, the Pentateuch. On the other hand, Jesus Christ had explicitly asserted that Moses had written of Him. If, however, there was no writing in Moses' day, obviously Moses did not write the Pentateuch, and Christ was plainly mistaken in what He had said.

It is an old objection, and one which even today is sometimes heard in ignorant attacks upon the Bible. However, it has lost its validity, because the discoveries of archaeology have proved beyond any shadow of a doubt that writing was known long before Moses' day. No educated person today would dream of declaring that, since the art of writing would have been unknown to him, Moses could not have written the Pentateuch.

This example is instructive and may serve as a warning. Difficulties in the Bible there are, and many of them we cannot now solve to our complete satisfaction; but that they are actual errors is another matter. There must always be kept in mind the limitations of human knowledge. Much that scholars of a previous day have pronounced to be in error is now acknowledged to be true. The archaeologist's spade has revolutionized many an opinion concerning statements of the Bible and attitudes toward the Bible.

In the nature of the case, then, inspiration extends only to the original manuscripts of Scripture. Since these manuscripts were inspired they were free from error. The originals are lost and we are today in possession only of copies, copies which contain textual errors and difficulties that no serious Christian can afford to ignore. These copies, however, do give the actual Word of God. No point of doctrine has been affected. The doctrine shines before us in all its purity. Why God was not pleased to preserve the original copies of the Bible, we do not know. Perhaps, in His infinite wisdom, He did not wish us to bow down to these manuscripts as unto images. Perhaps their preservation would have directed towards them veneration as relics and would have deflected one's attention from their message. One thing at least is clear. In His mysterious providence, God has preserved His Word. We do not have a Bible which is unreliable and glutted with error, but one that in most wondrous fashion presents the Word of God and the text of the original.

How good God has been to give us such a Bible! Whatever our need, here is the voice of the heavenly Father speaking to us. Nor must we search with great difficulty to discover this heavenly voice. Not merely here and there, not merely in some stray passage which we come upon after reading pages of error do we suddenly arrive at the Word of God. Rather, in its fullness and entirety this Word is before us. How rich and manifold it is! How well adapted to our every want and need! Gentle are its commands; tender its precepts; heavenly its doctrine. It is the Holy Bible, a "lamp unto our feet and a light unto our path."

The Human Writers of the Scriptures

"As light that passes through the colored glass of a cathedral window, we are told, is light from heaven, but is stained by the tints of the glass through which it passes; so any word of God which is passed through the mind and soul of a man must come out discolored by the personality through which it is given, and just to that degree ceases to be the pure word of God. But what if this personality has itself been formed by God into precisely the personality it is, for the express purpose of communicating to the word given through it just the coloring which it gives it? What if the colors of the stained-glass window have been designed by the architect for the express purpose of giving to the light that floods the cathedral precisely the tone and quality it receives from them? What if the word of God that comes to His people is framed by God into the word of God it is, precisely by means of the qualities of the men formed by Him for the purpose, through which it is given?"
BENJAMIN B. WARFIELD

3

The Human Writers of the Scriptures

There is one very important factor in the doctrine of inspiration which hitherto has been mentioned only in cursory fashion. That is the human side of the Scriptures. Peter stated expressly that "holy men who were borne along of the Holy Ghost spake." We have said little about these holy men whom God used in the composition of the Bible. We have simply sought to make it clear, since they themselves also emphasize this fact, that the Scriptures are from God. It is, we have contended, necessary to recognize the Divine origin of the Bible, and the implications of such recognition.

It is likewise necessary and important to do full justice to what the Bible has to say about its human side. This is today the more important because of the constant misrepresentations of this aspect of the doctrine. We are told, for example, that the human writers were mere pen holders whose hands moved under the direction of the Spirit. The historic doctrine is quite frequently parodied as being "static." The writers wrote as mere automata, so the parody runs, having received what was dictated to them and then placed it in writing. When modern authors proclaim, "We want no mechanical theory of inspiration," they give one the impression that they believe they are refuting an actual error. As a matter of fact, however, the idea of mechanical dictation is nothing more than a straw man. Recent conservative writers on the subject of inspiration have sought to do justice to the human side of Scripture; they have been far from advocating a mechanical dictation theory.

What shall we say about this word dictation in regard to the doctrine of inspiration? It was a word that Calvin, to take one example, did not hesitate to employ. "Whoever, then," he says, "wishes to profit in the Scriptures, let him, first of all, lay down this as a settled point, that the Law and the Prophets are not a doctrine delivered according to the will and pleasure of men, but dictated by the Holy Spirit."[1]   In speaking in such a vein, Calvin is simply following the thought of the Bible itself.   Paul, in writing to the Corinthians, did not hesitate to say, "Which things also we speak, not in the words which man's wisdom teacheth, but which the Holy Ghost teacheth; comparing spiritual things with spiritual" (1 Corinthians 2:13).   If we were to attempt to bring out more clearly the precise force of the Apostle's language, we might render, "in *words* taught of the Spirit."   Paul is saying as patently as he can that the words which he is employing are those which the Spirit has taught him, and this is precisely what Calvin also maintains.

At the same time, although the term dictation in itself is not objectionable and expresses forcefully the Divine origin of the words of the Bible, it is perhaps unwise to use the word today without some qualification.   A new connotation has come upon the term which it obviously did not have in the day of Calvin. When we speak of dictation, there immediately comes to mind the thought of the businessman dictating a letter to his stenographer, or the teacher dictating an exercise to her pupils.   In both these instances it does not make too great a difference who takes down the dictation.   One stenographer can probably do it as well as another, and if one is not available, another can easily be obtained.   Likewise, when the teacher dictates a passage to her class, the important thing is that the pupils take down precisely what has been dictated, and do not add to it or subtract from it.   The person of the stenographer or of the pupil is in reality a comparatively negligible factor.   Such, however, is not the situation with respect to the human writers of the Bible. True enough, the words which they employed were taught them by the Holy Spirit, but it is not the case that it makes no difference who wrote those words.   It is not true that Peter might just as well have written the Pauline epistles as the great Apostle himself.   It would serve the interests of clarity, therefore, if, in the discussion of this doctrine, we lay stress upon the fact that although the Bible teaches that its very words are from God, it most emphatically does not teach a mechanical dictation view of inspiration.

1. 2 Timothy 3:16, translated by William Pringle.

Men like Turretine, Calvin and others who have written on this subject have been as eager to do justice to the human side of the Bible as have some of the modern rejectors of the Biblical doctrine.   It is a sad thing that scholarly men of our day constantly erect a straw man and seek to attack it instead of coming to grips with the Scriptural teaching itself.   Those who believe the Bible and who wish to do justice to its teaching are as concerned as anyone to refute the notion that inspiration was a mechanical kind of dictation, that the human writers were mere automata whose personalities were entirely suspended in the writing of the books of the Bible.

Let us then proceed to notice in more detail the emphasis which the Bible places upon these human writers.   "How then," we read, "doth David in spirit call him Lord?" (Matthew 22: 43).   It is David who calls the Messiah Lord.   And there are particular conditions under which he does this.   It is while he is in the Spirit that he so speaks.   The implication is that there are also times when David is not in the Spirit, when, in other words, he is not inspired.   When David spoke of the Messiah as Lord, however, he did so being in the Spirit.   David, therefore, is the human author of the utterance; it is his, and it is as a conscious responsible human being that he speaks.   At the same time, the conditions under which the Psalmist spoke were not the normal conditions of everyday life; he spoke not as a normal man, but rather under peculiar circumstances; David was in the Spirit.

Of particular interest is the statement, "For David himself said by the Holy Ghost" (Mark 12:36).   Very strong is the emphasis that it was the man David who spoke.   This emphasis receives additional confirmation and strength from the passage, "And David himself saith in the book of Psalms" (Luke 20: 42).   Of unusual relevancy is this verse because it attributes the authorship of certain words to the man David.   In the place of saying that it was in the Spirit that he spoke, it substitutes the phrase "in the book of Psalms."

In the words addressed to God "who by the mouth of thy servant David hast said, Why did the heathen rage and the people imagine vain things?" a passage from the second Psalm is attributed to David.   It is God who uttered these words; they find their origin in Him; they are His; He, and He alone, is their author. Nevertheless, He spoke them by the mouth of His servant David. David spoke, but God spoke through him. Similar is the statement to the effect that the Lord received the name Jesus in fulfillment of the words which were "spoken of the Lord by the prophet" (Matthew 1:22). The tender and mysterious prophecy of the Virgin was of Divine origin, but God spoke it through the mouth of the prophet.

In referring to the passage about the burning bush which He says is in the "book of Moses," Christ quotes, "God spake unto him, saying . . . " (Mark 12:26). The words are regarded by Christ as those which God Himself has spoken, but they are to be found in a book written by the man Moses. In another place, however, no reference is made to the human author other than the question "have ye not read?" which implies that the words uttered by God are nevertheless to be found in a book where they can be read (cf. Matthew 22:32). In a similar type of statement the Apostle Paul makes reference to the Old Testament, "Well spake the Holy Ghost by Esaias the prophet unto our fathers, saying . . . " (Acts 28:25, 26a). Paul would here make it clear that the Holy Spirit spoke, yet at the same time it was through the mouth of the individual Isaiah that He gave His utterance. The prophet was the human author of the message, yet the one who was speaking through Isaiah was none other than the Spirit of God Himself.

A careful consideration of the above passages should make it clear that God, in revealing His Word, spoke through the instrumentality of men. In the first place, they were holy men; men who knew and loved their God. This does not mean at all that they were not sinful men; they were sinful, sometimes great sinners. David, for example, had committed sins which few, if any, men would forgive, but David, nevertheless, was one through whom the Spirit spoke. The writers of the Bible were indeed sinners, but they were men who, despite their sins, loved God and were used of Him in the composition of Scripture.

It would be most unjust to the data of Scripture to maintain that God merely looked about to see if here and there He could find a man through whom He might speak to the world. There is nothing in the Bible to support or to sustain this idea; in fact, everything teaches the very opposite. Did it matter, we may ask, through whom the Divine message was spoken? According

to the Bible it mattered very greatly. In the first verse of Amos'
rugged prophecy we read, "The words of Amos . . . which he saw."
Only nine short chapters, yet from them we learn something of
the man who wrote them. How different they are from the
quiet tenderness of Hosea! How unsuited was Amos to have
undergone the sad experiences of a Hosea! At the same time,
different as each was from the other, each was clearly conscious
of speaking forth the words of God.

The same is true when we turn to the pages of the New
Testament. Do not the human writers of the New Testament
also differ greatly one from another? It would seem that God
had chosen specific men to write specific portions of His Word.
And such was indeed the case. Not only, however, did the
Lord select certain men to write certain portions of His Word
but, more than that, they were used as real men. Their
personalities were not held in abeyance; their talents were not
obscured; they were not somehow placed in a state of suspended
animation. Rather, God used them as they were. All their
gifts of training and native talent God called into play.

The matter may be very clearly illustrated by the case of the
Apostle Paul. God very obviously did not look about to discover
if there were somewhere on the face of the earth a man who
might be used in the composition of those writings which we now
call the Pauline Epistles. There was only one man that could
have written those Epistles, and that man was the Apostle himself.
The Apostle, however, required training and preparation before
he could commit to writing the glorious epistles which now bear
his name. His very birth and upbringing in the city of Tarsus
were of importance. The instruction which he received at the
feet of Gamaliel and his indoctrination into the tenets of the
Pharisees served as a background which stood him in good
stead throughout the remainder of his life. Not the least of
his talents was his ability to use the Greek language both in
speaking and preaching. After his conversion he spent three
years in Arabia, years, we may well suppose, in which he engaged
in study and meditation.

Did all this, however, occur simply through chance? Not at all;
it was God who was at work in the events of Paul's life, shaping
him so that he would be precisely the man whom God wanted
and whom He needed to write the great epistles. It was a provi-

dential preparation; a schooling and training conducted at the hands of God Himself through the ordinary course of His providential working.

Similar was the case with Moses. Here again we note the long years of preparation. In childhood and youth Moses learned of the afflictions of his people in Egypt. He knew well the Egyptian mind, and how to deal with the taskmaster. Then came the period of training in the desert, where, in the stillness of the wasteland, he might mediate and reflect. Thus, through this time, followed by his own participation in the events of the Exodus, Moses came to the place where he was prepared for the task of writing the first five books of the Bible. It is clear that these books represent a unified plan and that they are the work of a great mind. Only a mind such as that of Moses could have composed them. And for this work of writing, Moses, in the providence of God, had been prepared and equipped. How graciously did the Lord deal with His recalcitrant and stubborn servant! How wondrously He led the man on, step by step, until Moses was ready to write.

Very wondrous was God's providential preparation and equipment of those men whom He had appointed to be the human instruments in the writing of the Scripture. Thus He prepared and raised up an Isaiah, a Jeremiah, a John, and a Paul. His work of providence and His special work of inspiration should be regarded as complementing one another. Those through whom the Spirit desired to give the Scriptures were individuals who had been equipped for the task in the providence of God. When, therefore, the Spirit bore a holy man of old (2 Peter 1:21) it was not *any* man who happened to be on the scene, but rather, just *that* holy man whom God, through years of training, had prepared to speak and to write precisely that portion of the Scripture which He desired to have him write.

The question may very well be raised how the Spirit actually controlled the writers of Scripture so that they wrote expressly what He desired and yet at the same time were responsible individuals whose personalities were not stifled. How, for example, could the prophet write, "The words of Amos . . . which he saw?" Does not this verse contain a glaring contradiction? If the words are truly those of Amos, how could they at the same time be those which had found their origin in God? If

God was the Author, how could Amos also be regarded as an author?

Legitimate as such questions are, however, they cannot be fully answered. God has not seen fit to reveal to us the mode by which He communicated His Word to His servants, placing that word in their mouths and "carrying" them until the Word was accurately committed to writing. We have come, in other words, into an area of mystery. There is much about this precious Scriptural doctrine which God has not revealed. The Scripture is silent as to the mode which God employed to preserve His Word from error. In this as in so many doctrines of the Bible there is mystery. It is of course, to be expected that such would be the case. We are but men and our understanding is at best limited and finite. We can only know as a created being knows. God, on the other hand, is the One who in His understanding is infinite. We cannot probe into His dealings in such a way as to obtain full and comprehensive knowledge thereof. He is not such a One as can be brought down and placed under the scrutiny of the microscope of the human mind.

In the doctrine of the Trinity likewise there is mystery. He who thinks that he can remove that mystery and fully understand the doctrine deceives no one but himself. This deep truth must be received in faith, and the believing heart rejoices simply because God has revealed this mystery in His Word. How wondrous is this revelation which God has given of Himself! How great, we are compelled to say, is our Holy God! When the mind delights itself in the thought that He is the one living and true God, it finds itself suddenly brought face to face with the fact that He is also Triune. Likewise, when it contemplates the Father, the Son, and the Holy Spirit, it is worshipping Him beside whom there is no other. The One reminds us of the Three, and the Three bring us to the One. Before Him, the one God in three Persons, we bow in adoration. We praise Him, we worship Him, we extol His matchless Name, we meditate upon His infinite attributes and perfections. Never, however, can we remove the mystery that adheres to the revelation which He has given of Himself as Triune.

It is the same with the doctrine of inspiration. When we have set forth all that the Scripture has to say, we can go no further. It may well be that questions arise in our minds, but they are questions which, at present at least, we cannot answer. Our duty is to believe all that God has revealed and to bow in humble acceptance of the truth which He has given. Scripture has spoken; it has permitted us to learn much concerning its inspiration. It has not, however, told us all. We may then freely acknowledge that there are difficulties in the Scriptural position, and also that there are questions which we cannot at present answer. Our portion is to be believers. God has spoken. Let us hear His voice, and beyond that let us not seek to go.

At this point, however, it is necessary to consider in some detail and with some care an objection to the above teaching which is frequently being voiced in our day. When the Word of God came through human personality, it is very often maintained, the Word was obscured to some extent. God was limited in His choice of available instruments through whom His Word might come to us, and therefore He did the best that He could with the personalities and means that were at His disposal. Consequently, the character of the revelation which we have depends not only upon God but also upon the human media through which it came.

Since the Word did come through human agents and instrumentality, it is claimed, there must adhere to it some of the error and imperfection which is found in everything human. It is just like plunging one's arm into muddy water: in withdrawing the arm some of the mud will adhere to it; or it is like rays of sunlight which are less bright when shining through a dirty window than a clear one.

The character of the Divine revelation, therefore, according to this view, depends not only on God, but also on those media through which that revelation came. If those media were fallible, then the revelation itself partook of that fallibility. God Himself was limited by the means at hand. He could communicate Himself and His truth to men only in so far as men themselves were spiritually mature to receive His revelation. Men with spiritual failings could mar and prevent that revelation from coming to mankind.

Those, who insist that the Word of God in coming through human instruments has itself been affected and has acquired imperfections, for the most part believe that they can themselves detect these imperfections. Generally they wish to limit the errors and flaws which have supposedly crept into the Word of

God to minor matters of fact or history. Sometimes a comparsion is made with the incarnation of the Lord. The Word which became incarnate was subject to all the limitations and hardships of human life, it is sometimes maintained, and likewise the embodiment of the spoken Word of God in the history of a people such as the Hebrews involved all the crudities and the errors that such a people would probably make.

One need not look far today for a statement of this position. It is to be found in much that is written on the subject. Whenever someone writes on the Bible, he seems to feel the necessity of pointing out that it contains errors, and that these errors are a result of the human agents who were employed in the writing down of Scripture. It seems to be taken for granted that error must in the nature of the case be found in whatever is written by human hands.

As we hear this objection to the Scriptural teaching, there are several questions which arise. In the first place, we would ask, What kind of a God is He who cannot reveal to the world a message that is free from error? Surely, He must be limited and restricted indeed! Those of us who from time to time engage in a bit of writing are happy to have a stenographer who types our work accurately. If we discover that the stenographer is constantly making mistakes in her typing, and these mistakes are of so serious a nature that our work is actually obscured and marred thereby, we shall probably change stenographers. God, however, if the position which we are now considering is correct, cannot even do this. God is far more limited than are we mortals. We have the ability of hiring someone who will do our work for us as we desire it done; God, on the other hand, cannot even do that. When God would speak to mankind in writing, He cannot get His message across without having it cluttered up with irritating errors.

It is well to consider this question carefully. God, we are being told, had to use the means at His disposal. Those means were human beings. Therefore, when God revealed His Word, that Word, in passing through the media of human writers, acquired the characteristics of those writers, including their error, their ignorance, their crudities. Well may we exclaim at the poverty and weakness of such a God! If indeed man can thus thwart Him, it is pertinent to ask, Is He really worth knowing after all?

One thing, however, is clear. Such a God, limited as He is by the human agents through whom He gives His Word, is not the God of the Bible. He may very well serve as the god of modern theology, but he is not the Creator of heaven and earth, the one true eternal God. If it were really true — and thank God that it is not — that the Father in heaven were restricted in His power by man and were limited in His ability to reveal His Word, we could then be sure that at the best he was only a finite being like ourselves. He might be more powerful than we, yet, since we can clutter up His revelation with our error, even that assumption is questionable. Since He is limited by His creatures, such a God is no God at all.

Very different is the God of whom Scripture speaks. This God, whom the Christian worships as the Creator, is One who doeth according to His will, "and none can stay his hand, or say unto him, What doest thou?" (Daniel 4:35b). This God, in whom are hid all the treasures of wisdom and knowledge, is One who can take up and bear the writers of Scripture so that what they have written is exactly what He desired to have written. He is One who in His infinite power can use as His agents and instruments fallible human beings, who can bring into His employ all the gifts, talents, and characteristics of those human beings, and yet can cause them to pen His own Word, and keep that Word utterly separate and distinct from their own sinful nature and the consequent imperfections which are the result of that nature.

There is, however, another point which must be raised in this connection. Those who believe that there are errors in the Bible, as we have seen, seek to account for the presence of these supposed errors upon the assumption that their origin is to be attributed to the human writers. Since human authors are fallible, they reason, the Scripture itself must therefore partake of fallibility. If this is actually the case, it follows that not merely part of Scripture partakes of fallibility, but all. Whatever is the Word of God has passed through human instruments. Whatever passes through human instruments, so this argument runs, must therefore partake of fallibility. All Scripture has passed through human instrumentality; consequently, all Scripture has become fallible. There is no escape from this position. It will not do to say that fallibility has attached itself only to statements of historical and geographical fact. To do that would be to guilty of gross inconsistency. Like a leach that cannot be removed, human fallibility attaches itself to all Scripture without exception. Whatever is the Word of God is also fallible; no part is free from error and imperfection.

It may very well be that this is not what modern writers believe but, be that as it may, it is the logical conclusion of their position, and it is well to note what that conclusion is. God grant that those who are so insistent that humanity must give to the Divine Word the character of fallibility, would realize what is involved in their claim. They have not solved any difficulties; rather they have created incalculably difficult questions and problems.

An example will reveal how dire are the consequences of this position. When we are called to a home where death has come, how inadequate we are. At such a time how trite and unsatisfactory are mere words of ours! How the heart grieves at the thoughtlessness and cruelty of those who have nothing more to offer than mere banality and platitude. Cold and unthinking they are indeed! Can we on the other hand, offer anything of greater comfort? We turn to the pages of the Bible and read, "I am the resurrection, and the life: he that believeth in me, though he were dead, yet shall he live: and whosoever liveth and believeth in me shall never die." (John 11:25,26). "Is that true?" asks the one in sorrow. "Is Jesus really the One who has taken my loved one to be with Him?" "Well," we reply, "we believe that it is true. Of course, this Word of God, like everything else in the Bible is tinged with fallibility. Like the remainder of Scripture it also has imperfection and error."

To speak in that vein would be mockery. It would offer no comfort to the soul who is in sorrow. Yet, how else could one answer? To the one in need there would be nothing better to say, since all Scripture is fallible. We could never be sure as to what it said about God, nor could we, for that matter, have any assurance that its prescriptions for our conduct upon this earth were free from error. Serious and tragic in the extreme are the consequences of adopting this modern error. We can only be thankful that its adherents are themselves inconsistent in their practice. For our part, we want nothing to do with a position which logically can lead to such results. Thank God that when it came through human agents His blessed Word was not coated with fallibility. Those agents did not control or circumscribe Him; they did not affect His Word, but rather, under His sovereign Spirit, were rendered the willing instruments to carry out what He wished accomplished.

Futhermore, if fallible human writers have given to us a Bible that is fallible, how are we ourselves, who most certainly are fallible, to detect in the Bible what is error and what is not? To this the answer is given that with the increase in knowledge, we can easily detect errors which the ancient writers made. They had crude ideas of geography and history, it is said, but we today have much greater knowledge. Where they went astray, we can furnish a check and correct their errors. To speak this way, however, is not to settle the issue at all. What about those parts of the Bible upon which we cannot check? How are we to discern what in those parts is error and what is not? How are we to separate the fallible from the inerrant?

To take an example, the Bible speaks of Palestine and Jerusalem. We may today travel to Palestine and Jerusalem, and thus we have a check. When the Bible mentioned these places, it was telling us the truth; such places do exist. The Bible also mentions certain customs of antiquity. Abraham, for example, took his concubine, Hagar, and from her a son was born. Archaeology has made it perfectly clear that this custom was as a matter of fact practiced in Abraham's day. Well and good, but what about those parts of the Bible upon which we cannot check? How shall we evaluate the God of Scripture? How do we know whether we can separate the wheat from the chaff in the Biblical teaching about God? The answer is that we simply cannot do so. If all Scripture is fallible, then all that Scripture says about God is fallible, and we have no way of detecting what is and what is not in accord with fact. We ourselves are likely to err. How then can we judge the Scripture? Judge the Scripture we cannot; we are left in a hopeless scepticism. It will not do to say that modern knowledge has made it possible to separate the wheat and the chaff in the Bible. It has done nothing of the kind. We are ourselves like the authors of Scripture and the only thing that can help us in an infallible Word from God. Since, however, God cannot give us an infallible Word, there is nothing that we can do. Here is the Bible, shot full of error, and we must make the best of it. Disastrous indeed is this conclusion. Disastrous as it is, however, it is the end at which we are bound to arrive if we adopt the view which we are now seeking to answer.

This brings us to another point which must be raised in opposition to the assertion that human fallibility precludes infallibility in the Scripture. It is that the advocates of this position are for the most part extremely inconsistent. Certain parts of the Bible, they tell us, are pure and true. For example, the injunction to love one's enemies is acceptable to modern theologians. There, certainly, is the Word of God. That we are to obey. In saying this, however, modern theology is in effect admitting the very case which it wishes to deny. In admitting that there is even one bit of Scripture that is the pure and infallible and trustworthy Word of God, the modern theologian is tacitly acknowledging that at least some of the Word of God has come through the medium of fallible human writers without itself becoming fallible. It was protected from error so that we today might regard it as trustworthy. It is the truth free from error; our duty in fact is to love our enemies. If, however, even a portion of the Word may have been transmitted through fallible human channels without error, why may not all have been so transmitted? To acknowledge that some may be preserved from error is to give the case away. If some may thus have been kept from imperfection, without doubt all may likewise have been so kept. Moreover, if it is true that humanity, because it is necessarily fallible, may thwart the revelation of God, so that that revelation comes to us marred, what is to be said about Christ? Jesus Christ was a true man, and if manhood necessarily involves fallibility, Jesus Christ was fallible. If humanity, simply because it is humanity, is characterized by error and imperfection, Jesus Christ is not our Savior.

From these consequences we cannot flee. We are not warranted in making an exception of the Person of our Lord, and if we have once adopted the position that the human necessarily entails imperfection, let us be consistent and admit that Christ also is imperfect. It is a sad conclusion to draw; sad as it is, however, it is one that we must draw if the premise which we have adopted is correct. If our Lord, in His human nature, was necessarily subject to fallibility, then, of course, He was not what He claimed to be; He was subject to sin. There is no escape from this conclusion, none whatever. If Jesus Christ was a sinner (for fallibility is the consequence of sin) we might as well face the fact that He is not, nor could He be, our Savior. As a matter of fact, however, this vicious premise is not correct. The God whom we worship is powerful enough to convey His revelation through human channels and to do so in such a manner that His revelation does not acquire the imperfections that adhere to sinful humanity. In the Person of His Son, He is able to take to Himself a true human nature which is not touched with sin. Although error and imperfection are found in sinful human nature they are not at all necessary characteristics of human nature as such.

Is it not, the charge is sometimes made, an illogical position to adopt, this position which asserts that God can give an infallible revelation through fallible channels? Man is fallible; man is the only instrument available to God through which this revelation can come. Simple logic demands that said revelation must then partake of fallibility. Thus the view for which we are contending is dismissed as "illogical."

But is this view, as a matter of fact, illogical? The charge, grave as it is, is based upon the premise that man is capable of qualifying or affecting the revelation which God gives through him. Is this premise, however, warranted by the facts? Can man, in truth, control God's revelation? Is God the Revealer subject to man? According to the Bible this premise is utterly and completely false. According to the Bible God has created man in His own image. Man therefore is subject to God and dependent upon Him. God, on the other hand, is utterly independent of man, and self-sufficient unto Himself. "For of him, and through him, and to him, are all things" (Romans 11:36a).

Man is entirely subject to the law of God. As created by God, Adam, although finite, was neverthless not fallible. Adam, however, sinned, and all mankind sinned in him and fell with him. Man, therefore, is a sinful creature and as a sinner is subject to error. God, since He is the omnipotent Creator, has absolute control over those whom He has created. In His good pleasure, which is a sovereign good pleasure, He may bear the human writers of the Bible, so controlling them, yet preserving intact their personalities, that they can write His revelation exactly as He wishes. If once we think rightly about God, other matters will appear in their proper perspective. Once we realize that God is in control of the situation, it will become clear that the Biblical doctrine of inspiration, mysterious as it may be, is nevertheless not illogical.

Thus we come to that which is basic in modern thought. In all this talk of the Word of God we would ask the question, What is it that modern theologians have in mind when they are speaking of the Word of God? Who is this God in whose Word they are so interested? It is difficult to identify Him. He seems to be a creation in the image of man, and not the Triune God who has spoken in the Bible. The issue involved is in reality that of theism. Who is our God? Are we followers of the King, or have we bowed the knee to Baal? Unless first we become as little children and acknowledge the true God in all our ways, we shall not speak profitably on the subject of that Word which has been breathed forth from His mouth. The modern god, created by man, lives and rules in the City of Destruction. From him and from his reign, however, we have been delivered by the God of Holy Scripture.

It should be clear from the discussion so far that the Bible is not to be regarded as a "joint" product, the combined effort of God and man. Surely the Bible itself does not make such a claim. There were indeed human writers of the Scripture, but they are not to be considered as co-authors with God. It is not that God contributed certain parts of the Scriptures, and men supplemented these, and it most certainly is not the case that men contributed the greater portion of Scripture to have it supplemented by God. Nor did God and man take counsel together as to what should be included in the Scripture. God did not consult man as to what should be written. The Bible is truly the Word of God. He is the final and the ultimate Author; the Bible comes from God. Without Him there could have been no Bible. Without men, however, there could have been a Bible. God could have given us His Word in some other manner than that which He actually did choose. As a matter of fact, He did choose to speak through inspired men but He was not compelled to do so. In no sense was He limited. That he employed human writers was an act of grace, and the heart of faith will ever adore and revere Him that He so honored the human race as to employ lost sinners as writers of His pure and holy Word. While the human authors were true authors, nevertheless they were not the originators of the words and the thoughts that are found in the Bible. They were holy men indeed, but they were holy men who were borne by the Spirit.

Were these human writers infallible, even when they were not borne by the Spirit? Obviously the Bible does not teach that this was so. They were men of their own day. No doubt their own views of astronomy, for example, were not one whit more advanced than those of their contemporaries. On the other hand, when they were the penmen of the Spirit of God, they were expressing the words of God. The thoughts which they were penning had been revealed to them by God; they were placed in their minds by the Spirit Himself. It therefore will not do to assert that they did not have a knowledge of modern astronomy and hence could not have written an account of the creation that was scientifically accurate. If Moses had depended only upon the wisdom of the Egyptians, he would have produced a rather clumsy account of Creation. If he had relied alone upon the thoughts and opinions of his own heart, he would have composed a first chapter of Genesis that for crudity and error might have equaled the writings of Babylonia. Moses, however, in writing the first chapter of Genesis was not drawing upon his own ideas and thoughts. He was giving expression to thoughts which he had learned by revelation of God. He was an inspired penman. What went on in his own mind as he wrote we can never tell, but he acted as a conscious, responsible human being. Without doubt he must have realized that he was writing far more deeply than he himself could fathom. However he composed, however he gathered his material and set it down in writing, whether he wrote and crossed out and polished, we do not know. Nevertheless he worked, and what was finally set down as the completed product was just what the God of Truth desired to have written down; it was the Word of God.

At other times, however, to continue our use of Moses as an illustration, what Moses may have said and done, and what he may have written down, was no more free from error, no more infallible, than any other purely human word or composition. Not at all times was he kept from error, but only when he served as the penman to write down the Divine oracles. The same is true of the other writers of the Bible. Hence, the folly of Reimarus' objection that the moral character of some of the human writers would preclude them from being the recipients of Divine revelation. In giving the Bible to mankind God did not make use of men who were free from sin. David was a sinful man, and yet through him God gave many of the Psalms. Moses was a murderer. Paul persecuted the Church of God. Yet God selected them to be His instruments of inspiration. That they were thus chosen in no sense condones or excuses their sins. If anything, it would seem to heighten their guilt. What they wrote, however, and what they said when they were not borne by the Spirit was not inspired; it was as subject to error as the utterances of anyone else. Only when borne of the Spirit were the authors infallible in what they wrote.

In the book of 2 Samuel there is recorded a letter which David wrote to his general Joab (11:15). When David penned this letter he was doing a despicable thing. It is a tragedy indeed that the man who had composed many of the Psalms should also have stand out against him the words of this letter: "Set ye Uriah in the forefront of the hottest battle, and retire ye from him, that he may be smitten, and die." Those words will ever stand to blacken the record of David. An evil thing indeed was the writing of this letter. Was David inspired when he wrote it? Most obviously he was not. It was something that was composed from his evil heart; this was the stratagem which he devised to cover up his own sin by removing the innocent Uriah from the scene. David did not write this letter under the impulsion of the Spirit of God.

Inspiration naturally extends only to that which the writers produced when they were under the impulsion of God's Spirit. How then, it may be asked, do we find a copy of this letter in the Sacred Scriptures? The answer must be that the writer of the book of Samuel was inspired as he recorded the letter. It was the intention of God to include this letter in the Scripture, and the author of Samuel, being borne of the Spirit, has given an accurate copy thereof. We have, in other words, a correct copy of the words which David wrote. To draw from this the conclusion that the letter had the approval of God upon its contents would be unwarranted indeed. In writing this letter David did an evil thing, and it was the will of God that we today should know of this evil thing; for that reason the letter was included in the Scripture. The writer has given an accurate copy of the letter, for inspiration secures accuracy. Inspiration does not, however, involve Divine approval of the contents of all that is inspired.

We may then say with assurance that the writers of the Bible were inspired only when they were actually engaged in composing the books of Scripture. Apart from that they were men of their times, and erred just as other men err. They were sinful human beings, and inspiration did not by some magical process keep them from error. It was only when the Spirit mysteriously came upon them as they wrote down His Word that they were in His power and so kept from making in their writings errors such as adhere to everything merely human.

Very remarkable is this doctrine of inspiration! It is remarkable above all because it is taught in the Bible itself. The Bible is God's Word, we may say, but the Bible is also the work of men. They were not, however, men who wrote under their own power and under ordinary circumstances. Great indeed was the honor which had been placed upon them. There were times when they were lifted from the ordinary level of human experience. There were times when what they set down in writing was free from error. There were times when they were under the compulsion of the Spirit of God. There were times when these chosen few of the human race were the writers of Scripture.

Some Reflections Upon Inspiration

4

Some Reflections Upon Inspiration

In what has been written thus far we have tried to set forth clearly and simply what the Bible itself has to say about its inspiration. There can be little serious disagreement over whether the Bible actually does teach verbal inspiration. The doctrine expounded in the preceding pages is nothing more than a digest of what Scripture itself teaches. Objection to the doctrine, therefore, is in reality objection to the Scriptures. This is not surprising, since men today do not wish to be guided by the Scriptures in their thinking. They may agree, and they probably will, that we have correctly expounded the Scriptural doctrine, but they protest against that doctrine. Many are the objections which they raise, and it becomes necessary at this point to face some of them. Such a procedure will by no means be without profit, for not only will it enable us to give an answer to many of the current criticisms of the Scriptural doctrine of inspiration but it will also enable us to understand that doctrine more clearly. To these objections, then, let us direct our thought.

One of the best ways to attack something is to demonstrate that it is unimportant, and that is precisely what some writers attempt to accomplish with respect to the Biblical doctrine of verbal inspiration. The originals of Scripture are lost, so it is argued, and we cannot completely reconstruct them. Therefore, these originals must have been unimportant. Evidently God did not think that it was necessary for us to have them. If a man wishes to do scholarly work on the Bible, he must use the Greek and the Hebrew texts which are available to him. He cannot obtain the original, and must be content with the texts at hand. More than that, the plain man who turns to the Bible for his devotional study must be content with a Bible in his own vernacular. He is removed from the original even a step further. Consequently, all this talk about an inspired and errorless original text is really beside the point. Futhermore, even if there were errors in the original, this would not hinder us from receiving a blessing from the Bible; and we would be foolish indeed if we were to maintain that, unless the original were free of error, we could receive no blessing from the Bible.

But is the doctrine of an errorless autographa of Scripture actually so unimportant after all? A little reflection, we think, will make it clear that such is not at all the case. Let us suppose that the Scriptures actually were given to us by a special revelation of God. In making this supposition we realize full well that we are going counter to the main stream of current thought. Grant, however that such is the case. If the Scriptures are indeed breathed forth from the mouth of God, does it matter whether they contain in them statements which are contrary to fact? To ask the question in this fashion is, of course, to answer it. It matters tremendously, for the veracity of God Himself is at stake.

How disturbing is the annoyance of tiny inaccuracies! Upon receiving a letter filled with trifling errors and misspelled words, we are displeased and annoyed; the letter casts reflection upon its writer. In fact, to send such a letter is to do a most discourteous thing. In writing a letter we want to spell our words correctly; also, for the sake of our own reputation, if for nothing else, we want to get our facts straight. If a person does not even take the trouble to do this he may justly be considered a boor or an ignoramus. It is difficult to maintain a high respect for someone who, in writing letters to us, is consistently careless. We do, of course, receive letters from people who are poorly educated, and their errors, even though regrettable, we are willing to pardon. When, however, an educated person writes, and permits minor inaccuracies to characterize his writing, we are disappointed in him and our respect for him is affected by it.

God has revealed to us His Word. What are we to think of Him if this Word is glutted with little annoying inaccuracies? Why could not the omnipotent and omniscient God have taken the trouble to give us a Word that was free from error? Was it not a somewhat discourteous thing for Him to have breathed forth from His mouth a message filled with mistakes? Of course, it was discourteous; it was down-right rude and insulting. The present writer finds it difficult to have much respect for such a God. Does He expect us to worship Him? What kind of a God is He if He has given such an untrustworthy Word to mankind? And this brings us to the heart of the matter. The Scriptures claim to be breathed forth from His mouth; if they partake of error, must not He Himself also partake thereof?

He, of course, tells us that His Word is pure. If there are mistakes in that Word, however, we know better; it is not pure. He tells us that His judgments are righteous, but we know better; as a matter of fact, His judgments are mixed with error. He declares that His law is the truth. His law contains the truth, let us grant Him that, but we know that it contains error. If the autographa of Scripture are marred by flecks of mistake, God simply has not told us the truth concerning His Word. To assume that He could breathe forth a Word that contained mistakes is to say, in effect, that God Himself can make mistakes. We must maintain that the original of Scripture is infallible for the simple reason that it came to us directly from God Himself.

It does not follow from this that only an errorless text can be of devotional benefit to Christians, nor do those who believe in the inerrancy of Scripture maintain such a position. Thousands have been brought to a knowledge of the truth and have come to know Him whom to know aright is life eternal, and they have had no inerrant text. When one reads some of the arguments that have been raised in opposition to the doctrine of inspiration, one very often receives the impression that there is a good bit of tilting at windmills. Of course an inerrant text is not necessary for the devotional life. There are those who through the King James Version have come to know Christ and have grown in grace daily, yet the King James Version is not inerrant.

Be this as it may, however, the serious student of the Bible will desire to approximate the original in so far as that is possible. We may revert to the illustration of the teacher who had received a letter from the President. When the original was destroyed (shall we say that it is unimportant whether the President of the United States made minor mistakes in his letter?), the teacher had only the copies which the pupils had made. As a result of the ignorance of the children who did the copying, these became imperfect copies. The teacher might have remained satisfied with these imperfect copies. She, however, had great respect for her President. Consequently, she endeavored to the best of her ability to correct each copy so that the exact wording of the original might be restored.

It would be foolish to maintain that, because they contained mistakes, the copies were therefore without any value. Anyone could read those copies and learn what the President had written. To obtain the President's message, all one had to do was to read a copy of his letter. So it is with the Bible. The copies of Scripture which are now extant are remarkably accurate, and hence, like the original, they are "profitable for doctrine, for reproof, for correction, for instruction in righteousness" (2 Timothy 3:16). Minor, indeed, are those errors which may be found in the copies of the Bible which we possess, and through careful, scholarly study they are being in remarkable measure removed. Very different, however, was the original. That was the actual God-breathed Word, true to fact in all its statements. Let no one say that it is a matter of indifference whether this original was inerrant; it is a matter of greatest importance, for the honor and veracity of God Himself are at stake. If there are actual errors in the original copies of the Bible, the Word which has come forth from the mouth of God is not a perfect Word, and the God of truth is guilty of error. If God has spoken falsely in His Word, He is not the God of truth, and consequently, the Christian religion is a false religion. This conclusion cannot be evaded. It is for this reason that those who embrace the Biblical doctrine are so zealous to maintain the absolute perfection of the Divine revelation in its original manuscripts.

It should be made clear, however, that if there actually are errors in the original manuscripts, we have no means of knowing where those errors start and where they stop. If God has erred in His speech at one point, how do we know that He has not done so at others? If He has denied the truth once, He might have done it more than once. If in minor matters He has given us falsehood, how do we know that in weightier things — — since He is the Author of His Word — He has not done the same thing? This conclusion cannot be avoided. Men may talk all they wish about the unimportance and irrelevance of minor errors in chronology and history; the real truth of the matter is that if God has blundered so badly on those matters in which we can check Him, how do we know that He has not also blundered just as badly in speaking to us of Himself? It is not an unimportant point. If the original manuscripts of Scripture contain mistakes of fact and statements which are contrary to the truth, then we cannot escape the conclusion that these original manuscripts, since they are inscribed with the outbreathed Word of God, are not trustworthy. If God has lied to us at one point, by what conceivable standard may we say that He has not lied to us at others? If the truth in what are sometimes called minor matters is of no importance to Him, how do we know that He has any regard for the truth in so-called major concerns? In fact, if He has violated the truth even in these small things, how do we know that He has any concern for the truth at all? If He is the God of truth, He has certainly taken a strange way of showing it. The so-called errors of the extant copies of Scripture, therefore, matters of chronology and the like, must be attributed to those human beings who made copies of the Bible. They are not from the God of Truth Himself.

Amazing indeed is the cavalier manner in which modern theologians relegate this doctrine of an inerrant original Scripture to the limbo of the unimportant. Discovering that it is possible for men to be blessed of God without an errorless text, men rush to the conclusion that therefore an infallible Bible is unnecessary and unimportant. So dogmatic are they in this procedure, so confident are their assertions that the doctrine of an inerrant Scripture is unimportant, that they seem not to realize what they are doing. It is obvious, we are sometimes told, that the great doctrines of the Christian faith can be formulated from the copies of the Bible which are now in our possession. The Church never had an infallible copy of the Bible with which to work. Consequently, it is asked, why should we bother with such a doctrine? We do not have the original copies of Scripture. How can we know what they were like? We can say nothing about them. Hence, the modern theologian is very eager to maintain his silence concerning them or, if he does not maintain it, to declare that even in the original copies of Scripture there were errors. He seems to be sure that the originals of Scripture were not infallible.

There is, of course, one means that is very widely adopted in order to escape from the difficulty of maintaining an originally inerrant Bible. It consists simply in equating the revelation of God with His ordinary providential working. In God's providence there have arisen, for example, those writings, the Iliad and the Odyssey, which we know as the works of Homer. Without entering into the question how much Homer actually had to do with their composition, other than to remark that we believe that they display the marks of one great mind, we may say that in a certain sense these works were given to us from God. Who can read the Iliad and the Odyssey without being greatly impressed by their magnificence? Surely the genius which went into their composition was a gift from none other than God Himself. Homer — assuming that he was the author — was a highly gifted and endowed man, and we may thank God for the talent that was given to him. At the same time, we would not say that the very words of either the Iliad or the Odyssey were taught to the poet by God. We certainly would not maintain that he, as he wrote, was borne by the Holy Spirit. Nor would we feel for an instant that, if there were serious errors in the original copies of the Iliad and Odyssey, such mistakes were a reflection upon God Himself. Rather, we do not particularly care whether there were errors in the originals of Homer. Whoever wrote those originals made the errors, and it is not too important who that author was. The originals were not given to the poet by a direct, special revelation. It is in similar fashion that some would also treat the Bible. They would regard its composition as a mere act of God's providence, and would in effect deny any special revelation. The composition of the Bible, therefore, on this view, would not differ in any essential respect from that of the great poetry of ancient Greece.

If this conception of the origin of the Bible be correct, it of course follows that the Bible is in reality no different from any other book. The men who wrote the Bible may indeed have been serious-minded men; they were not, however, borne by the Spirit of God as they wrote, nor were the words which they penned God-breathed. They were men of their own time, subject to the ignorance and limitations of their time.

Serious-minded these authors may have been; that they were good men, however, is open to question. The words which they wrote were given to the world as words which the writers received by direct revelation from God. If, in a matter so funda-mental as that of the origin of their words, the writers of Scripture did not tell the truth, how can we even say that they were good men? They were not good men, but deceivers. If the Bible arose as other books arise, merely in the ordinary providence of God, the Bible is not a good Book, for the Bible *claims* to be a special revelation of God.

These are the implications that one cannot escape if he is to accept the Bible as being no different in respect to its origin from other books. Those who thus treat the Bible say not a word that would lead one to believe that they themselves seriously consider the words of the Scriptures to be God-breathed. They do not come to grips with the question whether the original of the Bible was breathed forth from the mouth of God Himself. If the Bible came to us in the ordinary way through God's providential working — if, in other words, the Bible came to us just as other books do — then, it goes without saying, that it matters not one whit whether the originals of the Bible were free from error. If, on the other hand, (foreign and uncongenial as the thought is to the mind of the modern theologian) the Bible was given to man by special revelation of the one living and true God, it makes all the difference in the world whether the Bible came to us free from error. If the Bible is indeed the Word of God, is that Word free from error, or is God bound by the limitations and errors that adhere to sinful humanity? There is the issue, and it cannot be evaded.

If we are going to reject the Bible as God's special revelation, that is one thing. If, however, we are going to cleave to the doctrine of inspiration let us face the claims of the Bible honestly. The Bible asserts that it is the very Word of God. If we believe that assertion, let us accept it and follow its implications where they lead. It would be a great boon to the entire religious situation if those who no longer believe in the Scriptural doctrine of inspiration would cease speaking and writing as though they did so believe. When a man says that he considers the Bible to be the Word of God, the humble Christian will likely take his words at face value and think that he intends them in the same sense as does the Bible itself. Such, of course, is not the case at all. Merely for the sake of simple honesty, it would be a great advantage if in the present religious situation men would make it clear what they mean by their usage of Scriptural terminology.

If, however, we do accept the teaching of the Bible, God grant that we may not be ashamed of that teaching! The Bible, in manifold ways, has proclaimed and asserted its divinity. It has emphatically declared that in a unique manner it has come to us from God. If, in professing to believe the Bible, we are going to be serious, let us accept its claims and not try to explain them away! Let us follow our God who cannot lie; and since He cannot lie, let us believe that His Word is truth itself. Those copies of Scripture which came forth from God Almighty were infallible and inerrant. No matter what men may say to the contrary, no matter how much they may seek to obscure the issue, in the very nature of the case it could not have been otherwise.

AN OBJECTION

At this point it may be well to consider briefly an objection which is sometimes raised. Since, as we have maintained, God cannot err, the Word which comes forth from His mouth must also itself be inerrant. This conclusion, it is said by way of objection, need not at all follow. We might as well argue that, since Christ is the perfect Son of God, therefore He could not die. As a matter of fact, however, He did die. And because the sinless Son of God did die, we cannot maintain that the Holy Ghost could not have condescended to use the poverty, error and sin of the Biblical writers whom He employed. To this objection several things need to be said. Basically, however, it appears to confuse sin and the consequences of sin. All that God speaks, because God is Truth itself, must also be true and in accordance with fact. To maintain that God may have uttered words that are false or that do not square with the facts is in effect to make of God a liar. What, however, shall we say about the death of Christ? Jesus Christ, according to the Bible, is God become man. When the second Person of the ever blessed Trinity took to Himself our human nature, He took that nature apart from sin. Hence the importance of the doctrine of the Virgin Birth. That holy Babe which was born of Mary was the Son of God. Although He became flesh and dwelled among us, although He became man in the truest sense of the word, He nevertheless became a sinless man. Holy, harmless, and undefiled, He lived His blessed life upon this earth in our midst. Why, then, did He die? Does not death come only upon those who have sinned? But He was not a transgressor of the law. Why then did He die? The answer is that the guilt of our sin was laid to His account, and as our substitute He bore the penalty of our sin. He was, in other words, punished in our stead. It was our sin for which He was smitten. How wondrously the prophet has set it forth: "He *was* wounded for our transgressions, *he was* bruised for our iniquities: the chastisement of our peace *was* upon him; and with his stripes we are healed" (Isaiah 53:5). What Isaiah says is the same thing that the Apostle sets forth so beautifully in his second epistle to the Corinthians (5:21): "For he hath made him *to be* sin for us, who knew no sin; that we might be made the righteousness of God in him." If Christ had taken unto Himself a sinful nature, and so had died as a consequence of His own sins, then, indeed, there might be force in the objection which we are now considering. Such, however, was not the case. Not for His own sins did He die, but for the sins of others.

> *What thou, dear Lord, hast suffered*
> *Was all for sinners' gain;*
> *Mine, mine was the transgression,*
> *But thine the deadly pain.*

In those words we find the correct statement of the case. The transgression was not His but that of His people; the deadly pain, however, fell upon Him, for in their stead He was punished.

If He were a sinner, then, indeed, we should expect Him to die. Sin brings forth death, and sin also issues in error and fallibility. To say that God has erred is to say that He has sinned; to assert, however, that Christ died is not necessarily to say that He has died for His own sin. The death of Christ in no way implies that He Himself was a sinful man, and hence an appeal to the death of our Lord, such as we have just considered, in no wise militates against the Biblical doctrine of inerrancy.

A New View

Is not, it may be asked, this doctrine of an inerrant original text, comparatively new? Was it not developed during the last century by orthodox Protestant theologians? Luther and Calvin, it is often claimed, did not hold anything similar to it. More than that, the Fathers of the Church certainly did not teach it. Therefore, the conclusion seems to be, the doctrine is one which belongs not to catholic Christianity, but only to a small segment of the Church.

Modern writers like to cast their scorn upon this view and to declare how recent it is. Of course, it might as well be noted

in passing, a doctrine is not necessarily false because its implications were only recently realized. The Church existed for many
centuries before Luther saw the force of the Scriptural doctrine
of justification by faith. Despite that fact, however, men have
always been justified by faith. The doctrine was true long before
Luther saw its force and implications. If, therefore, it should
be true that only in recent years men have begun to see the
implications of the doctrine of inspiration, that in itself is no
condemnation.

Is this doctrine, however, something which has just been
developed during the last century? Our answer is, as we have
been seeking to show, that it is found in the pages of the Scriptures
themselves. It is perfectly true that its full implications were
not set forth before the Reformation. During the sixteenth and
the seventeenth centuries men who deeply loved the Lord Jesus
Christ and His Church worked out some of the implications of
the Scriptural teaching on inspiration. They did this, not because
they had a bent of mind inclined toward philosophical speculation
and sophistical niceties and wished to give satisfaction thereto,
but because they faced a powerful foe, a foe which would deny to
the Bible its position of supreme and final authority and would
substitute therefor the Church. That foe was Rome, and the issue
which was raised was vital, and one which struck at the very roots
of the Christian religion. To which ultimate authority is the
humble and devout believer to listen? Is he to listen to what the
Church has to say? Is the Church to tell him what he is to
believe and how he is to live? To these questions Rome said
yes, and its reply was fortified and buttressed by strong and
powerful arguments. To listen to the Church, however, would
be a return to the fiction of a merit-religion such as had characterized the Middle Ages and would close the door upon
the Gospel of the free grace of a merciful God and lead the
soul into that bondage against which the great Reformers,
Luther and Calvin, had so valiantly struggled.

There were those however, who refused to take the retrograde
step into the darkness and superstition of the Middle Ages.
To listen to the Church, they believed, would be to shut one's
ears to the voice of God. It must be shown that the Church was
usurping a place which did not belong to her, a place which was
God's alone. Was this blessed Book, this Book which had

led Luther out of the dark night of sacerdotalism and priestcraft into the glorious light of the grace of God, a Book whose claims could be trusted? The Book itself asserted, and that in no uncertain manner, that it was the Word of God. In what sense, however, was it the Word of God? Was it merely a secondary authority to be used as a support for whatever the Church thought men should believe? That was the way in which, in effect, it was regarded by Rome. Or was it the Word of God in a different sense? Was it the final court of appeal to which men must harken if they would be saved?

At this crucial period there were not wanting men whose hearts God had touched, who knew that Christ had died for them, who loved the Savior because He had delivered them from their sins, and these men could not sit by and watch the Bible be relegated to a secondary position. They were desirous that the Bible should receive its full recognition. Hence, they made earnest and careful study of the Bible in order to discover what it had to say for itself. As a result the Church has been enriched by their writings. We have, for example, the magnificent treatise on the Scriptures which Francis Turretin has left. There are those who could condemn that treatise and others of a similar nature by labelling them with the word "scholasticism." However, he who will take the trouble to work through what Turretin has written will make the discovery that here was a heart aflame with devotion to the Christ who had died for him, and seeking only to be true to what God had revealed concerning His Holy Word.

It is certainly true that during the sixteenth and seventeenth centuries the implications of the doctrine of Biblical inspiration were worked out more fully than before. And we may humbly give thanks to God that He gave men of such devotion to His Church. We could do far worse today than to study these great masters of Protestant theology.

This does not mean that we must agree with everything that they wrote. We must, rather, test what they wrote to see whether it actually is taught in the Bible. No doubt there are references and allusions in the writings of the Protestant scholastics which are not particularly relevant today. No doubt there may have been a tendency on the part of some to a certain formalism in statement, and possibly also to over-refinement in argument. With all their faults, however, these men rendered a great service, and we may thank God that He saw fit to give them to His Church.

It is also true that as a counter to the destructive criticism of the nineteenth century, a criticism which wrought such havoc in the Church of Christ, even further thought was given to the doctrine of inspiration. We may thank God for men such as Charles Hodge, A. A. Hodge, and Benjamin B. Warfield. If students for the ministry would study the writings of these men instead of those of the present neo-orthodox writers, the Church would find itself in a far healthier condition.

The two following quotations will give the reader an inkling of the penetrating insight and fidelity to Scripture manifested by A. A. Hodge and B. B. Warfield:

We believe that the great majority of those who object to the affirmation that Inspiration is verbal are impelled thereto by a feeling, more or less definite, that the phrase implies that Inspiration is, in its essence, a process of verbal dictation, or that, at least in some way, the revelation of the thought, or the inspiration of the writer, was by means of the control which God exercised over his words. And there is the more excuse for this misapprehension because of the extremely mechanical conceptions of Inspiration maintained by many former advocates of the use of this term "verbal." This view, however, we repudiate as earnestly as any of those who object to the language in question. At the present time the advocates of the strictest doctrine of Inspiration, in insisting that it is verbal, do not mean that, in any way, the thoughts were inspired by means of the words, but simply that the divine superintendence, which we call Inspiration, extended to the verbal expression of the thoughts of the sacred writers, as well to the thoughts themselves, and that, hence, the Bible considered as a record, an utterance in words of a divine revelation is the Word of God to us. Hence, in all the affirmations of Scripture of every kind, there is no more error in words of the original autographs than in the thoughts they were chosen to express. The thoughts and words are both alike human, and, therefore, subject to human limitations, but the divine superintendence and guarantee extends to the one as much as to the other.[1]

What a matchless statement of inspiration is found in the following words:

1. "Inspiration," by A. A. Hodge, and B. B. Warfield, in *The Presbyterian Review*, No. 6, April 1881, pp. 232-233.

The Bible, moreover, being a work of the Spirit for spiritual ends, each writer was prepared precisely for his part in the work by the personal dealings of the Holy Spirit with his soul. Spiritual illumination is very different from either revelation or inspiration, and yet it had under the providence of God a large share in the genesis of Scripture, contributing to it a portion of that Divine element which makes it the Word of God. The Psalms are divinely inspired records of the religious experiences of the writers, and are by God himself authoritatively set forth as typical and exemplary for all men forever. Paul and John and Peter largely drew upon the resources, and followed the lines of their own personal religious experience in the intuitional or the logical development of their doctrine, and their experience had, of course, been previously divinely determined for that very purpose. And in determining their religious experience, God so far forth determined their contributions to Scripture. And He furnished each of the Sacred writers, in addition to that which came to him through natural channels, all the knowledge needed for his appointed task, either by vision, suggestion, dictation or elevation of faculty, or otherwise, according to His will. The natural knowledge came from all sources, as traditions, documents, testimonies, personal observations and recollections; by means also of intuitions, logical processes of thought, feeling, experience, etc., and yet all were alike under the general direction of God's providence. The supernatural knowledge became confluent with the natural in a manner which violated no law of reason or of freedom. And throughout the whole of His work the Holy Spirit was present, causing His energies to flow into the spontaneous exercises of the writer's faculties, elevating and directing where need be, and everywhere securing the errorless expression in language of the thought designed by God. This last element is what we call Inspiration.[2]

Thank God for men who have been concerned to study the Church's doctrines and to discover what are the implications of those doctrines! Would that our present day could boast of such painstaking Bible study as that which characterized the labors of the men just mentioned. Let us freely grant and rejoice in the fact that there has indeed been development in the understanding of this precious doctrine.

What, however, about the period before the Reformation? As we read over the history of the Christian Church, there is one

2. *Ibid.,* pp. 230-231.

thing that impresses us, namely, the reverence in which the Holy Scriptures were held. Consider Justin Martyr as he appeals to the Scriptures to prove the deity of Jesus Christ. Why should he thus employ the Scriptures, were it not that he believed them to be the final court of appeal? Or hear Origen as, from the Bible, he endeavors to refute the specious attacks of a Celsus upon Christianity. Whatever errors Origen may have entertained, and he certainly had his share of them, the Scriptures, as his own practice makes clear, were to him the last and ultimate court of appeal. He may in effect have nullified this fact by the allegorizing with which he covered the Scriptures but, nevertheless, he at least thought that he was appealing to the Bible. Where they spoke, he was willing to listen; what they enjoined, he would put into practice. And it might be noted that the tremendous labor which he expended upon his six-fold version of the Bible, the Hexapla, is a tribute to his devotion to the Bible. More than that, however, the twenty-odd years in which he was engaged in this study, and particularly, his careful transcription of the Hebrew Old Testament in Greek characters is, say what one will, a remarkable tribute to his belief in the verbal inspiration of the Bible.

This monumental work of Origen's was no mere antiquarian pursuit, wrought for the sake of scholarship as such. Origen was not interested primarily in scientific research. Rather, it was as a servant of Jesus Christ, a minister of the Gospel, that he labored. By means of the Hexapla, he hoped that the church would have a better text of the Bible and, consequently, that the Gospel might be more faithfully preached. From such deep devotion to the text of Scripture and its actual words, one receives the impression that Origen, were he alive today, would be one of the staunchest defenders of verbal inspiration.

Nor does Origen stand alone in his devotion to the Scriptures. One might find example after example of trust in the final authority of the Bible. The question is not what books of Scripture were regarded as inspired; there were indeed differences of opinion as to the extent of the Canon. What is at issue is that throughout the course of Church history men appealed to that which they regarded as Scripture. If they considered a book to be Scripture, then they knew that they were bound to that book as to the very Word of God.

Valiant is the stand which Luther took upon this question. Hear him as he asserts, "Arguments based upon reason determine nothing, but because the Holy Ghost says it is true, it is true."[3] Well known are his brave words, spoken at Worms:

> Unless I am convinced by testimony from Scripture or evident reason — for I believe neither the Pope nor the Councils alone, since it is established that they have often erred and contradicted themselves — I am conquered by the writings cited by me, and my conscience is captive to the Word of God; recant I will not, since it is neither safe nor honest to do ought against conscience.[4]

And again,

> I have learned to ascribe this honor (i.e., infallibility) only to books which are termed canonical, so that I confidently believe that not one of their authors erred, but the other authors, no matter how distinguished by great sanctity and teaching, I read in this way, that I do not regard them as true because they themselves judged in this wise but in so far as they could convince me through the authority of the canonical writings or other clear deductions.[5]

From the time of the Apostles until the present God's people have loved His Word. In times of sorrow, they have found solace in its promises, in days of sadness, they have been comforted and strengthened by its testimonies; in the midst of happiness, they have rejoiced in its commands, and always has this been so because they have regarded this Word as God's Word; its words, indeed, have been a blessing to their souls. Thus, even though many of its implications have only been worked out since the days of the Reformation, the idea of verbal inspiration has been present from the beginning. One thing at least is clear: the doctrine of verbal inspiration, which Bible believers are defending today, is a doctrine which has been defended since the days of the Apostles. It is indeed the very view which the Apostles and, above all, our Lord Himself maintained. The views of modernism, neo-orthodoxy and destructive criticism do not represent a natural development of the attitude toward the Bible which has characterized the Church since the time of its inception. Those who espouse the doctrine of verbal inspiration and Scriptural infallibility are in a true apostolic succession.

3. M. Reu, *Luther and the Scriptures*, 1944, p. 16.
4. M. Reu, *op. cit.*, p. 28.
5. M. Reu, *op. cit.*, p. 24, referring to Augustine's statement.

Is the Bible Infallible Only in Faith and Practice?

Another objection, however, lies ready to hand. In stressing the fact that the Scriptures in matters of historical and geographical detail are infallible, we are charged with going too far. The Bible, it is acknowledged, is of course the only infallible rule of faith and practice, but that is as far as its infallibility goes. There are those who are willing to subscribe to the statement that the Scriptures are the only infallible rule of faith and practice, and by that declaration they mean, if we may employ the language of Charles A. Briggs,

> . . . they are infallible in all matters of divine revelation, in all things where men need infallible guidance from God. We do not thereby claim that a writer dwelling in Palestine had an infallible knowledge of countries he had never visited, of dates of events beyond his own experience where he had to rely upon tradition or doubtful or imperfect human records. We do not affirm that he gave an exact and infallible report of words spoken centuries before, which had never been previously recorded; or an infallible description of events that happened in distant lands and ages; removing from the traditional report every excess of color and every variation in detail. We do not thereby claim that the writer of the poem of the creation knew geology and astronomy, and natural history better than the experts of modern science, but to teach us the science of God and redemption, and the art of living holy, godlike lives. The Bible is the only infallible rule of faith and practice.[6]

In the words of this quotation Briggs has stated, perhaps as well as anyone, the objection of those who think they can limit the infallibility of Scripture to faith and practice. The objection, however, does not get at the root of the matter. It is an objection that has a certain pious ring to it and appears to possess a certain amount of plausibility. Plausible as it is, however, it cannot stand. Several things must be remarked concerning it.

In the first place, it is an objection that does not understand the true nature of faith. We do not believe, say these objectors, that the Bible is infallible in anything but faith and practice. It is not infallible in philosophy; it is not infallible in astronomy; it is not infallible in other sciences; it is infallible only when it tells us what we are to believe. When, however, we come to

---

6. Charles Augustus Briggs, *The Bible, The Church and The Reason*, 1892, pp. 93, 94.

examine the question what we are to believe we discover that the doctrines which Scripture commends are rooted and grounded upon that which was done in history. The Christian faith, as it is revealed in the Bible, is not a mass of abstractions divorced from history. It is not eternal truths and ideals, but rather the account of something that God did for us upon this earth in history. Hence, it becomes very important to us to know whether what the Bible has to say about these historical matters is correct or not.

According to the Bible our salvation depends upon the death of Jesus Christ at Calvary and upon his subsequent resurrection from the dead. Now, it is quite important to know certain details about the tomb in which He was laid. Was that tomb empty upon the third day? Was there an actual historical resurrection or not? Questions such as these intrude themselves into our consideration and will not be pushed aside. Is the Bible, therefore, correct in what it has to say of these historical details or not? If the historical framework in which the great redemptive acts of God took place is a framework which is not to be trusted, how do we know that we have a true and correct account of those redemptive acts themselves?

History and faith cannot be divorced, the one from the other. Remove its historical basis and faith vanishes. To understand our faith properly we must study history, and this history is offered to us in the Bible. To say that what the Bible relates of history is fallible, but what it relates of faith is infallible is to talk nonsense. Apart from history there is no faith. The separation between the two which some seek to make is impossible. The only faith that can legitimately bear the name Christian is one that is rooted in historical events. From these it cannot be separated.

This brings us to another consideration. Who is to say what is faith and what is not? Those who claim that the Bible is infallible only as a rule of faith do not define where faith begins and where it ends. This fact may be illustrated by an appeal to the first chapter of Genesis. With respect to this chapter, how far does the infallibility of the Bible extend? Is everything that is related in this important chapter necessarily in error? Or, are some statements true and some false? What is infallible and what is not infallible? Where does "faith" end and historical details begin? What, in other words, are the precise limits of "faith" in this first chapter of Genesis? What are the matters of "faith" herein revealed concerning which we may say that the Bible is infallible? And more than that, we would ask, who is to tell us what is and what is not a matter of faith? On these important questions the advocates of the view that the Bible is infallible only in matters of faith and practice are strangely silent. It will probably be acknowledged that in telling us that God is the Creator the Bible is infallible. No doubt Dr. Briggs, from whom we have just made a rather lengthy quotation, would at least maintain such a position. Others, however, do not wish to join Dr. Briggs in this belief. They are indeed willing to employ the words of the first verse of Genesis and they are also willing to speak of God as the Creator. Their language, however, bears a different connotation from that of Dr. Briggs, for they also make it clear that they do not believe in creation in the sense intended by Genesis 1. Both Dr. Briggs and those who reject the first verse of Genesis would doubtless wish to be known as Christians. Dr. Briggs, we think, would say that the doctrine of creation as taught in the Bible is a necessary article of faith. Others, on the contrary, would say that as it is taught in the Bible, the doctrine is not necessary at all to faith. Not only is it not necessary, they would furthermore maintain, but it is even positively harmful. Who, then, is to settle the issue? Who is to tell us what is and what is not of faith? Dr. Briggs may have certain ideas as to what faith is; others however, have quite different ideas. When, therefore, it is declared that the Bible is an infallible rule of faith, we may be pardoned if we ask the simple question, What is this faith? It should be clear that those who assert that only in matters of faith and practice, as distinguished, for example, from historical statements, is the Bible infallible, are in fact erecting the human mind as the ultimate judge of what is and what is not faith. We are, of course, far from maintaining that the human writers of the Scriptures were of themselves infallible in all their knowledge. We are far from holding that Moses, to take an example, possessed advanced knowledge of modern science. If Moses had depended upon his own ideas of science, he would have produced an account of creation that would have been anything but infallible. In writing of creation, however, Moses did not depend upon his own ideas, but wrote only that which was revealed to him by God.

Thus we come to the heart of the objection which we are now considering. Those who assert that only in matters of faith the Bible is infallible do not seem to appreciate the fact that the Bible is a revelation of God. In asserting that the Bible is infallible, we are not basing this infallibility upon the knowledge of the human writers of Scripture. It may be that Moses, Isaiah, John and Paul were all men whose views of astronomy are today outmoded. Probably they held opinions on many other matters which would now be regarded as out of date. The Bible, however, is not simply the work of Moses and Isaiah, John and Paul. If it were, what a jumble of confusion and error it would be! It might then be little better than the works of other great men of antiquity. The Bible, however, is the revelation of God. The information which it offers to us is information which was communicated to its human writers by God. The reason, therefore, why the first chapter of Genesis reads as though it were written only yesterday is that the information contained therein was revealed to Moses by God. Much as men today like to talk about the pre-scientific character of the Bible, there is no one who can prove the presence of an error in the first chapter of Genesis.

The Bible, it is often said, is not a textbook of astronomy. That we freely grant. The Bible nowhere claims to be such a textbook. It is, however, a textbook of the philosophy of astronomy; when the Bible speaks, as in Genesis 1, upon astronomical matters, it is absolutely in accord with fact in what it says. It may be that through misunderstanding and fallible interpretations of our own we have obscured what the Bible has to say. When, however, the true meaning of the Scripture is obtained, we have the truth upon that particular subject about which the Scripture is speaking. The Bible is not a textbook of geography; when, however, it speaks upon a geographical matter, it speaks with absolute authority. The Bible is not a textbook of geology; when, however, it speaks upon matters of geology, it is infallible in what it says. Human theories of astronomy, geology, and geography have changed and do change. The Bible, in what it says upon these subjects, is not in any sense in disharmony with the facts. That it may disagree with certain theories is, of course, granted; it does not disagree with the facts, since those facts also were given of God. The Bible, we must conclude, is infallible in all that it says, or we cannot be sure that it is infallible in anything. We cannot with any consistency maintain that only in the realm of faith and practice is it without error.

Do Protestants Misuse the Bible?

One frequently hears the assertion these days that Luther set Christendom free from the Roman Pope and now the time has arrived for some one to set Christendom free from the paper Pope. Until the time of the Reformation, it is maintained, the Church was considered infallible; now, however, the Bible has taken its place. The Bible is given the position of authority which once was occupied by the Church. In rejecting an infallible Church Protestantism has simply substituted an infallible book. This is bad, we are told, because the Bible does not claim such a place for itself. There is only One who should have supreme authority, namely, Jesus Christ. Protestants have put the Bible in the place of Jesus Christ, and that is one of the great weaknesses of Protestantism.

Plausible words are these; plausible, but utterly false. Before a little sober reflection they lose their force entirely. Despite that fact, however, they are often voiced in such a way as to give the impression that those who are uttering them had made some new and great discovery. They must not stand unchallenged, however, for they represent a perversion of the facts.

In the first place, it must be insisted that the picture offered by this objection is an oversimplification of the facts. It will not do to declare that until the time of the Reformation the Church was accepted as an infallible authority, and then with the Reformation the Bible was presented as a substitute. A modern writer sets it forth thus:

> "When the Reformation set the cat among the ecclesiastical pigeons, it was almost inevitable that the Bible should before long be given as spurious an eminence as the Church itself had enjoyed."[7]

It is true, of course, that through the long years of development the authority of the Church was receiving ever greater and more prominent recognition. At the same time, the Church claimed to reverence the Scriptures, and in her definition of doctrine did

7. William Neil: *The Rediscovery of the Bible,* London, 1954, p. 31.

appeal to the Scriptures. The supreme authority of the Bible, however, was more and more pushed into the background. What the Reformation did was simply to clear the air and re-establish the Scriptures as the sole authority. One has but to read the writings of the New Testament in order to see that the Church had begun with the belief that the Scriptures were that sole authority. Tradition, however, slowly but surely, began to usurp the place that at the beginning had belonged to the Bible. The Reformation swept away that tradition and once more called men to the Scriptures as the infallible authority. In other words, what the Reformation did was nothing more or less than to re-establish the rightful position of the Bible as the sole authority. The Reformation, in the providence of God, was a mighty purifying process. Gone was the error of human tradition and superstition which had grown during the Middle Ages, and in its place shone forth, once again, in all its purity, the infallible Word of God.

In calling men back to the Bible, however, did the Reformers place the Bible in a position which belonged to Jesus Christ? Did they, in their endeavor to unite Protestantism against Rome, set up an authority other than Christ Himself? Did they, in effect, supplant Christ with the Bible? Has the Bible, therefore, come between Christian faith and its Author? Has a false Biblicism engulfed Protestantism? Strangely enough, through what we believe to be a misunderstanding of his teaching, Luther is sometimes omitted from the charge which we are now discussing. Be that as it may, we are told that the Reformers, at least Calvin and some of the others, were guilty of attributing to the Bible a position of priority which belonged to Christ alone.

How, we should like to ask, can the Bible possibly supplant the authority of Christ? We today would probably know nothing of Christ were it not for the Bible. Where do these modern theologians who claim to be zealous for the absolute authority of Christ receive their knowledge of Him? They receive it, humbling as the thought may be, from the *words* of the Bible. They do not receive it from some mysterious, nebulous Word which is to be separated from the actual words of Scripture. Much as modern theology may dislike the words of the Bible, it is from those despised words, and from them alone, that we learn of Jesus Christ. It would be well if that rather evident fact were kept in mind as we discuss this question.

What we are saying is so patent that there would seem to be no cause for discussion. Little children sing from the heart what the modern theologian seems unable to comprehend:

> "Jesus loves me, this I know,
> For the Bible tells me so . . . ,"

It is but a child's hymn, but it has a far more profound insight into the truth of the matter than has many a modern theologian who thinks that he can make a disjunction between Christ and His God-breathed Word. Were it not for the *words* of the Bible we would know nothing of the love of Jesus for lost sinners, nothing of His atoning death and His triumphant resurrection, nothing of the gift of His blessed Spirit, nothing of the promises of His sure return. Is it any wonder that children love to sing:

> "Holy Bible, Book divine,
>   Precious treasure, thou art mine:
> Mine to tell me whence I came;
>   Mine to tell me what I am.
>
> Mine to chide me when I rove,
>   Mine to show a Saviour's love,
> Mine thou art to guide and guard;
>   Mine to punish or reward"?

There may be some who will regard these words as expressing a mere bibliolatry. Those, however, who, because this Book has told them of Him, know Jesus Christ, will dismiss all such cries as vain. Is this bibliolatry? Do Protestants worship a Book? For our part we know of none who do. Protestants do not worship the paper and ink and the leather cover that goes to make up a Bible. It is true enough that the very form of the Word of God means a great deal to the true believer. Do we not all possess Bibles that have been with us throughout our lives? At home and abroad, they have been our constant companions, and a certain attachment, no doubt, is to be found in our hearts toward them. But our love for the Bible is something far deeper than the attachment one has toward an ancient and comfortable piece of furniture. We love this Book because of its message. Its very words are treasured in our hearts because we believe that these words were given by God Himself. How deeply our love to

God has grown when we could meditate during the early hours
of the morning upon passages of the Scripture! We have
repeated the words to ourselves over and over again, rejoicing in
the blessing of the truth which they bring. Is this to dethrone
Jesus Christ from His position of absolute authority? Those
who speak thus evince little understanding of the true relationship between Jesus and His Word. It is through these blessed,
divinely revealed *words* that our sinful hearts are brought closer
to the Lord Jesus Christ.

The Reformers did not substitute the infallible Bible for an
infallible Christ. By giving to the world an open Bible the
Reformers preached Jesus Christ. When Calvin wrote his classic
Institutes, he simply opened up the way for a serious and devout
soul to come to a deeper knowledge of the Lord of Glory. And
what about Luther; did he obscure Jesus Christ? When, after
his vigorous stand at Worms, he was kidnapped and shut up in
an old castle, what means did he employ to preach Jesus Christ
as the absolute authority? If the modern theologians are correct,
Luther did a very foolish thing. Thank God, however, that
Luther did such a foolish thing. Luther translated the New
Testament into the German language so that the people might
hear the very words which Jesus Christ spoke. Luther knew
nothing of this modern distinction between the Word of God and
the words of the Bible. Luther, honest soul that he was, thought
that the best way to get Christ to the people was to give them
the Bible in their own language. And since the people had this
Word of God they came to know Jesus Christ as their Lord and
Savior. By giving his people the Bible Luther thus gave them
Jesus Christ.

We have a suspicion that those who are so concerned lest
the Bible occupy a position which belongs to Christ have also
themselves an "absolute" or "infallible" authority which they,
whether they realize it or not, would themselves place upon the
throne. It is the "infallible" mind of man. Not an infallible
Church, and not an infallible Bible, they tell us. Do they not,
however, in their turn, demand an infallible "human mind" before
which our Christianity must bow? Also, who is this Jesus Christ
whose position has supposedly been dethroned by the Bible?
We do not know him. Is He the eternal Son of God, the second
Person of the Holy Trinity, who, for our salvation, took unto
Himself human nature, without sin, being born of the Virgin

Mary, to live upon this earth a sinless life, and, as our High
Priest, to die upon the cross in our stead and to rise from the
dead? Is that the Christ about whom the modern theologian is
concerned? Has the position of this Christ been usurped by the
Bible? We think not, for that blessed Christ is the One of whom
the *words* of Holy Scripture speak. No, it is not that historic
Christ which the Bible displaces, but some Christ whom we
know not. There are many who say, "I am Christ." Is he
for whom modern theologians seem so concerned one of these?
If so, we know that he is at best but a fabrication of the human
mind; he is not the Divine Christ of Scripture. Is he but a
name for worldly urbanity, for sentimental good cheer; is he
but a slogan; is he the majority vote of the church council?
We know him not, nor do we have any particular desire to
know him. He cannot save us from our sins, sins which we
have come to know through reading the words of the Scripture.
Concerning all false Christs the Scriptures have said, ". . . see that
ye be not troubled: for all *these things* must come to pass, but the
end is not yet" (Matthew 24:6). Any Christ other than the
historic Savior, the Christ of the Bible, is a Christ whom man
has devised; and may we be spared from an "infallible" human
mind which will tell us what Christ we are to worship.

The issue in the Church today is not between those who
maintain that the original manuscripts of the Bible were inerrant
and those who believe that the original manuscripts may have
contained errors, but who, nevertheless, are ardent believers in
the doctrines of an evangelical, supernatural Christianity. If
that ever were the situation in Christendom, it certainly is not
so at the present day. It may have been that at one time there
were staunch believers in the other doctrines of Scripture who
nevertheless held that the original copies of the Bible contained
errors. If there were such, however, they have given way.
Certainly there are few today who hold to such a position. The
errors of the Bible which men now say they find are not minor
at all. If they were only minor the situation would not be so
desperate. The time has come, however, when men do not want
to accept the Biblical witness to itself, but rather would be guided
by the dictates of human reason.

There is, consequently, a refusal to do justice to the Biblical
doctrine of inspiration. The real reason why men oppose the
doctrine of an infallible Scripture is that they are not willing

to embrace the Biblical doctrine of inspiration. There is no such thing as inspiration which does not carry with it the correlate of infallibility. A Bible that is fallible — and we speak of course of the original — is a Bible that is not inspired. A Bible that is inspired is a Bible that is infallible. There is no middle ground. Many are the attempts, indeed, which have been made to discover such a middle ground. They are, however, vain. Futile indeed are the efforts of those who wish to hold to some doctrine of inspiration without at the same time accepting belief in infallibility. It soon becomes apparent that the type of inspiration to which they are cleaving is not one that is taught in Scripture itself.

In the city of Geneva, there is a monument to the Reformation, and on this monument are carved the figures of some of the great Reformers. Underneath their figures are inscribed the words, "Post tenebras lux" — After the darkness light. It is a stirring inscription. After the darkness of the Middle Ages, when, to all intents and purposes at least, the Bible was a closed and chained Book, light came. And light came in a most strange manner. Light came when the pages of the Bible were once more opened and its truths preached and believed in the hearts of the people.

Today also darkness is covering the land and gross darkness the people. If light is to come, it will not be through the work of man, but through the work of God's Holy Spirit. And light will come, we believe, when the Spirit once more causes the men of our day to turn from the superficiality of so much of modern religious life to the Word of the one living and true God. Then will the pages of the Bible once more be opened and men will turn to its life-giving words, for, being the words of God, they are "profitable for doctrine, for reproof, for correction, for instruction in righteousness: that the man of God may be perfect, throughly furnished unto all good works."

What Is Inerrancy? (I)

"Therefore all Scripture is God-breathed, and in every way profitable so that one may best and most profitably to the soul search out the Divine Scriptures."
                                        JOHN OF DAMASCUS

"Let no one separate the Old from the New Testament, let no one say that one Spirit is there, and another here. . . . We know the Holy Spirit who has spoken in the prophets, and at Pentecost has come down upon the apostles."   CYRIL OF JERUSALEM

"The entire Scripture is divided into two testaments . . . the Jews use the Old, and we the New; but nevertheless, they are not contrary, because the New is the fulfillment of the Old, and in each the Testator is Christ."
                                        LACTANTIUS

5

What Is Inerrancy? (I)

In what has been said hitherto the words inerrancy and infallibility have been frequently employed. We have contended that the Scriptures, because they come from God Himself, must like their Divine Author, be infallible. What, however, is meant by this word infallibility? In present discussions of the Bible, both the words infallibility and inerrancy are often used without attempt at definition. The result is that much confusion has adhered and does adhere to current discussions of inspiration. There is not much point in talking of an infallible and inerrant Bible, unless we know what the words mean. Sometimes men say that they cannot believe in an inerrant Bible, because there are errors of grammar, or poor style, or the quotations do not always agree. Are statements such as these justified? Whether they are justified or not, they are often made, and they cause us to ask again the question, What do we mean when we speak of an inerrant and infallible Bible?

By the term infallible as applied to the Bible, we mean simply that the Scripture possesses an indefectible authority. As our Lord Himself said "it cannot be broken" (John 10:31). It can never fail in its judgments and statements. All that it teaches is of unimpeachable, absolute authority, and cannot be contravened, contradicted, or gainsaid. Scripture is unfailing, incapable of proving false, erroneous, or mistaken. Though heaven and earth should pass away, its words of truth will stand forever. It cannot be changed nor destroyed.

Closely related to this concept is that which is expressed by the term "inerrant." By this word we mean that the Scriptures possess the quality of freedom from error. They are exempt from the liability to mistake, incapable of error. In all their teachings they are in perfect accord with the truth.

In what way then shall we discover how the terms "infallible"

113

and "inerrant" can be applied to the Bible? We might conceivably approach the matter with an a priori idea as to what infallibility should be and then proceed to make the Bible fit into that idea. If we were to proceed in that way, we should not be alone. There are those who do just that. They approach the Bible with a preconceived idea as to what inerrancy and infallibility should be. That is one way of obtaining an answer to our question. Popular as it may be, it is a method that cannot have satisfactory results. There is a much better way to follow, namely, that of turning to the Bible itself to learn what infallibility is. If we follow this latter method we shall obtain the Biblical view of the matter and, since the Bible is the Word of God, that is all-important.

We may the better understand the Biblical teaching on inerrancy if we contrast it with an example of an a priori approach to the problem. The late Dr. Henry Preserved Smith once wrote, "The natural theory concerning an inspired book is illustrated by the Mohammedans."[1] Concerning the Koran, according to Dr. Smith, the Arabs maintain belief in the following:

1. The Koran is eternal in its original essence and a necessary attribute of God.

2. It is written down in heaven on a 'treasured tablet,' from which it was communicated piecemeal to Mohammed by the angel Gabriel.

3. It is written in an Arabic style, which is perfect and unapproachable, 'The best of Arab writers has never succeeded in producing its equal in merit.'

4. Every syllable is of directly Divine origin. This includes the unintelligible combinations of letters put at the head of certain Suras.

5. Its text is incorruptible, 'and preserved from error and variety of reading by the miraculous interposition of God Himself.' To account, however, for the slight variants which actually exist, the Koran is said to have been revealed in seven dialects.

6. As being the truth of God, it is the absolute authority, not only in religion and ethics, but also in law, science, and history.[2]

With respect to this attitude of the Arabs toward the Koran, Dr. Smith makes the following observation:

1. Henry Preserved Smith: "Biblical Scholarship and Inspiration" in *Inspiration and Inerrancy*, 1891, p. 197.
2. *Op. cit.*, pp. 199, 200.

This is the kind of Bible we should like to have God give us, and when we construct for ourselves a theory of revelation we do it along these lines.[3]

We can be grateful indeed to Dr. Smith for having given so succinct and capable a summary of what the Moslems believe concerning the "inspiration" of the Koran. If anyone should construct his view of inspiration along such lines as these, we believe that he would be guilty of approaching the question with an a priori concept of what inspiration should be. Surely those who have sought to defend the Scriptural doctrine of inspiration have not thus been guilty. Perhaps no one has written quite as deeply and profoundly on the subject as has the late Benjamin B. Warfield. To the sympathetic reader it is obvious that the doctrine of inspiration was one in which his heart delighted. Yet he had no a priori theory of what inspiration should be. He did not frame what he believed to be a "natural" theory, and then proceed to manipulate the Bible in order to make it conform to that theory. What Dr. Warfield did do, was to go to the Bible to discover what the Bible itself taught. If, on the other hand, one approaches the Bible with a previously adopted "natural" theory as to what an inspired book should be, he has in effect decided the question in advance.

It is true that the Moslems regard the Koran as ". . . written in an Arabic style, which is perfect and unapproachable." Does anyone, however, have the warrant to approach the Scriptures with the conception that they must also be written in a "perfect and unapproachable style?" If one believes in the infallibility of the Scriptures, does that mean that he must also insist upon an impeccable and unapproachable style? The question can be answered, and it can only be answered by an examination of the phenomena which the Scriptures themselves present.

One need not read far in the Bible to make the discovery that its style is indeed majestic. Majestic and lofty as it is, however, it soon becomes apparent that the Bible is not written for the sake of style, but in order to convey information to the reader. The Bible is an intensely practicable book, and one soon finds himself in agreement with the Apostle Paul: "For whatsoever things were written aforetime were written for our learning, that we through patience and comfort of the scriptures might

3. *Op. cit.*, p. 200.

have hope" (Romans 15:4). What is contained in the Scriptures has in view the benefit of the reader. There is no exaltation of style for style's sake. At the same time, the very content of the message lends force and beauty to the words in which it is expressed. In the Bible there is a variety of styles. Who is to say that one is superior to the other? In the book of Deuteronomy, for example, there is a smoothness and flow of language that is a delight to read. In other parts of the Old Testament, however, the language is rough. Certain portions of the Hebrew of Daniel, for example, are in a style quite different from that found in Deuteronomy. The same is true of the Psalms. In the same Psalter is to be found the quiet tenderness of the Twenty-Third Psalm, the rugged style of the Ninetieth, and the majestic acrostic of the One Hundred and Nineteenth Psalm. Here is no mechanical or slavish uniformity but rather a grand diversity of style.

The acrostic, it is true, is at times criticized as a somewhat mean device, not worthy of a dignified content. Let one, however, examine the One Hundred and Nineteenth Psalm and he will discover what a forceful device the acrostic actually is. A mere glance at this Psalm shows that it is divided into twenty-two divisions, each consisting of eight verses. Over the first division, in many of our English Bibles, there is printed the first letter of the Hebrew alphabet, *Aleph,* which may be said roughly to correspond to the first letter of our own alphabet. In the Hebrew each of the first eight verses of the Psalm begins with that first letter of the Hebrew alphabet. Each verse in the second commences with the second letter and so on down through the twenty-two letters of that alphabet.

True it is, that in translation the full force of the acrostic is lost. It is, however, an impressive device, and as one reads and rereads this Psalm, the impression is brought home to his mind and heart that the entire language, as it were, represented by its alphabet, is brought into play in order to emphasize and render prominent the central theme of the Psalm, the grandeur and majesty of the Word of God. The Psalm stands in a class by itself; remove from it its acrostic and the force is greatly diminished.

In the New Testament also variety of style is found. The late J. Gresham Machen, for example, used to delight in pointing out to his students the remarkable contrast in style which appears in the first chapter of Luke.[4] The first sentence of the Gospel which, in our English Bibles, occupies four verses, is a remarkably constructed sentence. It works its way up to a majestic climax in the words, " the certainty." It is Greek in its construction and characteristics; and to read it is pure pleasure. Suddenly, however, as one makes the transition from the fourth to the fifth verses of the chapter, he finds himself thrust into another world. Here is no classical Greek but rather the simplicity of the Semitic: "There was in the days of Herod, the King of Judaea, a certain priest named Zacharias, . . . " Not only does one admire the artistry of Luke and the beauty of his language, but one also thanks God that He has given to His written revelation such variety and sheer charm and beauty.

Varied and manifold indeed are the styles which are to be found in the Bible. How we may thank God that His Word is not confined to the monotony of a Koran. The more we study the Bible, the more does the richness and luxuriance of its style bring delight to our hearts. It is clear, then, that infallibility and inerrancy do not involve monotony and sameness of style. He who thinks that the monotony of the Koran should serve as an example of what Biblical infallibility is has no proper conception of the facts. Infallibility does not need to be equated with monotonous style.

The question, however, may be asked, Are there not barbarisms or grammatical errors in the Bible? In the last book of the Bible, the Prophecy of Revelation, does not a word which is usually construed as feminine appear as a masculine? And what about the Hebrew language? Are there not many errors of grammar in the Hebrew of the Old Testament? How can we maintain that the Scriptures are inerrant, when there are grammatical errors, errors which without any doubt were to be found in the original? If the Bible were infallible, it might be claimed, these grammatical errors would not appear in it.

In answer to this several remarks need to be made. First of all, what do we mean by an error of grammar? An error of grammar, it would seem, is, after all, nothing more than a departure from customary usage. Sometimes, that which is regarded as an

4. J. Gresham Machen, *Is the Bible Right About Jesus?* 1941.

error of grammar at last comes to be an accepted manner of speech. When it has thus been accepted it can no longer be considered a mistake. If someone asks me, "Did you see him?" and I reply, "Yes, I saw him," I have simply employed the customary form of the verb. If, on the other hand, I reply, "Yes, I seen him," I may be charged with ignorance. When someone thus employs the past participle without an auxiliary, we consider him to be unlearned. Our judgment will probably be correct. A person who says, "I seen him" has not learned to use correct English, and such a usage will probably serve as somewhat of an index to his character. One who is careless in his habits of speech is likely to be careless in more important matters. On the other hand, this need not necessarily be the case. There are those who have not had the opportunities of a good education, and whereas in their speech they may violate grammatical rules, they are otherwise careful people. One who uses the past participle without an auxiliary may be careless or he may be ignorant; has he, however, committed an error or a sin? What he has done is to deviate from the standard usage, and that is all. In time this standard usage may change even to its opposite. In some languages it is, as a matter of fact, perfectly good practice to employ a past participle without an auxiliary. Certainly, one who does so has not done anything morally wrong; he has merely deviated from what is at the time a widely accepted practice.

When therefore we find in the Bible departures from the so-called standards of speech — and we *do* find them — we need not be surprised. God gave His Word to men that they thereby might come to know and to serve Him. He employed the language which men themselves used. Not a stilted textbook of grammar, but the living speech of the people is what we find in the Holy Scriptures. Inerrancy does not involve a mechanical and stilted formality of style. All that it involves is that in the original manuscripts we have the language which God wished us to have.

The variety which is found in the special revelation of God may be compared with that which occurs in the created world. All that God made was good, but how great is the variety that God has placed in the world. All is not level and uniform. Rather, in mountains and valleys, the rough places and the smooth, we may behold the wonder of God's creative activity. Not monotonous regularity but grand variety meet us on every hand. And so it is with the Bible. God gave us His Word in human speech; the speech of the educated, the speech of the herdsman and shepherd, the speech of poetry, the speech of prose. Here are statistical records, yet here also is prose of incomparable beauty and dignity. Here is poetry and here is symbolism. Marvelous indeed is that variety which is found in the language of the Holy Scriptures. And all is invested with a dignity and majesty which mere language could never possess were it not the vehicle which conveys the message of salvation.

Parallel Passages

The Koran, as Dr. Smith has indicated, does contain slight variants in its texts, and in order to explain this it has been maintained that the Koran was revealed in seven dialects. Shall we assume that the Bible, also, in order to be infallible, must, wherever there are parallel passages, exhibit a word for word agreement? If we do make such an assumption, we have no Biblical warrant for so doing. Should we proceed upon the belief that whenever the Bible records an event or passage more than once there must be a slavish similarity? The facts of the Bible make it clear that such is not at all the case.

A good example for study is the great Messianic prophecy found in Isaiah 2:1-4 and Micah 4:1-3. If the reader will compare these two passages in his English Bible he will make the discovery that there are minor variations between the two. There are good reasons for believing that the text as found in the prophecy of Micah is the original and that Isaiah has based his version upon that of Micah. Why, however, if this be a true interpretation of the facts, did not Isaiah give a verbatim copy? Why did he take the liberty of making slight variations? The answer to these questions may be difficult; indeed, it may not be possible with our present state of knowledge to give an answer that is satisfactory. The fact is that these minor differences are present.

At this point we may note that in many respects the writers of the Bible wrote in accordance with the customs and practices of the day. In times of antiquity it was not the practice to give a verbatim repetition every time something was written out. There are, to take but one example, several copies of the annals of the Assyrian King Sennacherib. They are written down, not on paper or parchment, but on stone. They relate the same events, and yet, despite this fact, there are small differences in the various copies. The writers of the Bible likewise did not always think it necessary to give a verbatim copy, and often they permitted minor differences. Inerrancy does not demand absolute identity in parallel passages. That minor variations may, be found is in perfect harmony with inerrancy.

At this point an objection lies at hand. It may very well be, so the objection runs, that there are minor variations between two parallel accounts, but is it not true that there are also actual contradictions? To this question we would reply in the negative. We do not believe that there are contradictions between passages of the Scripture that are parallel. Those who maintain that genuine contradictions, and not mere minor variations, are to be found, often appeal by way of example to the first two chapters of Genesis. Here, they tell us, are two contradictory accounts of the creation. In fact, this is one of the fundamental dogmas of modern (and also of nineteenth century) "criticism." If one examines a textbook of introduction to the Old Testament composed during the last century, he will find it confidently stated that in the Bible there are two different accounts or stories of the creation. Likewise, if one turns to a "critical" introduction of the present century, he will make the same discovery. It is almost an axiom of modern criticism that there are two conflicting accounts of creation.

Those who hold this view believe that these two accounts go back to different origins and that, when the book of Genesis was finally compiled by a redactor, the two accounts were placed together side by side. Are these critics right, however? Are there two conflicting stories of the creation to be found in the book of Genesis? We for our part believe most emphatically that there are not. Bible-believing scholars for over a hundred years have been pointing out that there are not two "creation" narratives. Bible-believing scholars, however, are largely ignored by "critical" scholars, and their arguments are not given the serious attention that they deserve. We may first of all note that if the first and second chapters present conflicting views of creation, it was passing strange that the so-called redactor placed them together, side by side. Apparently, this redactor, whoever he may have been, did not notice any discrepancies.

Apparently also, no one else noticed any until the advent of "criticism" in the eighteenth century. Be that as it may, however, let us briefly examine the chapters to see if the alleged discrepancies are actually to be found.

It has been asserted that in the two chapters the order of the creation is different. In the second chapter the order is said to be man, vegetation, animals and woman. Obviously, this differs from the first chapter, and hence, we are told, the two conflict at this point. Is this, however, a valid observation? If one reads the second chapter carefully he will note that it is not. Whatever else it is intended to be, the second chapter does not purport to state matters in chronological fashion. To insist upon this would be to compel the chapter to teach nonsense. It would, for example, compel us to believe that God created man (verse 7) before there was any place to put man. It would indeed compel one to understand that God had twice placed man in the garden (cf. vv. 8 and 15). The order of this chapter, one is forced to conclude, is that of emphasis, not of chronology.

It is further maintained, and rightly, that there is a difference of style. A difference of style, however, does not necessarily imply contradiction. The difference in style is to be explained upon the basis of a difference in subject matter and in manner of treatment. The first chapter of Genesis is monumental and grand in style. The second chapter, on the other hand, deals with quiet forms of plastic beauty, the formation of the garden, the planting of its trees, the placing of man in the garden. Certainly, the style of writing differs, but that does not warrant the conclusion that here is a second and different account of the creation.

More important, it is maintained, are the divergent conceptions of God which appear in the two chapters. In Genesis 2 God is said to be conceived anthropomorphically (i.e., acting as a man acts), whereas in the first chapter this is not the case. In the second chapter, God fashions, plants, takes, breathes, builds, and walks. In Genesis 1, on the other hand, it is the majestic Creator who by the word of His mouth brings into existence that which He desires. It must be noted, however, that the conception of God given in the first chapter is also anthropomorphic. Here God is represented as saying, seeing, dividing, calling, blessing, deliberating, and resting. It is in fact impossible for the finite mind to conceive of God without conceiving of Him anthropomorphically. God Himself is an infinite Being, and hence a finite mind cannot conceive of Him unless it speaks of Him and thinks of Him anthropomorphically.

The key to the understanding of the proper relationship between the first and the second chapters is found in the following phrase: "These are the generations of the heavens and the earth" (Genesis 2:4a). A careful study of this particular phrase will clear up much difficulty and misunderstanding. The phrase, "These are the generations" occurs eleven times in the book, and always as a heading. It is as though the writer were to say, "These are the things generated," or, "These are the things begotten." This may be seen, for example, from the heading, "These are the generations of Noah" (Genesis 6:9). The following section does, of course, deal with Noah and the ark, but it works up to the three sons who were generated from Noah. The phrase, "These are the generations of the heavens and the earth," therefore, does not deal primarily with the heavens and the earth but rather with that which was begotten of or generated from them, namely, man. Here, in these words, there is a clue to the fact that Genesis 2, instead of being a second account of creation, deals rather with the creation of man. Indeed, all in the chapter centers about that very fact. Man is the center of the creation. The garden is prepared for him, the animals are to be his helpers, and the woman is to be the help that is like unto him. The second chapter tells of the preparation of the Garden of Eden, so that man can live in it. At the same time it also paves the way for the account of the temptation and the fall which are related in the third chapter.

When the proper relation between the first and the second chapters is thus seen, it becomes clear that there is no contradiction between them. Genesis 1 is the account of creation, Genesis 2 of the Garden of Eden and of the formation of man as the one to dwell in that garden. In adopting this view of the relationship of the two chapters are we closing our eyes to the evidence? Are we engaging in dishonest harmonization? Are we seeking to reconcile what cannot possibly be reconciled? To those who would answer these questions in the affirmative, we can only say that the arguments which they have adduced are not convincing. If the Bible is God's Word that Word must be in harmony and agreement with itself. To force passages of Scripture to contradict one another when they can and do harmonize is to engage in an unwarranted type of exegesis. That minor variants may appear in parallel passages of the Scriptures is consonant with inerrancy; that actual contradictions are present is not. This brief study of the relationship between the first and second chapters of Genesis may serve as a warning that we need not become alarmed whenever we are told that contradictions exist in parallel passages of the Scripture.

A proper study of the relationship which exists between the first and the second chapters of Genesis, will, we believe, make it clear that they do not present two conflicting accounts of creation but, rather, are supplementary and complementary, the one to the other. There are some parallel portions, however, where it is not easy to understand or to discern the proper relationship. It is necessary to say a word about such passages. In order to do this it will be well to choose one of the most difficult, namely, the two sections, 1 Kings 15:14 and 2 Chronicles 14:5. If we set them side by side the difficulty will immediately become apparent.

1 KINGS 15:14	2 CHRONICLES 14:5
But the high places were not removed.	Also he took away out of all the cities of Judah the high places and the images.

The difficulty is increased by the fact that in 2 Chronicles 15:17 we read, "But the high places were not taken away out of Israel." Here, it would seem, if ever, there is plain, unadulterated, downright error. One passage says YES; the other says NO. How then, without engaging in a good bit of intellectual slight-of-hand, can the two be harmonized? Before we face the difficulties, however, there are a few preliminary remarks which must be made. Certain critics, whenever they meet such a difficulty as the one which appears in these parallel passages, immediately cry out, "Here is error; error of such a nature that it must have been found in the original. Therefore, the Bible is not infallible." Such procedure, however, is entirely too hasty; it has not come to serious grips with the situation.

The Bible, according to its own claim, is breathed forth from God. To maintain that there are flaws or errors in it is the same as declaring that there are flaws or errors in God Himself.

On the other hand, the very phenomena of the Bible make it clear that there are weighty difficulties involved in the acceptance of the Bible's claim. For that matter, as we have already indicated, there are weighty difficulties involved in all the doctrines of our Holy Faith. We may go to the root of them all and ask why God, if indeed He is self-sufficient, created the heaven and the earth? We may toy with that question to our heart's desire, but we cannot answer it. We know that He created for His own glory. On the other hand, if He was utterly self-sufficient, why did He wish a further manifestation of His glory? We simply cannot answer the question. Are we therefore, since we are here faced with such tremendous difficulty, to throw overboard our faith in God? Shall we assert that, after all, inasmuch as He has created for His own glory, He is not self-sufficient? It is that type of procedure which is engaged in by those who, as soon as they encounter difficulty in the Scriptural doctrine of inspiration, immediately cry out that the doctrine is false, and that there are errors, after all, in the Bible.

When we meet difficulties in Scripture, it is well to be cautious about asserting the presence of error. We as Bible believers are not called upon to offer an answer to all the problems in the Bible any more than we are called upon to offer an explanation of the doctrine of the Trinity. It is perfectly true that our responsibility is to study the Biblical difficulties in order, if possible, to understand and to harmonize them. To explain them to everyone's satisfaction, however, or to provide a harmony in every instance, is not incumbent upon us. Hence, if in the light of our present state of knowledge there are some passages which we cannot yet harmonize, we need not become overly discouraged.

It may very well be that there are some passages which, save by strained and forced attempts, we cannot harmonize. If such is the case, by all means let us be sufficiently honest and candid to admit that we cannot harmonize the particular passages in question; for to employ strained and forced methods of harmonization is not intellectually honest. If we do employ such methods, we shall only bring upon our heads the deserved charge of intellectual dishonesty. Far better it is to admit our inability than to produce harmonization at the expense of honesty and integrity. Much as we might wish that we could explain all difficulties, we can console ourselves with the thought — and a true thought it is — that those who have rejected the Biblical doctrine of inspiration have far greater problems and difficulties to solve, and that, upon the basis upon which they proceed, these difficulties cannot be solved. We could indeed wish that those who so constantly and confidently reject the Biblical doctrine of inspiration would give evidence that they realize somewhat the implications of what they are doing.

It must also be remembered that the mere fact that we ourselves are unable to solve every difficulty and to answer every question does not involve the conclusion that therefore these difficulties are incapable of solution. One reason why we are unable to solve some of the Biblical difficulties may simply lie in the fact that we do not know all the factors involved. It is quite conceivable that with the increase of knowledge we may see the answer to some problems which for the present baffle and defy explanation. It is well, when we cannot explain, merely to allow the matter to stand. We have no right to declare that there is no answer. To say the least, such a conclusion involves considerable conceit. We cannot see the explanation of a particular problem; does it therefore follow that there is no answer? Such a conclusion is certainly not consonant with the Biblical doctrine of inspiration.

With these preliminary remarks in mind let us turn to the present question. Is there at this point a real and genuine contradiction between the books of Kings and Chronicles? At first glance it would seem strange if the author of Chronicles had allowed a glaring contradiction to stand in his text. It would have been strange if in 15:17 he had remarked that Asa had not taken the high places out of Israel, whereas only a chapter earlier he had stated the very opposite. One wonders what kind of an author he was if he permitted such a glaring contradiction to stand. On the face of it, therefore, it would seem very unlikely that such a contradiction should stand in the book of Chronicles. And this first impression, the more we consider the question, becomes stronger and more convincing.

One rather old interpretation of the difficulty maintains that the passage of Kings is speaking of the removal of legitimate altars or high places of the Lord. These were not removed To this effect both Kings and 2 Chronicles 15:17 are in agreement. On the other hand, the reference in 2 Chronicles 14:5 is said to be to heathen altars and images. This suggested harmonization is not a desperate device of conservatives at all costs to obtain a harmony. Among others, it was advocated by scholars such as Thenius and Bertheau who could not, by any stretch of the imagination, be accused of being actuated by harmonistic desires. According to this explanation, then, we are to understand one passage as teaching that King Asa did not remove the legitimate high places of the Lord, but did remove those that were dedicated to strange gods.

There is a strong objection — yet an objection by no means insuperable — to this interpretation, and that is that three chapters farther along, namely, in 2 Chronicles 17:6, the high places are said to have been removed by Jehoshaphat, and the reference would seem to include high places which were of the Lord. Of course, there is question about the precise force of the word in this passage, and therefore, it may be that after all 2 Chronicles 17:6 is no real objection to the explanation which we have been discussing. Fortunately, however, there is another solution which may serve. Asa and Jehoshaphat, it has been held, did indeed abolish the altars on the high places but did not carry through these reforms with thoroughness. They wished to be true to the Lord, but despite that fact did not consistently fulfil their desire to remove the altars. If this be the correct interpretation, we have the matter discussed from two different viewpoints. On the one hand, as in Kings and 2 Chronicles 15, the thought is presented that an entire removal of the high places in the land was not accomplished. In 2 Chronicles 14:5, however, mention is made of Asa's act in taking away the high places, an act, which, as the same author one chapter later points out, was not carried through perfectly. This explanation finds a support in that 2 Chronicles 15:17 asserts that the high places were not taken away out of Israel, whereas 2 Chronicles 17:6 states that they were taken out of Judah. The kings, we have said, were unable to carry through the reform as fully as they desired. In Judah, where they had authority, the high places were removed. In a wider sense, however, they could do nothing, and the high places remained.

Either one of these alternatives presents a satisfactory explanation of the difficulty and quite possibly one of them is correct. It is also possible that the true explanation lies elsewhere. A careful student of the passages, however, is compelled to acknowledge that, while there is difficulty here, and all is not as clear as one might desire, nevertheless, there is no warrant for the dogmatic assertion that there must be a contradiction.

PARALLEL PASSAGES IN THE GOSPELS

From this very brief consideration of two groups of parallel passages in the Old Testament we have concluded that we are not within warrant in asserting that actual contradictions have been found. Only two groups of passages have been examined, but it may safely and with confidence be asserted that other parallel passages in the Old Testament, while they may bristle with difficulties, cannot legitimately be regarded as exhibiting actual contradictions.

When we turn to the pages of the New Testament, however, do we find the situation to be the same? This question we may answer in the affirmative. There are parallel passages in the New Testament also, but whereas they may often contain difficulties they do not exhibit genuine contradictions. At this point, there is a new factor which must be introduced. It is the question of the reason for our desire to explain difficulties and to attempt harmonization of apparent conflicts. In the year 1891 the late A. B. Bruce wrote:

> The Gospels are the main theatre of harmonistic operations, and we cannot think without sadness of so much effort being wasted on the endeavour to bring the Evangelists into perfect accord in details, which might be more profitably expended in elucidating their grand common theme, the ministry of Love and the doctrine of the Kingdom. To the harmonists busy at their petty task we are inclined to say, Sirs, we would see Jesus. It may, indeed, be thought that the minor work of harmonizing may be combined with the major work of exhibiting the mind and spirit of Christ. But it is not easy; the moods that go along with the two kinds of work are so different. Theoretically, it may seem quite practicable to combine scrupulous payment of tithes even on garden herbs, with due attention to the great matters of the law, justice, mercy and faith. But a wide experience has shown that zeal for minutiae tends to undermine conscience, so that men who carefully strain out gnats are too often equal to the feat of swallowing camels. In

like manner it may be affirmed that it is not from the harmonists that we have got, or are ever likely to get, good 'Lives of Jesus.' To paint the image of the Great Master successfully, one must be set free from slavish solicitude about harmonistic problems, and feel at liberty to handle the materials with a fearless breadth of treatment.[5]

One wonders how it is possible for a man so completely to miss the point. Those of us who would fall under Dr. Bruce's condemnation as "harmonists" have no desire whatever to neglect the great matters of the Law. Rather, it is simply out of a concern for these great matters that we are also occupied with what Dr. Bruce calls "minor" matters. Dr. Bruce would cry, "Sirs, we would see Jesus." Very good, but how is Jesus to be seen? Are we to find Him in a record that is filled with blemishes? Possibly so, but one very annoying question keeps rising. If the Gospels are filled with minor blemishes and errors, how do we know that they do not also contain greater blemishes? If in so-called minor matters they have failed us, by what warrant may we declare that in so-called major matters they are trustworthy? To compare a desire to obtain a proper understanding of the relationship between parallel passages in the Gospels with a Pharisaic attitude toward paying tithes on garden herbs and neglecting the weightier matters of the law is to betray a sad ignorance of the true state of affairs. The quotation which we have made is valuable, however, inasmuch as it shows how far some men may depart from a proper grasp of the questions and issues involved.

In the light of this quotation let us face some of the alleged contradictions which are supposed to occur in the Gospels. One of these has been stated as follows:

Once more: In Matthew (xix. 17), where the ruler asked our Lord: "Good Master, what good thing shall I do that I may have eternal life?" Christ answered, according to the received text: "Why callest thou me good?" Mark and Luke both gave precisely, verbally, the same answer. So far the theory of verbal inspiration is safe. But, unfortunately here again textual criticism finds that Matthew's text should read: "Why askest thou Me concerning that which is good?" — a difference not only in the words but in the thought, and indeed in the point and pith of the answer. Thus we see that the ten-

5. A. B. Bruce, in *Inspiration and Inerrancy*, pp. 32, 33.

dency of a more exact knowledge of the text is to accentuate the individuality and variations of the records, so far as the nearest approach even to our original autographs enables us to judge.[6]

Here, then, we have the problem stated, and with it the implication that the closer we get to the originals the greater the differences between the records. To state the matter very baldly, Matthew reports Christ as saying, "Why askest thou Me concerning that which is good?" whereas Mark and Luke reported Him as having said, "Why callest thou Me good?" Here, if anywhere, it would seem is a contradiction. In our King James version all three evangelists reported the Lord as having said the same thing. At this point, however, the King James version follows inferior manuscripts, and it is now acknowledged that the correct reading, which does not appear in the King James translation, is that which causes the difficulty. What shall we say — what can we say to this? We could say that there is a hopeless contradiction here, and that we can do nothing about it. There are those who do make just that assertion. For our part, however, we cannot join them.

As we turn to the examination of this difficulty, we would first make it clear that we do not believe for a moment that the consideration of the relationship of these passages one to another is a waste of time or in any sense unimportant. We are dealing here with a record of the words which our blessed Lord spoke while He was upon this earth in the flesh. We can conceive of nothing more important than the endeavor to ascertain precisely what those words were and to understand them as best we are able. Those who would dismiss such study with a curt, "We would see Jesus" are simply closing their eyes to the one way in which it is possible to see Jesus. What did Jesus Christ say while He was here upon this earth? It is only through a careful study of His words and works that we shall come to know Him. Consequently, we believe that the study of the relationship which these various passages sustain one to another is of the utmost importance. It is only through such study that we shall come to a deeper understanding of that wondrous Figure whom we find in the Gospels. And, Dr. Bruce to the contrary notwithstanding, we do not see how a satisfactory "Life"

6. Llewellyn J. Evans, "Biblical Scholarship and inspiration," in *Inspiration and Inerrancy*, pp. 153, 154.

of the Lord could be written if it did not make a serious endeavor to come to grips with the things which He uttered.

The approach of the three Gospels to this particular incident is not characterized by slavish repetition and imitation. Each brings forth certain matters of his own; each goes his own way. Matthew, for example, simply says, "And behold! one came to Him and said, Teacher, what good thing shall I do that I may have eternal life" (19:16). Mark on the other hand reads, "And as He was proceeding along the road, one came running and bowed before Him and asked Him, Good teacher, what shall I do that I may inherit eternal life?" (10:17). Luke relates thus: "And a certain ruler asked Him saying, Good teacher, what should I do to inherit eternal life?" (18:18). (*Translations by the author.*)

The first question that arises is whether it was the intention of each evangelist to give a verbatim report of all the words of the rich man and of the Lord, or whether their intention was rather to give a summary of those words. This is not a question to be dismissed lightly, particularly since we today in relating an incident or conveying a message employ the same method. For example, Mr. A. says to me, "Will you please tell Mr. B. that I should like to see him as soon as it is convenient?" I go to Mr. B. and say, "Mr. A. says that he would like to see you as soon as you can make it." I have given correctly the message of Mr. A., but I have not given a verbatim repetition. It is quite possible that the evangelists likewise did not intend to report the conversations verbatim. He who would insist that they must so report those conversations would have a difficult time proving that such was their intention. In the second place, it must be remembered that the original conversation between the rich young ruler and the Lord took place in Aramaic, and that the three Gospels have given the narrative in Greek. In the nature of the case, therefore, the conversation comes to us in a translation.

In the light of the above two considerations, first, that it may not have been the intention of the evangelists to give a verbatim report of the entire conversation, and, second, that they give the conversation in a translation, we may well understand the minor divergencies in the Gospel accounts. These minor divergences are in fact an evidence of genuineness. If each of the three Gospels had given a word for word account which was identical with that of the others, we might possibly suspect that there had been a deliberate attempt to imitate. The minor divergences, therefore, are a sign of genuineness. What then shall we say concerning the answer which the Lord gave? In Matthew, in response to the question introduced by the one word, "Teacher," Christ says, "Why askest thou Me concerning that which is good?" In the other two evangelists, in answer to the question introduced by "Good teacher," Christ says, "Why callest thou Me good?" In all probability, the full question was, "Good teacher, what good thing shall I do that I may possess eternal life?" To this the complete answer of the Lord may have been, "Why callest thou Me good and why askest thou Me concerning that which is good?" (*Translations by the author.*) No one of the evangelists, however, has seen fit to give the complete question or the complete answer. Nor has any of them thought it necessary to give all the details and circum-stances of the meeting. Such was evidently not the intention, nor is there any particular reason why it should have been.

We may now note that Matthew probably purposed to summarize the basic thought of the ruler when he reported the question as "What good thing shall I do that I may have eternal life?" The form of the question in Mark, however, differs from that in Luke. In Mark, the question may be rendered literally, "What shall I do in order that I may inherit eternal life?" in Luke, "Having done what shall I inherit eternal life?" In both cases the meaning is the same. Both, however, are a translation from the Aramaic which the rich young ruler spoke. Both bring out the meaning correctly, just as does the question recorded in Matthew.

Very instructive indeed is this incident. It tells us much as to the manner in which the evangelists reported their messages. Each has introduced that which is germane to his purpose, and the study of each is very rewarding. No slavish imitation is to be found here, but variety of a useful and instructive kind. Differ as the evangelists may in their emphases, there is one thing that we must insist upon. Here is no contradiction; here is no error; here is nothing that is not true to fact. Infallibility and inerrancy do not demand servile imitation, but simply that what is recorded in Scripture be true to fact. In so far as he has dealt with the account, each of the evangelists has reported accurately. Each account is trustworthy and true, and each supplements the other. Here again, therefore, we may say that the parallel passages of Scripture do not contain error.

Such a conclusion, however, is not universally satisfactory. There are those who insist that the only possible explanation of minor divergencies in the parallel passages of the Gospels is that there are real contradictions. Let us hear Dr. Evans once more:

> Nay! every advance which criticism has made in the examination of the Gospel record has only made it more and more certain that the varying representations of the record can be accounted for only as being the inevitable accompaniments of human fallibility in the complex processes through which the record reached its final form. It is now as certain as anything can well be, as a matter of historical record, that, when one Evangelist says that two blind men were healed by Christ near Jericho, while another mentions but one; when one describes the healing as taking place on the way into Jericho, the other on the way out; these variations are to be taken at their face value, as representing diversities in the sources, as the honest, but immaterial contradictions of honest human testimony, when subjected to the complicated and trying conditions through which the Gospel witness has passed — divergences which, so far from discrediting the essential fact, the miracle, only corroborate it to every candid judgment.[7]

It is precisely this, however, which is not the case. Minor contradictions and errors, if they are actually such, do not tend to bring confidence to the whole. If anything, they lessen that confidence. If the evangelists were guilty of trifling errors and evidences of carelessness in so-called minor matters, we simply cannot escape the conclusion that they may have been just as careless in more important things. If the writers of the Gospels cannot even agree as to the number of those whose eyes were opened by the Lord, we may very rightly ask how we can know whether the eyes of any were opened? Since the accounts are so garbled, there may not have been any miracle performed at all. Are matters, therefore, really as Dr. Evans pictures them?

Matthew (20:29ff.) records that as the Lord and His disciples departed from Jericho, a multitude followed and two blind men were sitting by the way side. Mark (10:46) states that as

7. *Op. cit.,* pp. 147, 148.

Christ went out of Jericho with His disciples and a great number of people, Bartimaeus the son of Timaeus, a blind beggar, sat by the way. Luke, on the other hand, (18:35) relates that as He was approaching unto Jericho, a certain blind man sat by the way begging. Difficult indeed is this group of passages to reconcile the one with the other; difficult, however, as they may be, we are not warranted in declaring that there are present actual contradictions or errors.

Matthew alone makes mention of two blind men, just as Matthew alone had mentioned two demoniacs (Matthew 8:28). Luke, unlike both Matthew and Mark, places the miracle as Jesus approached rather than left the city. Here then, it would seem, there must be contradiction and error. Contradiction and error, however, there need not be. Whether a perfectly satisfactory solution to the problem can be given or not, we need not resort to the expedient of postulating error.

One possible solution is that after the Lord had passed through the old Jericho, the city which went back to Canaanitish times, the blind beggar Bartimaeus was healed, and the other who was with him. If this is the explanation, it is obvious that the evangelists are employing the word "Jericho" in different senses. In speaking of an approach to Jericho, Luke would then have reference to the new city which had been built recently during Herodian times; on the other hand, Matthew and Mark would have in mind the old city. If this were the case there would be no contradiction at all, since in speaking of Jericho the evangelists would not have the same thing in mind. Another possible explanation is that as the Lord approached Jericho the blind beggar Bartimaeus heard Him pass by and enquired of the crowd what was happening. Because of the throng that was about Him the Lord did not immediately hear the blind man, hence the latter changes his place so as to meet Jesus when He will leave the city. Emphasis is placed upon Bartimaeus, but it is quite possible that another blind man was also present. In this case, one writer mentions two blind men, whereas the others simply single out the more prominent for mention. We may recall Matthew Henry's comment to the effect that, if two blind beggars were present, there surely was one.

There is, of course, another possibility which must not be neglected. It is that we today do not know all of the circumstances, and that if we did, there would be no difficulty whatever.

If we knew all about the entrance of Christ into Jericho and His meeting with the blind beggars, the whole matter would be cleared up and we should be able to fit all the details into their proper places. As it is, however, God in His goodness has revealed to us enough so that we may see that there is the possibility of harmonizing the accounts. It is unwarranted dogmatically to proclaim that the Scriptures are here in positive error.

In Matthew 5:3 we read: "Blessed *are* the poor in spirit: for theirs is the kingdom of heaven." Slightly different, however, is the language of Luke, "Blessed *be ye* poor: for yours is the kingdom of God" (6:20). Says Nolan R. Best in a chapter which he entitles "The Mirage of Inerrancy"

> But here there is contrast not only of words but of sense. We should be able to tell very much more than we do now about the attitude of Jesus toward the economic conditions of life if we could be sure whether when He spoke of blessed poverty He was thinking of the lack of worldly goods or of the absence of religious pride among those whom He delighted to count as His friends.[8]

Must we here then throw up our hands in despair and cry, Here is contradiction, contradiction which is hopelessly irreconcilable?

Are we straining out a gnat and swallowing a camel if we show some concern about this matter? Is it after all a comparatively trivial thing with which we are here confronted? There may be some who would so dismiss it. We, for our part, cannot do so. We are here concerned with words which Jesus Christ, the Lord of Glory, uttered. We believe that it is all-important to know what He had to say on this subject. What kind of a Bible is it that cannot give us an accurate record of His own words? How can we have much respect for a Book which has garbled a matter of such complete and utter importance?

Is there, however, actually a contradiction in the Beatitudes? Are we not rather again faced with the fact that the evangelists write from different standpoints? Luke stresses the fact that the words are addressed to the disciples. Matthew makes them more general. Does either evangelist claim that he is reporting all that the Lord has said? May not Christ have made both these utterances? May He not even have expanded them beyond that which is preserved for us in the Scriptures?

8. Nolan R. Best, *Inspiration*, 1923, p. 74.

Perhaps the consideration of one more illustration will be instructive. It is maintained that there are serious contradictions in the order of narration of events in the Gospel records. To take but one example, we are told that the calling of the twelve Apostles by the Lord is given a different position in the narrative by Matthew from that which it occupies in Mark and Luke. Matthew, it is said, tells of the ordination of the disciples (10: 1ff.) and then relates that after this ordination (11:1ff.) Christ reproved the Pharisees for their blindness and on the Sabbath day healed the man with the withered hand (12:1-21). Mark and Luke, on the other hand, are said to give quite a different order of events. According to these two Gospels, Christ first reproved the Pharisees and healed the man with the withered hand (Mark 2:23-2:5; Luke 6:1-12) and then ordained His disciples (Mark 3:14-19; Luke 6:13-16). Here, it would seem, the order is indeed not in harmony. If Mark and Luke are correct, does it not follow that Matthew must be incorrect? If one is right, must not the other be wrong? Both cannot be correct. The problem will become clearer if we list the order of events as follows.

MATTHEW	MARK AND LUKE
Ordination of disciples.	Pharisees reproved.
Pharisees reproved.	Man with withered hand healed.
Man with withered hand healed.	Ordination of disciples.

Before we adopt the position that there is irreconcilable conflict, it will be well to examine somewhat more closely the three narratives. Of particular interest is the account which is given in Matthew. In the address which the Lord delivers to His disciples there is a measure of fullness which is not paralleled in the other two Gospels. If now we examine passages such as Luke 12 and 21 we make the discovery that phrases and thoughts of the great Matthew discourse are therein incorporated. It would appear, then, that the Lord spoke these same words on more than one occasion, or else Matthew united these different sayings into one discourse, apparently regarding them as having an internal connection. May it not be that both of these suppositions are correct?

It may furthermore be noted that in the discourse recorded in the Gospel of Matthew, the Lord goes beyond the time then present to the future. Here is, as it were, a picture of times to

come and of the relationship which the disciples and the followers
of the Lord will have to sustain to those times.   One who will
read thoughtfully this wondrous passage will discover about it
an air of solemnity.   It differs considerably from the briefer
charges recorded in Mark and Luke.

The events recorded in the twelfth chapter of Matthew are
introduced by an "at that time."   It is difficult to see that this
phrase must demand that the events took place after the commission recorded in the tenth chapter.   When this fact, together with
the unique character of the commission to the Apostles in Matthew
10 is considered, why must one insist that the order of treatment
of the matter in the Gospels is erroneous?   There is much about
the question that, with our limited knowledge, we do not understand.   To say that there is obvious error, however, is to engage
in the unwarrantable.

From this brief survey of parallel passages in the Gospels we
may learn much as to what is implied in the term "inerrancy."
All that the Bible-believing Christian asserts when he declares
that the Bible is inerrant is that the Bible in its statements is
not contrary to fact.   It records things as they actually were.
The term inerrancy does not demand that each of the Gospels
or that each writer, in case there is a parallel passage, must
necessarily present his account in precisely the same words as
another writer.   Each, however, has told the truth.   He has
recorded matters accurately.   He has given a true picture.   He
has not necessarily told all that occurred.   One writer writes from
one standpoint; another from another.   One includes certain
details, and another includes others.

Very instructive is a study of such parallel passages.   From
it one learns much about the method of the individual writers.
To examine each instance of alleged discrepancy, however, is
not the purpose of this work, nor is such an examination necessary.
The consideration of only a few of these alleged discrepancies will
make it clear that there is not warrant for the assertion that
actual error is present.   In each case there is either apparent
some possible solution or if that solution is not apparent, one
must remember that if more were known than is now the case,
the solution would probably be clear.   Even, however, if that solution were not clear, it is perfectly legitimate to acknowledge that
we are unable to offer an explanation.   Nor are we required in
every instance to offer an explanation.   He who is bold enough to

assert the presence of actual errors in the original manuscripts is in effect saying that the Word which God has revealed contains errors. It is as though he were to say that God Himself has breathed forth an impure Word. It is an attack upon the integrity of God. With such a position the Christian who desires to be faithful to the Scriptures and to honor His God can have nothing to do.

Literal Interpretation

Before we conclude these brief remarks on the subject of inerrancy, there is another matter which must be included. It is the objection that the Bible should not be interpreted in a strictly literal sense. This idea of literal interpretation is, it would seem, equated by some scholars with the doctrine of infallibility. We confess that for our part we cannot see why this should be so. That such is the case, none the less, becomes readily apparent. Men do not want to believe in a literal interpretation of the Bible, and it is in these terms that they characterize the view which the Bible believer holds.

That such an unfortunate and unjust characterization of the Biblical doctrine is made may in part be laid to the door of the Bible believer himself. Unfortunately there is much loose talk and much careless writing upon the subject of inspiration. Not infrequently one hears remarks such as, "I believe that the Bible means exactly what it says." When such sentiments are uttered, and no further qualifying explanation is offered, one may readily understand how false impressions can arise. That such false impressions have arisen is not, of course, to be laid to the account of the great defenders of the Biblical doctrine of inspiration. Men such as Gaussen, Lee, Bannerman, Turretin, Calvin, Luther, Hodge, Warfield, Machen, men such as these are not responsible for the erroneous impression that only a literal interpretation of the Bible is to be admitted. Very clear and very careful also have these great theologians been in their writings. It is not to men such as these that we refer when we assert that the responsibility for the rise of the erroneous view which we are now considering is to be attributed. Not to men such as these but to men who have not made a careful study of the subject is this responsibility to be attributed. It is a sad thing when men who name the Name of Christ are slovenly and careless in their speech. They do untold harm, and the present writer fears that such individuals have been the cause for misunderstanding upon this subject.

It is all very well to assert that the Bible means precisely what it says, but one must go on to ask, "What does the Bible say?" It is impossible to know the meaning of a passage of Scripture unless one first knows what that passage says. Those who constantly talk about the necessity for a literal interpretation of Scripture give the impression that all Scripture must be interpreted literally.

For our part we believe that the Bible is to be interpreted in the sense, and only in the sense that was intended by its authors. In other words, to be true to the proper interpretation of the Bible, we believe that it is necessary to engage in grammatico-historical exegesis. Where the Bible presents prose, we must interpret as prose, where poetry, as poetry. The language of prophecy has its own canons of interpretation. In the work of exegesis, our constant aim and endeavor must be to ascertain, in so far as we are able, the meaning which the writers of the Bible and, basically, the meaning which the Holy Spirit intended to convey. One who would ascertain that meaning must do justice to figures of speech, and to all metaphorical and symbolical expressions.

In daily life one constantly engages in exegesis. In reading the newspaper one does not try to interpret literally whenever possible. One simply seeks to understand what the writer had in mind. It is that which Bible-believing Christians would do in the interpretation of Scripture. The Bible is to be understood in the sense in which its writers intended.

There may be, and there doubtless are, those who claim that only a literal explanation of Scripture will suffice. There are, however, conservatives who insist upon the importance of correct exegetical methods and procedures. There are Bible-believing Christians who demand that their ministry be well trained. For the very reason that they appreciate the importance of correct methods of interpreting the Bible, they insist that their ministers be capable students of theology, Greek, and Hebrew. No one regrets more than do serious Bible believers the present decline in classical studies and in the study of Biblical Greek and Hebrew. Bible believers have been responsible for founding many universities, for they realize full well that a proper knowledge of the Bible and ignorance cannot go hand in hand.

The doctrine of inerrancy for which we contend does not demand the literal interpretation of all parts of Scripture. It does not demand that the writers of the Bible be regarded as mere automata; it does not insist that the writers, whenever they happen to record the same event, must be in actual verbal agreement with one another. It does not necessarily require that events be narrated in the same order. Sometimes, for reasons of emphasis, where the order is not intended to be chronological, that order may vary in differing accounts of the same events. Inerrancy does not demand that when two writers translate from another language, their translations should be in verbatim agreement. It allows them freedom of expression, as long as they represent accurately the thought of the original. Inerrancy does not insist that each writer should give the details, or even as many details of the same event, as another writer. It does not demand that each writer must view the same event from precisely the same standpoint. Inerrancy, in other words, allows for the full employment of the gifts and talents with which God endowed the human writer. All that it postulates is that each writer who was borne of the Holy Spirit has recorded accurately that which the Spirit desired him to record. The Bible, in other words, is a true account of those things of which it speaks. This is the claim that Bible-believing Christians make for it, and this claim is taught by the Bible itself.

It is thus a wondrous Word that God has given to man. Its depth and beauty will largely be missed by those who read only with an eye to criticize. On the other hand, he who reads believingly, and he alone, will not only behold the richness and variety of Scripture, but, of infinitely greater importance, will hear the voice of the heavenly Father. Varied indeed are the styles and approaches used by the human writers of the Bible. Living over a period of some fifteen hundred years, and differing as they did among themselves, they yet uttered one harmonious message concerning God and man's relationship to God. Not a congeries of conflicting opinions is given in the Bible but one harmonious account of God's gracious plan of redemption. And the reason for this deep unity is to be discovered only in the fact that the Bible is the Word of God.

What Is Inerrancy? (II)

"*Matthew might have said, 'The generation of* Jesus *was on this wise,' but the Holy Spirit foreseeing the corruption of the truth, and fortifying us against their deception, says, by Matthew, 'The generation of* Christ *was on this wise."* IRENAEUS

" *. . . look carefully into the Scriptures which are the true (utterances) of the Holy Spirit."*

CLEMENT OF ROME

"*Though various elements are inculcated in each, still the faith of believers differs not, since everything concerning the Nativity, and Passion and Life is declared in all of them by one and the self-same guiding Spirit."*

FRAGMENT ON THE CANON

6

What Is Inerrancy? (II)

In the previous chapter we have engaged in a consideration of the proper import of the word "inerrancy." In this consideration we have sought — whether successfully or not, the reader must judge — to reject any a priori theories as to what inerrancy must be, and instead to examine the phenomena of Scripture itself for our answer. This examination has been necessary in order that we may make it clear that our conception of "inerrancy" must be determined by the Scriptures. We have rejected what Dr. H. P. Smith was pleased to denominate a "natural" theory of inspiration, for we believe that man is not, nor can he be, the judge as to what is and what is not a "natural" theory of inspiration. It has been our contention that the only legitimate theory of inspiration is that which is presented by the Bible itself. Our view of inspiration must be derived from the Bible.

It is necessary to stress this point, for sometimes even those who hold to the high view of inspiration are guilty of approaching the question with ideas already formed as to what the doctrine should be. The late James Orr,[1] for example, who held a high view of the Bible, fell into this error. Thus, he defined "inerrancy" as "hard and fast literality in minute matters of historical, geographical, and scientific detail." Our concern at the present is not so much with the definition itself, mistaken as we think it to be, but with the question, What right has Dr. Orr to impose this particular definition upon the word "inerrancy"? Much confusion has been occasioned because of such a priori approaches to the subject.

In the previous chapter therefore we have sought to make a modest attempt to consider some of the phenomena which the Bible itself presents. Modest as the attempt has been, however, it has at least enabled us to see that the Scriptural conception is

1. James Orr, *Revelation and Inspiration,* reprinted 1952, p. 199.

not at all what one himself might be inclined to entertain. In the study of inerrancy there is one matter which calls for particular comment. It is a subject which has often seemed to be a stumbling block to those who wish to hold to the infallibility of the Bible. The doctrine of an inerrant Bible, it has been maintained, collapses when one considers the manner in which the writers of the New Testament make their quotations from the Old. If inerrancy were true, would not the writers of the New Testament give verbatim quotations from the Old? The fact that they do not do this is sometimes thought to be clear evidence that verbal inspiration, and in particular inerrancy, must go by the board.

The practice of making quotations is indeed very interesting, and there are several methods by which it may be accomplished. Thus, to take the most common method, one may write: Dr. A. A. Hodge says of the books of the Bible that they " . . . are all one and all, in thought and verbal expression, in substance and form, wholly the Word of God, conveying with absolute accuracy and divine authority, all that God meant them to convey, without human additions or admixtures."[2] In this quotation, in order to set off the words of Dr. Hodge, the common device of quotation marks has been employed. Furthermore, the exact words of Hodge have been given without any change or modification. In addition, certain other devices have been employed. Inasmuch as an entire sentence of Dr. Hodge was not given, the quotation began with three dots, in order thereby to show that certain words were omitted. This is, of course, the standard procedure which we employ for making a verbatim quotation, and by such stylistic devices no one can confuse Dr. Hodge's words with those of the one who makes the quotation.

A second way of quoting Hodge would be to assert that he believes the books of the Scriptures in their entirety to be the Word of God and therefore free from any error which might be caused by human admixture. In such a method of quotation only the substance of Hodge's words would be given. His actual words would not be repeated verbatim, but no one can deny that the substance of what Hodge believed about inspiration would have been correctly presented. Dr. Hodge would truly have been quoted, but not verbatim. Another manner by which the

2. A. A. Hodge, *A Commentary on the Confession of Faith*, 1869, p. 51.

thought of Hodge may legitimately be conveyed is as follows. The question is asked, "Does Dr. Hodge believe that the Scriptures are absolutely infallible?" In answer to this question it may be asserted, "He certainly does so believe." In this reply Hodge has again been accurately represented. The substance of his belief on the subject of inspiration has been stated, yet his actual words have not been given. Each one of these different methods of representing the thought of an author is recognized as legitimate. They are practices in which all of us, from time to time, engage and it is well to keep them in mind as we consider some of the methods which the writers of the New Testament employed in their usage of the Old.

MATTHEW 1:21

The first quotation of an Old Testament passage found in the New is in Matthew 1:21, "Behold the virgin shall have in the womb and shall bear a son, and they shall call his name Immanuel." One can see immediately that this quotation differs slightly from the original. The prophecy in Isaiah may be rendered, "Behold the virgin is with child and shall bear a son and shall call his name Immanuel." It is well to note the differences. Isaiah said, "is with child," whereas Matthew, substituting the future tense for the present, says, "shall bear in the womb." Isaiah furthermore says, "She shall call his name," whereas Matthew has, "they shall call his name." How are these differences to be explained?

The Greek translation of the Old Testament which is known as the Septuagint renders the verse, "Behold the virgin shall have in the womb and shall bear a son, and thou [i.e., Ahaz] shalt call his name Immanuel." As soon as we examine this ancient Greek translation it is apparent what Matthew has done. Matthew has followed it rather than the Hebrew and has substituted "shall have in the womb" for the present tense of the original. He has furthermore made the subject of the verb indefinite. Instead of the "she shall call" of the Hebrew or the "thou shalt call" of the Septuagint, Matthew has rendered, "they shall call." Why, it may be asked, has Matthew made these changes? It would seem that he believed the Greek to be more suitable for his purposes than the Hebrew. Apparently, he also regarded the indefinite "they" as a satisfactory expression of the thought of the passage. Matthew of course wrote under Divine inspiration and the very form in which he wrote was a revelation from the Spirit of God. The Spirit, therefore, who is the Author of all Scripture, evidently wished Matthew to present this particular prophecy in a form slightly different from the original Hebrew.

It is well to note the manner in which the passage is introduced, ". . . that there might be fulfilled that which was spoken by the Lord through the prophet, saying, , , , " (*Translations by the author*). The original had been uttered by the Lord, and the thought of this original, after the brief introductory words just given, is then stated by Matthew. It is this message which the Lord spoke. The actual word, "saying," is employed, but it does not therefore follow that Matthew is compelled to give the verbatim words of Isaiah. There is nothing in the introduction to the quotation which demands a word for word repetition of the language of Isaiah. In fact, such slavish following of Isaiah's actual words would be impossible for the simple reason that Isaiah wrote in Hebrew and Matthew in Greek. Matthew, in other words, was compelled to translate, and all the problems involved in translation were faced by him. He has, however, despite that fact, accurately rendered the thought of the prophet. He has told us just what the Lord did as a matter of fact say through Isaiah. He does not contradict Isaiah.

The original Hebrew of the Old Testament employs an adjectival form which can be rendered "is with child," but which is also capable of being translated, "will be with child." Matthew has followed the Greek rendering, and has used the future. Apparently, he thought that thus he could best bring out the message of the original.

In its quotation the first Gospel employs the word "virgin." Now the Hebrew Old Testament, so far as the present writer is aware, does not possess any word which always bears the connotation "virgin." The term which is found in Isaiah 7:14 (*almah*) is one for which there is no precise equivalent in English. Probably we may most closely approximate it with the expressions "damsel" or "maiden." Generally speaking, these two terms would not be employed of a married woman but only of one that was single. The Hebrew word is never, as far as the present writer knows, either in the Old Testament or outside, used of a married woman. In the light of these facts, and in the light also of the fact that the ordinary Hebrew word for virgin, (*bethulah*), can sometimes be employed of a married woman, it would seem that Matthew was very judicious in his choice of a word to render the Hebrew. He employed the Greek term for "virgin," namely, *parthenos,* and in this we believe that he acted wisely. Had he done what some of the early translators did, namely, translate the Hebrew by the Greek word *neanis* (young woman), he would have obscured the meaning of the original; he would not then have been faithful to the Old Testament. Matthew, however, writing under the inspiration of the Holy Spirit, employed just that Greek word which most accurately and justly sets forth the meaning and import of the original. Hence Matthew shows himself to be a responsible and faithful translator.

It is of course perfectly in order to ask why Matthew substitutes "they shall call" for the Hebrew "she shall call." Possibly, however, we cannot give a fully satisfactory answer to this question, but it may be that Matthew merely wishes to make the verb impersonal, removing stress from the person who does the calling to the fact of the calling itself. This supposition is strengthened by the fact that in verse 21 the angel, in speaking to Joseph and announcing to him the fact of the virgin birth, had employed the precise language of the Greek Old Testament, "thou shalt call." The important thing, then, is not so much who is to name the Child as the fact that He shall be named. Matthew follows the Septuagint in spelling out the name, Emmanuel, but, to avoid any misunderstanding, he also interprets it, "God with us."

In all this Matthew has been very faithful to the message of the original. He has not, to be sure, given a verbatim quotation of Isaiah. Inasmuch as he is translating, that would, in the nature of the case, have been impossible. He has, however, brought out the meaning of the prophecy clearly; he has given a true presentation of that which the Lord did as a matter of fact say when He spoke through the mouth of the prophet Isaiah.

At this point an important question intrudes itself. In quoting from the Septuagint, did Matthew regard the entire Septuagint as inspired, and did the fact of his quoting therefrom cause the Septuagint to become inspired? Questions such as these are sometimes, indeed quite frequently, asked, and it is well to consider them. They do not, however, actually come to grips with the Scriptural conception of inspiration.

Inspiration, as we have been contending, has to do with the original manuscripts, and with those alone. That which was breathed forth from the mouth of God, and that alone, may be regarded as inspired. The Hebrew Old Testament which is now in our possession is a copy of the inspired original, and the Septuagint is a translation of that copy. Strictly speaking, neither the present Hebrew Old Testament nor the Septuagint is inspired any more than, let us say, the familiar King James Version is inspired. On the other hand, in so far as the Hebrew approximates the original — and it is a remarkably close approximation — it is the infallible and inerrant Word of the living God. Likewise, in so far as the Septuagint is a correct translation of this Hebrew, and in so far as it correctly and accurately sets forth the thought of the latter, it also may be called, and rightly so, the infallible and inerrant Word of God. The same is true with respect to any translation of Scripture. In so far as the Authorized Version, to take the translation that is most familiar and loved among us, sets forth the truth of the original Hebrew, it also is the infallible and inerrant Word of God. There are extant today many Bibles in many languages of which we may truthfully say that they are the infallible and inerrant Word of God, yet of which we cannot say that they are inspired.

Matthew, therefore, when he employed the Septuagint as adequate for his purposes, did not thereby grant "inspiration" to it. Nor does his usage of the Septuagint imply that he regarded it as inspired. All that his action implies is that he found it to be suitable for his purposes. As an inspired penman he used the Septuagint when it was the wish of the Spirit of God for him to do so. It does not follow that the passage which he quotes is inspired as it stands in the Septuagint. It simply means that that particular passage of the Septuagint was a faithful representation of the thought of the Hebrew. By way of summary we may say that the original Hebrew manuscripts were inspired. The Septuagint was not inspired, but in so far as it correctly represented the original it was the infallible Scripture. When the New Testament writers quoted the Septuagint, they did not thereby render it inspired. Nor did they even constitute as inspired the particular words of the Septuagint which they themselves employed. The words which they employed in their quotations were inspired, not because they came from the Septuagint, but rather, because they were written down by the New Testament authors, who, as they wrote, were borne of the Holy Spirit.

The New Testament, as well as the Old, is the Word of God. The choice of words employed by its writers was given to them by God Himself. He revealed precisely what it was that He desired them to set down in writing. He guided them in their usage of the Old Testament. He made known to them how they were to employ the Septuagint. As they penned their words, they were inspired of the Spirit, so that the first copies of what they wrote, like the first copies of the Old Testament books, are the inspired Word of God.

From this instance of Matthew's usage of Isaiah there are several conclusions which we may legitimately draw.

1. In employing the Old Testament the New Testament writers were compelled to translate either from the Hebrew or the Aramaic.

2. In making their translation the New Testament writers did not seek to give a slavishly literal rendering, but rather, by the use of suitable Greek words that were at their disposal, to bring out the true sense of the Old Testament passage.

3. In making their quotations the New Testament writers do not necessarily reproduce the Old Testament verbatim. They often prefer merely to give the sense of the Old Testament.

4. In their usage of the Old Testament the writers of the New often prefer the ancient Greek translation which is commonly known as the Septuagint.

5. When they so desire and it better suits their purpose the writers of the New Testament have no hesitation in deviating in minor matters from the exact language of the Septuagint.

6. The New Testament usage of the Septuagint does not secure inspiration for the latter.

7. From the fact that the writers of the New Testament employed the Septuagint as suitable for their purposes it does not follow that they regarded it as inspired.

8. The words which the New Testament authors use from the Septuagint do not suddenly become inspired portions of the Septuagint.

9. The Spirit of God guided the writers of the New Testament in their general usage and in their choice of language from the Septuagint, so that what they wrote was inspired of Him. It was inspired, however, not because it was taken from the Septuagint, but rather, because it was breathed out by Him and written down by those whom the Spirit bore as they composed the New Testament writings.

MARK 1:1-3

Very instructive is this usage which Matthew makes of the prophecy of Isaiah. A careful study thereof will free the mind from many a misconception. From this first quotation given in the Gospel of Matthew let us turn to the first quotation of the Old Testament which appears in Mark. Here we enter into a type of problem that is quite different from that which the Matthew passage had presented.

The quotation which we are now about to consider is as follows. "As it is written in Isaiah the prophet, Behold! I send my messenger before thy face, who will prepare thy way; The voice of one crying in the wilderness, Prepare the way of the Lord, make straight his paths" (*translation by the author*). The difficulty — for in comparison with our frequent usage of quotation marks it seems to be a difficulty — is that after the words, "as it is written in Isaiah the prophet," there follows a verse taken from Malachi 3:1, and only then does the quotation from Isaiah appear. One's first reaction is to regard this as an error, and there are many who do just that. Mark tells us that he is referring to Isaiah, but before he gets around to Isaiah he introduces some words from Malachi. A harmless error, we sometimes are told, but an error nevertheless. Perhaps, it has been maintained, there was an anthology in which the two passages were found together. Mark might have been employing this anthology, and so the error would very naturally have arisen. Whatever be the method in which it arose, however, there are those who insist that it is an error.

Before we too hastily conclude that there is an error here, it will be well to examine the passage more closely. To one who reads the King James' version, the difficulty is not apparent, for that version introduces the quotation with the words, "As it is written in the prophets." This translation removes the difficulty entirely. When, however, we must make a choice between an easier and a more difficult reading, we must remember that the more difficult reading is likely to be correct. And that is the case here. Not only is the more difficult reading here more likely to be correct, but it is also attested by better manuscripts. The correct reading, we may safely assume, is, "As it is written in Isaiah the prophet."

The question then which we must face is this, Did Mark erroneously attribute to the prophet Isaiah a passage which was actually written by Malachi? In quoting Malachi did Mark think that he was quoting from Isaiah? If these questions must be answered in the affirmative, then, very obviously, Mark was mistaken, and it simply follows that here is an error in the Bible, and the whole Scriptural doctrine of inspiration with all that is involved therein must go by the board. Was Mark therefore actually in error in his procedure? That is the question which we must now face.

It is evident that Mark desires to introduce his readers immediately to the work of John the Baptist in the wilderness. In fact, the words, "in the wilderness" (verse 3) appear almost as a key phrase. The messenger who heralded the coming of the Savior was one who was to appear in the wilderness. Apparently Mark named Isaiah as the author who had employed this phrase (Isaiah 40:3) and at the same time had thought that it was suitable to include an introductory quotation from Malachi. Turretin suggests a solution which is worthy of very careful consideration.[3] Mark mentions Isaiah, he says, because Isaiah was the older of the two and from him the younger prophet had drawn. Indeed, it cannot be denied that the words from Malachi are very similar to those from Isaiah, and it is quite likely that there was on Malachi's part conscious reflection upon the prophecy of Isaiah.

What Mark has actually done then is to name Isaiah as the author of the quotation in which the desert is mentioned, the quotation which is the most immediately applicable to the work and ministry of John the Baptist. If it should be objected that Mark uses the phrase "as it is written," we may well reply that we are evidently to understand these words as having reference to the message itself rather than to a verbatim presen-

3. Francis Turretin: *Institutio Theologiae Elencticae,* vol. 1, 1847, p. 75.

tation of what Isaiah had said. That this is the case becomes immediately apparent if we place the three sources together, one after the other.

THE HEBREW OF ISAIAH

Make straight in the wilderness a highway for our God.

THE SEPTUAGINT

Make straight the paths of our God.

MARK

Make straight his paths.

In the light of what Mark actually does, it is perfectly clear that by the word "it is written" he did not intend his readers to receive the impression that he was giving a verbatim quotation of Isaiah. In the nature of the case, inasmuch as Mark must engage in translation (he was writing Greek, and Isaiah Hebrew), he could not give verbatim what was written in Isaiah. Very obviously, then, by the phrase "it is written" he must have desired his readers to receive a different impression. What was it then that he wished them to understand?

It would seem that the first and second verses of Mark belong together. The first verse calls attention to the beginning of the Gospel. What was that beginning of the Gospel of Jesus Christ? It was, Mark tells us, as it was written in Isaiah. He then proceeds to recount what Isaiah had written about the beginning of the Gospel. That which was written, then, is, according to Mark, the beginning of the Gospel, and it is this beginning to which the evangelist would direct the attention of the readers. The ministry of John the Baptist in the wilderness is the beginning of the Gospel of Jesus Christ, and that beginning was already set forth by Isaiah.

If this interpretation is correct, there is then at hand an answer to the question why Mark employed words from Malachi. These words, although they are found in the text of Malachi, nevertheless do indeed reflect the ideas of the fortieth chapter of Isaiah. The sentence, "Behold, I send my messenger before thy face," corresponds to Isaiah's phraseology, "The voice of one crying in the wilderness." Likewise his "who shall prepare thy way" corresponds to Isaiah's "prepare the way of the Lord." The thought of Malachi is based upon that of Isaiah. Apparently

Mark deliberately introduced this language from Malachi because it lent itself so well to the matter in hand.

We are far from maintaining that there is no difficulty for the modern reader in this usage of the evangelist. It is so different from our usual practices that we are likely on that account to condemn it offhand. Difficult as it is, however, and differing as it does from our common practices of the twentieth century, it is not on that account to be regarded as an actual error. We are not in a position to maintain that at this point the second evangelist was actually guilty of error. Those who insist that Mark made a mistake have read too much into the words "it is written." Mark would have us understand that the beginning of the Gospel was written in Isaiah; the deniers of Mark's accuracy apparently think that he meant that the actual words which are quoted were therein written. This is to be over-literal; if the advocates of this position were consistent, they would be compelled to assert that nothing of what appears in the Greek text of Mark was written in Isaiah, for all that is written in Isaiah is Hebrew. It is not Mark, but the literal-minded critics of Mark who at this point are in error.

Acts 15:14-18

From what has been said thus far it should be clear that each usage which the New Testament makes of the Old must be examined and studied by itself. It is first of all necessary to determine, in so far as it is possible, what the purpose of the New Testament writer is. Then, and then only can one have a proper understanding of the procedure in which the New Testament writer has engaged. Very instructive for this purpose is the usage which James at the Apostolic Council makes of the Old Testament. The relevant passage is found in the fifteenth chapter of Acts. A word is in order about the background which called forth this utterance.

In the early Church the question had arisen whether the Gentiles were to be received without circumcision. One group, the Judaizers, had insisted that circumcision was necessary unto salvation. The others, under the leadership of the Apostles, vigorously rejected this position. Peter arose and courageously attacked the stand of the Judaizers. His words will ever remain as a ringing declaration of the truth of salvation by grace. "We know," he said, "that by the grace of the Lord Jesus we shall be saved even as they" (Acts 15:11). Peter made it very clear that he was unalterably opposed to the idea that circumcision or any other requirement, save faith in Jesus Christ, should be demanded of the new converts. When he had finished speaking, Paul and Barnabas took exactly the same side in the debate as did Peter. Between Peter and the other two there was the greatest harmony. Paul and Barnabas told how through them God had wrought signs and wonders among the Gentiles. When they had finished, James arose to speak. Now at last, it might have been thought, a voice would be raised in defense of the necessity of observing the ceremonial law as a condition of salvation. In James, the strict Jew, one might have thought, Paul, Barnabas, and Peter would surely have a strong opponent. But not only did James not oppose the others, he most heartily agreed with them. He was not at all concerned to insist upon the necessity of the ceremonial law for salvation; rather, he pointed out that he was in perfect agreement with the others. He made a favorable reference to Peter's speech, and then appealed to the Old Testament in support of that speech.

He recounts how Peter had called attention to the fact that at the first God took from among the Gentiles a people for His Name. He adopts the same position as that for which Peter, Paul, and Barnabas were contending. Salvation is not to be restricted to the Jews, but God has also taken from the Gentiles a people for His Name. To support his statement James appeals to the Old Testament. "To this fact," we may paraphrase his thought, "namely, that God has visited to take for Himself a people from the Gentiles, agree the words of the prophets, as it is written." With these words, "as it is written," we are brought to the Old Testament itself. Then follows a remarkable summary of the Old Testament teaching. (*Translations by the author.*)

"After this I shall return and build again the booth of David that is fallen, and its remnants I shall build again and make it straight.

"In order that the remnant of men may seek the Lord and all the Gentiles upon whom my name is called upon them,
"Saith the Lord, who doeth these things, known from eternity."

The general import of the entire quotation is sufficiently clear. Without question it has reference to the outcalling of the Gentiles to be a people unto God's Name. The upbuilding of the fallen booth of David finds its fulfillment according to this passage in the calling out of the Gentiles, that is, in the work of the Church of Christ. James has thus very aptly brought forth from the Old Testament, references to the preaching of the Gospel in this present age in which we now live.

When, however, we compare James' quotations with the Old Testament text itself, we may well ask, What procedure has he followed? As we read this account of the Apostolic Council in the book of Acts, we must remember that we are reading a narrative which was written by Luke in Greek. In his fifteenth chapter Luke is reporting the words which James employed. First of all, therefore, the question arises, Did James employ precisely these words which Luke has recorded? Did he, in other words, speak in Greek or in Aramaic? It is probably not incorrect to assume that he spoke in Aramaic. If that were the case, Luke's narrative is a translation of what James has said. It is well, as we proceed, to bear this thought in mind.

From what portions of the Old Testament does James derive his quotations? He begins with the words, "After this I shall return and build the booth of David that is fallen." In Jeremiah 12:15 we read, "And it shall come to pass after uprooting them I shall return and have mercy upon them." With the verse in Jeremiah, James' words have a formal similarity. James omits "and it shall come to pass" and simply employs the word "after." In place of Jeremiah's "I have uprooted them" he simply says, "these things." He continues with "I shall return" and then substitutes for Jeremiah's "and have mercy upon them" the words "and build up . . . . " If we set the two passages side by side, James' procedure will be more clearly seen.

JEREMIAH	JAMES
And it shall come to pass	
after	after
my uprooting them	these things
I shall return	I shall return
and have mercy upon them.	and build up.

So much, then, for the beginning of the quotation. James commences with a reference to Jeremiah. He soon leaves Jeremiah, however, and takes over from the ninth chapter of

Amos. Here, for the most part, he follows the Septuagint. If the three passages are set side by side James' procedure will be more readily grasped.

HEBREW	SEPTUAGINT	JAMES
I shall raise the booth of David that is fallen	I shall raise up the tent of David that is fallen	And I shall build up the tent of David that is fallen,
And I shall fence up its breaches, and its ruins I shall raise	And I shall build up its fallen places and I shall raise its ruins	and its ruins I shall build up and make it straight
And I shall build it as the days of old	And I shall build it as the days of eternity	
To the end that they may possess the remnant of Edom, and all the Gentiles upon whom my name is called upon them, saith the Lord who doeth this.	To the end that the remnant of men may seek, and all the Gentiles upon whom my name is called upon them, saith the Lord God, who doeth these things.	In order that the remnant of men may seek the Lord, and all the Gentiles upon whom my name is called upon them, saith the Lord who doeth these things.

The comparison of these three passages is quite interesting. It is clear that James finds the Septuagint suitable for his purpose. Furthermore, he does not follow the Greek translation in any slavish fashion. He adapts it to his own purposes. In fact he seems to give a running summary of the thought of the Septuagint. It must be remembered, however, that there is another possibility always to be kept in mind. In his speech, James, we have said, probably employed the Aramaic language. Employing the Aramaic he may have adhered more closely to the Hebrew than does Luke. If that had been the case, James would have given to us a summary in Aramaic of the teaching of the prophets. Luke recorded the material in Greek, and he may have believed that the Septuagint presented a satisfactory summary of the thought of James. If such were the case Luke must be understood as intending to report not the verbatim words of James — that he could not have done, inasmuch as James spoke Aramaic and Luke wrote in Greek — but rather a summary of James' words which would accurately have represented his thought. If such were Luke's intention, there can surely be no legitimate objection to it. We do the same thing today.

James closes his summary with a thought from Isaiah. The words "known from eternity" are based upon Isaiah 45:21. They are not, however, nor are they intended to be, a direct quotation of the language of the prophet.

It should be clear that James has done just what he said he was doing. "To this agree the words of the prophets," he had asserted, and then, to prove his assertion, he adduced some of the words of the prophets. He does not claim to give a precise, word-for-word quotation from the prophetical books. All he claims is that what the prophets have spoken agrees with the fact that now God has visited to take from the Gentiles a people for His Name. When the purpose of James is kept in mind no legitimate objection can be raised against it.

From the usage which James here makes of the Old Testament we may learn that he has no hesitation in engaging in a free paraphrase of the Old Testament language. He even adapts that language to suit his own purpose. This is clearly seen in his treatment of Jeremiah. The words of Jeremiah would have been well known to Jewish hearers. Jewish hearers would have rightly seen in them the blessed promise that after the punishment of the exile God would again manifest mercy to His people. As they heard James use these words, they would have linked up the building of David's fallen booth with God's once more showing mercy to the people. They would have realized that in the Gospel of God's grace, the Gospel which Peter, Paul, and Barnabas had so stoutly defended, there was indeed seen, in a sense far more wondrous than in any mere return from Babylonian exile, the mercy of God once more manifested to His people.

With respect to the passage from Isaiah, it is difficult to know precisely what James' purpose was. It would seem that he desired merely to allude to that passage of Scripture without making any particular quotation of it. His words call to mind the language of Isaiah, and possibly that was all that he intended to do. The reader who will carefully compare the procedure of James with both the Septuagint and the original Hebrew will learn much concerning the method which the New Testament writers, in their use of the Old Testament, permitted themselves to employ.

ISAIAH 6:9-10

From what has been remarked hitherto it should be abundantly clear that in applying to the Scriptures the term inerrant, we do not at all insist that New Testament quotations must be verbatim reproductions of the Old. Each reference to the Old Testament must be examined individually, and thus one may come to an understanding of the principles which the New Testament writers employed. All that we, as believers in the inerrancy of

Scripture, need maintain is that the writers of the New Testament, in making their quotations, have not contradicted the Old Testament. What they have written is true; it is an accurate representation of the Old Testament thought.

That all doubt may be removed, however, it will be well to consider one of the more difficult examples of quotation. It is the usage which the New Testament writers make of the familiar words of Isaiah 6, revealed to him concerning the callousness of those to whom he is to preach. It will tend toward clarity if first we give a rendering of the Hebrew and place it side by side with the Greek. We may then note the various forms of the prophecy as they appear in the New Testament.

HEBREW	SEPTUAGINT
9. And he said, Go and thou shalt say to this people, Hear, hearing, and do not perceive, and see, seeing, and do not know.	9. And he said, Go, and say to this people, In hearing ye shall hear and will not understand, and seeing ye shall see and will not behold.
10. Make fat the heart of this people, and its ears make heavy, and its eyes smear over;	There has become fat the heart of this people, and with their ears they have heard heavily, and their eyes they have smeared over;
Lest it see with its eyes, and with its ears it hear, and its heart perceive, and it turn and there be healing to it.	Lest they see with their eyes and with their ears they should hear and understand with their heart and should turn and I should heal them.

The attentive reader will find it profitable first to note the differences which exist between the Greek and Hebrew. He may then examine the quotations which appear in the New Testament.

MATTHEW 13:14, 15

14. And this prophecy of Isaiah is fulfilled for them which sayeth,
   Hearing ye shall hear and not understand,
   And seeing ye shall see and not behold.
15. The heart of this people has become fat,
   And with the ears they have heard heavily,

And their eyes they have smeared over,
Lest they should see with the eyes
And with the ears hear,
And with the heart they shall understand and turn [i.e.,
repent]
And I shall heal them.

MARK 4:11,12

11. And he said to them, To you is given the mystery of the
kingdom of God, but to those that are without all these
things are done in parables, that

12. Seeing they might see and not behold,
And hearing they might hear and not understand,
Lest they should turn and it should be forgiven them

LUKE 8:10

12. But he said, To you it is given to know the mystery of the
kingdom of God, but to the rest in parables, that seeing
they may not see and hearing they may not understand.

JOHN 12:40

He hath blinded their eyes and made fat their heart, that
they might not behold with their eyes and understand with
their heart and turn, and I shall heal them.

ACTS 28:26, 27

26. Saying, Go to this people and say,
In hearing ye shall hear and not understand,
and seeing ye shall see and not behold,

27. The heart of this people has become fat
And with their ears they have heard heavily,
And their eyes they have smeared over;
Lest they should ever see with their eyes
And with their ears they should hear,
And with the heart they should understand and turn,
And I shall heal them.

Here indeed is a variety of divergences. And it must be
acknowledged that if the reader were to make the comparison in
the original languages he would discover yet more variety, which
cannot well be represented in an English translation. It is not,
however, germane to our purpose to discuss each of these minor
variations. One point, nevertheless, cannot be passed by. A
mere glance at the language used in the Gospel of John makes

clear that it differs from the other New Testament quotations. In all these other references it is simply stated that the heart of the people has become fat whereas in the Gospel of John the Agent of this hardening is plainly said to be God. Now, is it not alleging something quite different from what was declared by Isaiah, to assert that God is the One who has hardened the hearts? Has not the author of the fourth Gospel added a thought that is found neither in the other parallel quotations which occur in the New Testament nor in the original text of Isaiah itself?

At first sight this might seem to be the case. When, however, we examine more closely the context in John, we discover that such a first impression is incorrect. The quotations which John makes are indeed remarkable. The beloved disciple points out that the sad unbelief which was manifested by the Pharisees was, as a matter of fact, in accordance with Old Testament prophecy. He then appeals to the prophecy in Isaiah 6 with the words, "For Isaiah said again. . . ." It is perfectly obvious that he is not giving a verbatim reproduction, either of the Hebrew or of the Septuagint. He is, rather, bringing out the deep meaning of Isaiah's words. He is stressing the point that the unbelief of the Pharisees was to be traced to the fact that they could not believe, because God Himself had rendered them incapable of belief. Their eyes were blind, but it was God who had blinded their eyes; their heart was fat, but it was God who had made it so. Is this, however, as John claims, what Isaiah really said? One need but consider carefully the actual words of Isaiah to discover that John has in no wise misrepresented him. In the prophecy itself, the command is given to Isaiah to go to the nation and to command it to hear but not to perceive. By his preaching the prophet is to make the heart of the nation callous lest it repent and God heal it. The ministry of the prophet is such that it produces hardness in the hearts of the hearers, a tragic fact that was revealed almost immediately in the refusal of the stubborn king Ahaz to believe the message which was preached to him.

It would be a grave mistake to think that the preaching of Isaiah, in itself, could harden the heart of the hearer. It was the Lord who worked through the prophecy and it was the Lord who hardened the heart. In advance, before any preaching whatever had been done, the Lord had announced to Isaiah that the outcome of his ministry would be the destruction of his hearers.

This destruction was to be wrought by God through the instrumentality of His servant. It is therefore not primarily a prediction that the people will not believe, but rather a prediction that they cannot believe. Their heart is to be made fat lest, were it not fat, it might repent. The outcome is foretold in advance. In the light of these facts is it not clear that the One who does the hardening is none other than God Himself? Difficult as is the doctrine that faces us, we cannot escape the plain statements of the Scripture. Here is the doctrine of reprobation; and John the Apostle, as the spokesman for the Holy Spirit, has gone to the heart of the matter in interpreting as he did. John has given a fair representation of the message of the prophet Isaiah. Isaiah said just what the Apostle claims that he did.

With respect to the other quotations, they differ from John in that they follow more closely the letter of Isaiah than did John. With respect to the content, however, they do not at all differ essentially from John. In both, the actual message of Isaiah is found. When the purpose of the writer in each instance is taken into consideration, we may safely say that justice has been done to the Old Testament.

It may be that the examination of these passages has been somewhat tedious to the reader. However, it is only by means of such an examination that one comes to understand and to appreciate the true nature of the quotations which the New Testament writers make of the Old. It is only by such an examination as this that one can guard himself from the false conceptions of inerrancy that are abroad in our day.

Here in the New Testament is no mechanical, parrot-like repetition. Here, however, we see the human writers of the Bible acting as responsible agents. Here we begin to understand the true nature of verbal inspiration and also of inerrancy. Here there opens to view a broad vista and a fruitful field for further investigation. Here is diversity, rich and instructive. Here in the age of fulfillment, is the Spirit of God, bringing to clearer light the deep truth which He had formerly revealed unto the writers of the Old Testament.

Are There Errors in the Bible?

". . . the Gospel cannot stand in part and fall in part . . ."
                                            CYPRIAN

". . . of which [i.e., the Scriptures] *not one tittle shall pass away without being accomplished; for the mouth of the Lord, the Holy Spirit, spoke it."*
                                CLEMENT OF ALEXANDRIA

[The Scriptures] *"breathe the Spirit of fullness, and there is nothing, whether in the Law or in the Prophets, in the Evangelists or in the Apostles, which does not descend from the fullness of the Divine Majesty."*
                                            ORIGEN

7

Are There Errors in the Bible?

In what has been said before we have sought to make clear what the phenomena of the Bible permit one to believe concerning inerrancy. Now it is possible that one may agree with all of this, and yet there may be one consideration which might cause one to hold back from accepting in its entirety the Bible as the infallible Word of God. It is the assumption that there are errors in the Bible.

There are good Christian people who would like to believe in the absolute trustworthiness of the Bible, yet who hesitate because they are convinced that there are mistakes in the Scriptures. With such people we have great sympathy. In serious Bible study one often encounters difficulties, and the solution of these difficulties is not always readily apparent. Foolish indeed is the man who thinks that he has an answer to every problem in the Bible. On the other hand, an honest and inquiring soul will of course be troubled by some of the problems which are met in the study of Scripture.

If, however, it is rash to profess to solve all the problems which the study of the Bible brings upon us, it is yet more rash to make the dogmatic assertion that there are actual errors in the Bible. The proper method of dealing with difficulties is not to dismiss them as positive errors, for if the Bible is indeed God-breathed, it follows that it must be true and infallible. To assume that God could speak a Word that was contrary to fact is to assume that God Himself cannot operate without error. The very nature of God therefore is at stake. If we assert that the autographa of Scripture contain error, we are saying that God is guilty of having told us something that is not true. It may be a matter which we ourselves would call minor, but in this case a minor error is no less an error than a major one. A person who continues to make so-called trifling mistakes is not one whom we can trust. And one who constantly slips up in lesser points is one whose words may well be brought into question when greater matters are involved. If God has communicated wrong information even in so-called unimportant matters, He is not a trustworthy God. It is therefore the question of Biblical theism which is at stake. If the autographa of Scripture are not infallible, we can never be sure at what points they are trustworthy and at what they are not. We would then have no sure position for the defense of Christianity. If, as a matter of fact, the revelation of God is not free of error, the message of Christianity must ever remain in doubt.

With these considerations in mind, let us examine briefly some of the alleged errors which are supposedly found in the Bible. At the very outset we are told that the early chapters of Genesis are the product of a prescientific age and hence cannot today be accepted as genuine history. This is a charge that is frequently made, and it is one to which our attention must be directed. The first three chapters of Genesis, which are the object of much modern criticism, relate the creation of the heaven and the earth, the making ready of the earth for man to inhabit, the creation of man, the preparation of the Garden of Eden, and the temptation and fall of Adam. Here, we are told, there may be legend or myth, but not sober history.

What, on the other hand, is the claim which these chapters make for themselves? Obviously, they purport to be historical. They tell a straightforward narrative, which is without any of the characteristics of legend. Apparently the writer believed that he was relating something that had actually occurred. It is certainly thus that the holy and infallible Christ understood him. "Have ye not read," He asks, "that he which made *them* at the beginning made them male and female?" (Matthew 19: 4). Not only did the Lord quote this verse from Genesis but He proceeded to base upon it His infallible teaching, "What therefore God hath joined together, let not man put asunder" (Matthew 19:6). If in its assertion that the early chapters of Genesis are not historical, modern scholarship is correct, how grossly mistaken Jesus Christ was! The apostle Paul likewise regarded the Genesis narrative as historical and upon it he bases a great deal. He contrasts the fall of Adam with the redemption and obedience of Christ. Indeed, it is by no means going too far to say, despite some modern assertions to the contrary, that if the fall of Adam was not historical for Paul, neither was the redemption of Christ. Paul regarded the early chapters of Genesis as historical and although he did not have some of the "insights" of modern theology nor the "gains" of nineteenth-century "criticism" at his disposal, he has not been surpassed among men as an interpreter of the Old Testament.

The early chapters of Genesis must be interpreted as historical narrative. They purport to tell of something that actually occurred. According to them God did create the heaven and earth; Adam and Eve were actual historical persons who lived upon this earth and who, by eating of the forbidden fruit, disobeyed God. Their tragic act of disobedience brought with it dire consequences for the entire world. He who says that, although these early chapters purport to be history, he himself does not believe that history, is a far better and more trustworthy exegete than is he who asserts that they are "profoundly true" but that they were never intended to be understood as history.

If then we may arrive at the position (and it is the only position at which one may legitimately arrive) that the early chapters of Genesis purport to be history, let us next ask the question whether, as a matter of actual fact, they are filled with the errors which inescapably accompany a pre-scientific age. The answer to this question must be in the negative. In their statements these chapters are scientifically accurate. They do not teach anything that is not in accord with the facts. Can anyone point out an actual error, for example, in the first chapter of Genesis?

Particularly interesting does this question become when one compares the first chapter of Genesis with the so-called Babylonian account of creation. Are there errors in the Babylonian account? To ask this question is to give the answer. No one would think seriously of defending the Babylonian narrative from the charge of error, for the simple reason that it is so full of it. In the midst of the polytheism and superstition of that ancient world the first chapter of the Bible, on the other hand, stands out like a fair flower in a barren wilderness. The Genesis account differs completely from the cosmogonies of the ancient world. In it there is a robust and vigorous monotheism; the Creator is glorified and His wondrous work in creation exalted. Here God is honored in such a way that the reader may come to marvel at the greatness of Him who by the word of His mouth brought all things into being.

Are there errors in the first chapter of the Bible? Let us say without fear of contradiction that no one has been able to demonstrate the presence of error in this majestic opening chapter of Scripture. Some have said that the mention of the presence of light without the sun is error. Light, however, need not be concentrated in the sun. There can be light bearers apart from the sun, and if we read the chapter carefully, we must conclude that at one time such was the case. Another objection is from the side of evolution, which, contrary to the narrative in Genesis, teaches that man has evolved from lower animals. To this we would simply reply that such an assumption is an assumption only; it is not based upon fact. It is contradicted both by the Bible and by other evidence. There is no evidence that man came from lower animals, but rather much evidence to the contrary. If man came from the animals whence did he receive his ability to reason, to speak, to communicate, to say nothing of his capacity for religious worship of God? These are questions which antitheistic theories of evolution cannot answer. What settles the matter, however, is the plain declaration of the chapter which we are now considering that creation was "after its kind." In our opinion the hypothesis of evolution has been so convincingly exploded that it is a wonder that men still toy with it. The arguments against the hypothesis are extremely cogent. The difficulties which are found in an acceptance of the first chapter of Genesis seem almost trifling when compared with those which are found in any hypothesis of the evolution of man.[1]

Another objection brought against the first chapter of Genesis is that it is geocentric, whereas, as a matter of fact, we know that the sun is the center of the universe. To this objection we may reply that the first chapter of the Bible is indeed written from a geocentric standpoint. It does tell its story from the position of one who lives on this globe, and it also points out how the other heavenly bodies serve the earth. Is this, however, out of accord with the facts? Although the emphasis in Genesis 1 is geocentric, it is clear that this emphasis is for a religious purpose. Man is to live, not upon some other planet, but upon the

1. Cf. Dewar and Shelton, *Is Evolution Proved?*, London, 1947.

earth, and here also is to be the scene of his redemption. Is it any wonder that Genesis lays stress upon this earth? What would be the purpose in emphasizing what took place on some other planet? What Genesis says is perfectly in accord with fact. It does not teach that this earth is the center of the universe, and so does not at all conflict with any facts of science. It teaches that the sun and the moon serve this earth, and in so teaching it is perfectly correct. As a matter of fact, whatever other purposes they may have, the sun and moon do serve this earth. The geocentricity which is found in the first chapter of the Bible is perfectly in accord with scientific fact. Genesis does not claim to give a description of the relation of the heavenly bodies one to another, but to state that the earth on which we live is benefited by the sun and moon. When, therefore, the purpose of Genesis is taken into consideration it will be seen that there is no error whatever. And if anyone objects to the thought that even in a religious sense the emphasis of Genesis is geocentric, then in all consistency he must himself stop talking about the sunrise or the sunset. One who lives upon the earth, no matter how many advanced degrees in physics or astronomy he possesses, cannot help speaking of the universe from the standpoint of an earth dweller. This obvious fact should be kept in mind when the charge of the geocentricity of Genesis 1 is raised.

Surely, however, it will be said, Genesis is in error in declaring that the heaven and the earth were brought into being in six days. To this we may reply that there is serious question whether we are to understand the reference in Genesis to six days such as we know them now or whether the writer rather desired us to understand the days as longer periods of time. There is good evidence to support the latter position, although it must be insisted that God certainly could have brought all things into being in the space of six days. We cannot understand the reason for an objection that would so deny the Lord's power. The long ages of geology may indeed have occurred, and yet, in itself, this does not disprove the doctrine that the earth may have been brought into existence in six days such as we now know them. For our part, we incline toward the view that the days were periods of time longer than twenty-four hours. We do this, however, not in order to find an expedient for harmonizing Scripture with geology but simply upon exegetical grounds. We are inclined to think that the Bible itself implies that the days were longer than twenty-four hours in length. One thing, however, is sure, whatever the length of the days may have been, science has not proved, nor can it prove, that there is error in the account of creation contained in Genesis.

Of an entirely different nature is an objection to which we must now give brief consideration. It is sometimes asserted that the idea of creation cannot be expressed in terms of science. For that reason, it is said, Genesis must not be taken as a scientific account, since it was never intended to be such. The idea of creation, rather, can only be expounded in terms of myth. There are, we are told, basically two reasons why this is so. In the first place, if Genesis 1 is taken as scientific, then we are faced with the problem of conceiving of time before time, which, of course, is impossible and inconceivable. In the second place, the idea of an infinite time which had no beginning is claimed to be impossible. Hence, in Genesis, we must realize that truths which in themselves transcend time and space are presented in the language of space and time.

Objections such as this, however, are really irrelevant; they do not come to grips with all the factors involved. If the Biblical account compelled one to think of time before time or to conceive of infinite time which had no beginning, we would well acknowledge that it was not correct. Does the Biblical account, however, make any such demands? Very obviously, it does not. Objections to the Biblical account such as these leave God out of the picture, or else they bring Him to the level of the creature and subject Him to those same limitations which bind man. It is because men fail to make the distinction between God and man that they are unwilling to accept the account of creation as historical.

The issue which is at stake is in reality that of theism. The Bible does not ask us to believe that a god who is subject to time and space brought the heavens and the earth into existence. It tells us rather that God Almighty is the Creator, and He is not subject to time and space as we are. Before God created the heaven and the earth, He was. There is no such thing as infinite time without beginning, nor does the Bible say that there is. Rather, time and space were brought into existence by God Himself. "But, beloved, be not ignorant of this one thing, that one day *is* with the Lord as a thousand years, and a thousand years as one day" (2 Peter 3:8). In these words the Lord tells us that He is not bound by time. "Before the mountains were brought forth, or ever thou hadst formed the earth and the world, even from everlasting to everlasting, thou art God" (Psalm 90:2). The language of Scripture is anthropomorphic, as indeed it must be, but its meaning is amply plain. God is not subject to time.[2]

It is therefore the grossest misconception to assume that the Bible teaches that there was a time before present time, or that there is such a thing as infinite time without a beginning. The Bible simply teaches the eternity of God. God, an infinite Being, has no beginning nor ending. He is. In His infinite and inscrutable wisdom He brought into existence that which previously had no existence, and His creation He made subject to time and to space. Indeed, He brought time and space themselves into being. Someone may reply, that it is impossible to conceive of existence without time and space. Granted that we certainly have difficulty conceiving of *finite* existence or existence on the level of the creature without the conditions of time and space, does it therefore follow that God the Creator cannot exist without time and space? The Bible certainly teaches that He can and that He does so exist. When we bring the infinite God down to the level of the existence of the creature, we fall into error most grave, for God is utterly independent of His creation. The creation is subject to Him, but not He to the creation.

The objection therefore which we are now considering is one which obliterates the distinction between the Creator and the creation, and is for that reason irrelevant. When the book of Genesis states that God created the heaven and the earth it is scientifically correct. It is teaching that God, He Who is utterly sufficient unto Himself, by the Word of His power, brought into existence that which previously had no existence. We may grant full well that if the Bible related this of a man or an angel, one could not believe it. The Bible, however, does not say that man or that any other creature created; it tells us that God created. When therefore we read the exalted language of the first chapter of Genesis we believe it to be scientifically accurate for it is a revelation from Him of whom it speaks. To say that creation can be told only in terms of myth is to

2. Cf. Cornelius Van Til, *Why I Believe in God.*

deny creation in any genuine sense. If creation must be recounted to us in the language of myth we are then perfectly justified in asking whether there actually has been a creation. Creation can and has been related in the language of science, language which is not symbolical or mythical but a straightforward account of what actually took place. God did as a matter of fact by His own fiat, bring this world into existence. "For He spake and it was done; he commanded, and it stood fast" (Psalm 33:9). We may then read the first chapter of Genesis with the assurance that we are reading a scientifically accurate account of that which actually transpired.

MATTHEW 27:9

It is now necessary to turn our attention briefly to a different type of alleged error. In Matthew 27:9 we read, "Then was fulfilled that which was spoken by Jeremiah the prophet, saying, And they took the thirty pieces of silver, the price of him that was valued, whom they of the children of Israel did value." As it stands in Matthew this quotation is attributed to the prophet Jeremiah, whereas, as a matter of fact, the quotation seems to have been taken from Zechariah 11:13. Here, indeed, is a difficult problem; here, some would even say, is a positive example of error. It will be well to place side by side a translation of the Hebrew text of Zechariah and of the Septuagint and then to give again Matthew's words.

HEBREW

And the Lord said unto me, Cast it unto the potter, a goodly price at which I was valued from them. So I took the thirty (pieces) of silver and cast it in the house of the Lord unto the potter.

SEPTUAGINT

And the Lord said unto me, cast them unto the furnace, and I shall see whether they are worthy, in the manner that they have been esteemed by them. And they took the thirty (pieces) of silver and they cast them in the house of the Lord unto the furnace.

MATTHEW

And they took the thirty pieces of silver, the price of him that was valued, whom they of the children of Israel did value; and gave them for the potter's field, as the Lord appointed me."

With these three passages before us we may note that all that

Matthew has actually taken from Zechariah is to be found in the following:

a. *and they took the thirty pieces of silver* — this is from the Septuagint. It should be noted, however, that in the Septuagint the phrase *thirty pieces of silver* is masculine whereas in Matthew it is neuter.

b. *the price of him that was valued* (these words are clearly based upon the Hebrew of Zechariah, *a goodly price at which I was valued from them*).

c. *and gave them for the potter's field* (this is a very free rendering of the Hebrew, *and I cast it unto the potter*).

At least the burden of the quotation is from Zechariah. Why, then, does Matthew attribute the passage to Jeremiah? To this question several plausible and possible answers have been made. In the Babylonian Talmud (the section is in *Baba Bathra* 14) Jeremiah is placed at the head of the prophets. It is possible that this tradition of the priority of Jeremiah was far older than the Talmud. Thus, when the disciples reported to the Lord what men said concerning Him, they mentioned "Jeremiah or one of the prophets" (Matthew 16:14). It may be that the name Jeremiah was in this instance singled out inasmuch as his work was commonly regarded as standing at the head of the prophetical books. In mentioning Jeremiah, therefore, Matthew may have in mind the entire prophetical section of the Old Testament. A similar parallel is found in Luke 24:44 where Christ designates the third part of the Old Testament canon by the term Psalms. As a matter of fact, the book of Psalms was only the first book of this division, but evidently the Lord thought it sufficient to name only the first book as a suitable identification of the entire third section. Possibly this is the procedure which Matthew also is following. If so, he is simply doing what the Lord Himself, on another occasion, saw fit to do.

A second suggested solution is to the effect that Matthew has primary reference to the events mentioned in Jeremiah 18 and 19. The eighteenth chapter of Jeremiah relates the visit of the prophet to the potter's house. The prophet compares the power of the potter over the clay to God's absolute power and sovereignty over the nations. In the following chapter the Lord commands Jeremiah to take the potter's earthenware bottle and to break it, using the action as a symbol of the manner in which the Lord would break the sinful nation of Judah. It should be apparent that apart from these two chapters the language of Matthew's quotation "and gave them for the potter's field, as the Lord appointed me" does not seem to reflect Old Testament language. The words "as the Lord appointed me" probably have reference to the action of Jeremiah in obedience to God. Those who adopt this explanation think that the evangelist was calling attention to the heart of the message as presented by Jeremiah, but that he also used the specific wording of Zechariah in part. This is a possible solution and is not lightly to be rejected.

Another explanation is that Jeremiah 32:6-8 offers the clue to the difficulty. Upon this view Matthew takes the form of his expression from Jeremiah who speaks of the purchase of a field. Matthew wishes to stress not the thirty pieces of silver, but simply the fact that a price was paid for the field. Hence, it is argued, he finds Jeremiah suitable for his purpose. Still another possible answer to the difficulty is that the word Zechariah stood originally in place of Jeremiah. This is a conceivable solution, because the Syriac translation does not have the word Jeremiah. Lastly, it may be noted that the Jews believed that the spirit of Jeremiah had passed over to Zechariah. This thought was based upon the fact that a passage such as Zechariah 1:14 clearly reflected upon Jeremiah 18:11 and 35:15 and Zechariah 3:8 reflected upon Jeremiah 23:5.

The basic question which is involved is that of the intention of Matthew, and the answer to this question is not as simple as at first sight it might seem to be. Did Matthew intend to quote from Zechariah? If he did, why did he include in the quotation the words, "and gave them for the potter's field, as the Lord appointed me"; words which are not found in Zechariah, and which for their proper understanding presuppose acquaintance with Jeremiah 18 and 19? Considerations such as these make it perfectly legitimate to ask the question, Did Matthew then actually intend to quote from Zechariah? On the other hand, if the evangelist's intention was to refer to the book of Jeremiah, it is perfectly in order to ask why the frame of the quotation is based upon a passage found in Zechariah. The question is indeed a difficult one, and it may not be possible with our present knowledge to present an answer that is entirely satisfactory. The present writer inclines to the view that originally the word Zechariah stood in the text, and that sometime, very early indeed, the word Jeremiah, by a copyist's error, was substituted for it. Toy, for example, thinks that a copyist may have mistaken one abbreviation for another, writing *-iriou* instead of *-zriou,* a solution which is perfectly possible.[3] It may also be, however, that the evangelist himself originally wrote the word "Jeremiah." Matthew adds the word "field" which is of great importance for his own message. This word and the thought involved in it come, of course, from Jeremiah. The evangelist apparently finds that a reference to two Old Testament passages is necessary for his purpose. Hence, on this view, he mentions Jeremiah as being the older and greater of the two prophets and the one who furnished the word which gave the basic point of his quotation.

The more one ponders the procedure of the first evangelist, the more he realizes how difficult is the question under consideration. One thing, however, is clear. There is no warrant for the assertion that Matthew has made a mistake, that he has simply attributed to Jeremiah what as a matter of fact was actually from Zechariah. How glib such an objection is! It sounds convincing only to those who have not taken the trouble to study carefully the facts. Whether Matthew himself originally wrote Zechariah or Jeremiah, we may not today be able to state with positiveness. However, we may state with assurance that, whichever word he wrote, he wrote the truth. There is a certain sense in which it may be said that the quotation is from Jeremiah; likewise there is a sense in which it may be said to have come from Zechariah. There is no error here.

The Speech of Stephen

a. The call of Abraham

Very different is the case, we are told, with the speech of Stephen. It is in the highest terms that Luke speaks of this first Christian martyr. Stephen was "full of grace and power" (Acts 6:8) and his opponents "were not able to resist the wisdom and the spirit by which he spake" (Acts 6:10); but, be that as it may, he is said to have made some serious historical errors in his speech. It is important, however, to note that Stephen himself believed that he was reciting historical events correctly. His entire speech, recorded in the seventh chapter

3. Crawford H. Toy, *Quotations in the New Testament,* 1884, p. 71.

of the book of Acts, is in answer to the question of the high priest, "Are these things so?" Stephen very clearly believed that they were so.

What then are these serious errors which Stephen is supposed to have made? The first alleged error is found in verse 4, which states that Abram left Haran after the death of Terah his father. If one studies the figures of Genesis, we are told, he will discover that Terah must have lived at Haran at least fifty years. When Terah was seventy years old, we are told in Genesis 11:26, Abram was born. At the age of seventy-five (Genesis 12:4) Abram departed from Haran; therefore when Abram left Haran, Terah must have been one hundred and forty-five years of age. We are told, however, (Genesis 11:32) that Terah lived, all told, two hundred and five years. Hence, according to Genesis, when Abram left Haran, Terah had sixty years to live before his death. Stephen says that after Terah's death Abram left Haran; according to Genesis, however, Terah lived sixty years after Abram departed from Haran. Here, if anywhere in the Scriptures, it is claimed, is a contradiction.

Professor Evans has visualized an opponent bringing up this and other such objections before Stephen and concludes that these would not have silenced Stephen. "Such a criticism on such a speech would have been like flinging a feather in the teeth of a cyclone" (op. cit., p. 167). We, for our part, are unable to take such a light view of the matter. Nor do we think that Stephen would have taken a light view. It is a disturbing thing to have called to one's attention flaws in one's speech. If we are seeking to give a defense of ourselves or of our position, we try to present matters in as favorable a light as possible. We try to be as accurate as we can. We realize full well that if we make obvious errors, to a great extent we lose the respect of our hearers. It is certainly difficult to believe that a man like Stephen, who was on trial for his very life, would have been as careless as some critics seem to think he was. The Old Testament history was well known to the Jews of that day. They would have been quick to detect and to point out any error that Stephen might have made. The very fact that the Jews who heard Stephen did not make any outcry against him on the basis of his recital of the events of Old Testament history is most significant. True enough, they did make an outcry; they "were cut to the heart, and they gnashed on him with *their* teeth" (Acts 7:54). Why, however, did they do this? Was it because he had made errors in his recital of the events of Old Testament history? Not at all. With that recital of events they had no quarrel whatever. What aroused them was something quite different. What aroused them was Stephen's accusation that they had been the betrayers and murderers of the Just One, even Jesus. It was not Stephen's recital of history, but his application of that history, which caused the Jews to turn upon him.

Did Stephen, however, as a matter of fact contradict the book of Genesis? To say that he did would be indeed an easy solution of the problem. Stephen, one might say, had simply made a mistake, and Luke, the inspired writer of Scripture, accurately recorded the speech of Stephen, just as the latter gave it, mistake and all. Stephen, on this view, was not an inspired speaker, and hence there were errors of fact in his speech. Surely, this would be an easy solution of the problem. Defenders of the verbal inspiration of the Bible would here find a simple way out of the difficulty. Easy, however, as the solution might be, it is not, we think, a legitimate one. Everything in the account points to the fact that, as he spoke, Stephen was truly inspired. We read that he was full of the Holy Spirit, and that those who beheld him saw his face as it had been the face of an angel. In the light of the entire context in the book of Acts we dare not assert that it was as an uninspired man that Stephen spoke. Sometimes what at first sight looks like the easiest solution of a difficulty, turns out, upon further reflection, not to be so easy after all, and surely a solution which flies in the face of the clear statements of Scripture must be rejected. Better to admit that one cannot solve the difficulty than to take refuge in a solution of this kind.

Several other proposed answers have been offered. For one thing, it has been suggested that the correct age of Terah, the father of Abraham, as given in Genesis 11:32, should be simply one hundred and forty-five instead of two hundred and five. There is an ancient translation of the first five books of the Bible, known as the Samaritan Pentateuch, in which the numeral one hundred forty-five is found. It is not likely, though, that this is the original reading, and—it- is not wise to emend our Hebrew text upon the basis of this reading in the Samaritan Pentateuch.

It has again been thought that the reference of Stephen is not to the physical but rather to the spiritual death of Terah who, according to an old Jewish tradition, went back into idolatry after his departure from Ur. This can hardly commend itself as a serious interpretation of the difficulty. Another proposal is to assume that the order of statement in Genesis 11:26, where the three sons of Terah are mentioned, does not list the sons in the order of age but rather of prominence or importance. Hence, we read in Genesis 11:26, "And Terah lived seventy years, and begat Abram, Nahor, and Haran." The verse does not mean therefore that Terah begat all three sons when he was seventy years of age, nor does it mean that he even begat Abram at that age. All the verse, on this interpretation, would say is that at this age Terah began to beget sons, and of these the most important was Abram. Now, it could be that Abram was not actually born until Terah had reached the age of one hundred and thirty. If that is the meaning, the difficulty is cleared up easily. Is that, however, the meaning? There are some considerations which make it quite unlikely that we are so to understand the passage. Such an age was extremely advanced for childbearing. If Abraham had been born when his father was so old, he would not have been sceptical about a son being born when he himself was at the age of one hundred. With what incredulity Abraham asks the question, "Shall *a child* be born unto him that is an hundred years old?" (Genesis 17:17). Had his own father been one hundred and thirty years of age at Abraham's birth, it is not likely that the father of the faithful would later have exhibited such incredulity toward the promises of God.

Another explanation that has been offered is that the phrase "after the death of his father" which Stephen employs does not refer to physical death, but rather to the fact that from this time on Terah was actually dead to Abraham, inasmuch as Abraham never saw him again. This is possible, but it is not likely; Stephen seems to have reference to an actual, physical death. Yet another explanation is that Stephen is simply referring to the order in which the events are narrated in Genesis. Hence, upon this view, his words "after the death of his father" would simply be the equivalent of "after the account of the death of his father." In Genesis the death of Terah is first narrated (11:32) and then Abram's departure from Haran (12:4). It may be that Stephen has reference merely to the order in which these events are presented in Genesis. This is possible, but it is a solution which is not free from difficulty.

It is therefore the part of wisdom to acknowledge that the true solution of the problem is not yet known. Luther once remarked that he would be extremely grateful to the man who was clever enough to discover the solution of the problem. It may be, however, that cleverness is not what is required. In all probability, the reason for our difficulty lies in the fact that we do not know all that is involved. It is most interesting that the thought to which Stephen gives expression, namely, the departure of Abram from Haran after Terah's death, is also found in Philo. It is also most interesting to note that none of those who stood about, ready to condemn Stephen, found any flaw in his interpretation of the Old Testament history.

Another point needs to be emphasized. Stephen's language suggests that there may have been two calls given to Abram. "The God of glory appeared unto our father Abraham, when he was in Mesopotamia, before he dwelt in Charran." In these words (Acts 7:2) the first call is clearly stated. It came to Abram before he had left Ur to journey unto Haran. We then read, "and from thence, when his father was dead, he removed him into this land, wherein ye now dwell" (Acts 7:4). According to this verse, therefore, it was God who removed Abram from Haran unto Palestine. When one reads the account in the Old Testament, however, it would seem as though there was only one call. It may be that Genesis relates events not in strictly chronological order, but rather in the order of emphasis. Difficulties of this kind sometimes also occur in secular history. It would surely be the part of presumption to assert that at this point there is positive error in the Scripture. Far wiser is the course of candid acknowledgment that, with our present limited knowledge, the answer to this particular difficulty is not known to us.

b. The Length of the Egyptian Bondage

A further difficulty in Stephen's speech has to do with the length of the Egyptian bondage. In verse 6 we read, "And God spake on this wise, That his seed should sojourn in a strange land; and that they should bring them into bondage, and entreat *them* evil four hundred years." Here Stephen sets the limit of the Egyptian bondage at four hundred years. With this numeral two other passages of the Bible agree. In Genesis 15:13 the affliction is also said to endure for four hundred years, and in Exodus 12:40 the sojourning of the Israelites is said to be four hundred and thirty years. The one who supposedly is in error, however, is not Stephen, but none other than the Apostle Paul, for in writing to the Galatians, he said, "And this I say, *that* the covenant, that was confirmed before of God in Christ, the law, which was four hundred and thirty years after, cannot disannul, that it should make the promise of none effect" (3:17). Here, so the charge runs, Paul has made a mistake of some two hundred years. As a matter of fact, the time from the giving of the covenant to the exodus from Egypt was six hundred years. Paul, it is charged, has simply overlooked two hundred years, and so is guilty of a gross blunder. Let us again hear what Dr. Evans has to say:

> According to the Hebrew Bible, and according to Stephen Paul's chronology is at fault by about 200 years. And, unfortunately, we are precluded from falling back here on that convenient abstraction, the original autograph, by the unquestionable fact that, according to his customary rule, Paul is here following the Septuagint, which has added certain words to the Hebrew text in Exodus (l.c.) so as to make the 430 years include the sojourning in Canaan, along with the sojourning in Egypt. Now, as a question of criticism, Biblical and historical, I cannot help believing that the Hebrew text and Stephen are right here, and that the Septuagint and Paul are wrong. What am I to do? If I instruct my class that Paul's statement is infallibly inspired, I put Stephen in the wrong, I have the Old Testament passages to explain, and I have serious historical difficulties to remove.[4]

Much as we may admire the sincerity of Dr. Evans we believe that he has not actually come to grips with the problem. For one thing, we certainly cannot lend our agreement to the suggestion that the original manuscripts of the Bible are a "convenient abstraction." It is difficult to understand how a serious scholar, such as Dr. Evans was, could speak in this way. It must be evident to the reader that those who wish to be loyal

4. *Inspiration and Inerrancy*, pp. 158-159.

to the Bible do not at all use the idea of original copies of the Bible as a convenient abstraction. Disregarding this remark, however, we may go on to point out that whatever be the explanation of the alleged discrepancy between Paul and Stephen, there is no actual error.

That some sources employ the numeral four hundred and others four hundred and thirty is not to be explained as a contradiction. As has long been recognized, the difference is simply that in one instance a round number is employed, whereas in the other the exact number is found. As to the greater difficulty, however, namely, the supposed discrepancy of two hundred years, we may note a very old explanation and attempted reconciliation that has long been at hand. This old explanation goes back to Josephus, and would interpret Exodus 12:40 as having reference not merely to the time of sojourn in Egypt but also to the previous period in the land of Canaan, so that, as a matter of fact, the entire length of time from the giving of the promise to the exodus is thought to be four hundred and thirty years. On this view, even the period of time in Canaan would be regarded as one of sojourning, when the people were not actually at home in the land. The Septuagint text of Exodus and also the old Samaritan, add the words "and in the land of Canaan." On this construction the thought would be that the entire period of time in which the people were excluded from actual possession of their land was four hundred and thirty years. That this ancient interpretation is a possible one cannot be denied. If correct, it removes the difficulty at one stroke. Is it, however, correct? For our part, we have great hesitancy in accepting an interpretation which appears to be somewhat unnatural. The verse in Exodus apparently intends us to understand that four hundred and thirty years was the actual period of time spent in Egypt. Moses speaks of the sojourning of the children of Israel "who dwelt in Egypt." On the face of it then, this solution, attractive as it doubtless is, is not actually the way out of the difficulty.

Perhaps, if we examine the purposes of the Apostle, we may find a clue to the solution. Paul is making a contrast between the giving of the promise to Abraham and the giving of the law. It is when we consider the emphasis that the Apostle places upon these two termini that we realize that his intention is not to state precisely the length of the sojourn of the Israelites in Egypt. His purpose, therefore, differs from that of Stephen, from the passage in Exodus, and also from that in Genesis. It is well to keep in mind this consideration that Paul is not primarily concerned, as was Stephen, to state the length of the sojourn in Egypt. Before one asserts that there is a positive contradiction between the two, he must take into account the fact that the intentions and purposes of the two were not the same. According to Exodus (12:40ff.) the beginning of the exodus took place precisely at the expiration of four hundred and thirty years. The giving of the law, we learn from Exodus 19:1, did not occur until three months later. Therefore Paul must be using an approximate number. Unlike the book of Exodus, he is not concerned to tell the precise time that existed between the giving of the promise and the law. Paul's great concern is to stress the contrast between the promise and the law, not the length of time that existed between the two.

It should also be noted that whereas Paul speaks of the promise being given to Abraham, he also mentions Abraham and his seed, and this seed he interprets of Christ. It is quite possible, then, in the light of his purpose, and his mentioning Abraham and his seed, that Paul simply wishes to set in contrast the whole period of the giving of the promise, namely, the so-called patriarchal period, with that of the giving of the law. Between these two there was approximately four hundred and thirty years. The great period of separation which kept these two apart was the period of four hundred and thirty years during which the nation was in bondage in Egypt. Thus, on this view, the two termini mark the period of the patriarchs, the period of the giving of the promise, and the period of the giving of the law. If this is the purpose of the Apostle, no fault can be found with his method. It is a perfectly possible construction, and if we have interpreted Paul correctly, there certainly is no conflict between what he says and the other passages with which he is alleged to stand in contradiction. Once the purpose of the writer is taken into consideration, the difficulty disappears. He who would assert that there is an actual contradiction between Stephen on the one hand and Paul on the other must first of all prove that the intentions of Stephen and Paul were precisely the same. Obviously, such was not the case. Difficult as this present example may appear, it is surely clear that there is no error of fact or contradiction.

c. Other Difficulties

The seventh chapter of Acts, the chapter in which Stephen's remarkable speech is found, contains several rather notable difficulties. In verse 16, for example, mention is made of ". . . the sepulchre that Abraham bought for a sum of money of the sons of Emmor, *the father* of Sychem." In the book of Genesis, however, (33:19) Jacob is said to have made the purchase. Abraham, on the other hand, according to Genesis 23:3-20, had bought a burial place near Hebron from Ephron and the Hittites. Here, it would seem, is confusion indeed! It will be of interest to note some of the solutions which have been proposed. One view is to take the word "Abraham" in Acts 7:16 as having the force of a genitive, *i.e.*, "the descendant of Abraham." Thus, for example, when in 1 Kings 12:16 the Israelites ask, "what portion have we in David?" they are not concerned with David but with Rehoboam, a descendant of David. Again, in 1 Kings 14:13, Rehoboam is used for Abijah; and in Jeremiah 33:9, David for Christ. Another solution is to regard the word "Abraham" as a gloss which was early inserted in the text by a scribe in place of Jacob. This last supposition would seem to offer the least difficulty; possibly it is correct.

MARK 2:26

One further example of an alleged error may be examined. In Mark 2:26 we find the words, "How he [David] went into the house of God in the days of Abiathar the high priest, and did eat the shewbread, which is not lawful to eat but for the priests, and gave also to them which were with him?" The difficulty here, we are told, is that, as a matter of fact, at this time Abiathar was not the high priest, but rather Ahimelech (see 1 Samuel 21:1-6). The Old Testament says that Ahimelech was high priest, whereas the New makes Abiathar to be high priest. Is there an answer to this difficulty? It may be that here also there is a textual error, and that the word Abiathar was later inserted into the Greek text of Mark. It may be, too, that there is no textual error at all; that even in the days of Ahimelech, who is not actually called the high priest in Samuel, Abiathar was already exercising priestly functions.

Abiathar later came to prominence, and hence, the purpose of Mark may simply have been to mention the priest who came to greater prominence. In speaking of Abiathar as high priest Mark may have been calling him this by way of anticipation. In other words, when David entered the temple, at the time Ahimelech may have been the high priest, and yet at the same time Abiathar may also have been exercising priestly functions. Mark, wishing to mention the more prominent, names Abiathar, calling him high priest by way of anticipation. Such at least is a possible solution of the difficulty. It should be noted that when Doeg the Edomite accused Ahimelech to the king, Saul commanded that not only Ahimelech but the "priests" should be slain (1 Samuel 22:17).

Among those who escaped the sword of Doeg was Abiathar, the son of Ahimelech (1 Samuel 22:20). It would then seem that Abiathar was actually performing the function of a priest at the time when David entered the house of God and sought food. If, therefore, because of the later prominence of Abiathar, Mark chose to mention his name, no error was made. At the same time, we must acknowledge the possibility that this is not the correct explanation of the difficulty. If all the facts were known, the answer would be apparent.

There are some who would say, Why not simply grant that Mark made a slip of the memory? Why not admit the presence of an error here? What serious harm could be occasioned by the presence of a minor error such as this? Simple as this solution of the problem may seem to be, it is not trifling. If actual error is found in the Bible, it is God, not the human writers, who is responsible for that error. From this conclusion there is no escape.

The Bible is inerrant. That Word which the Holy God gave to man is a Word that in all its statements is to be trusted. Upon its utterances we may fashion our lives and actions. He who dogmatically proclaims the presence of error in the Bible has, as a matter of fact, arrogated to himself an amount of knowledge which he does not actually possess. We today are living almost two thousand years after the latest books of Scripture were written. Can we transport ourselves back to the days of Scripture and speak with such positiveness upon those days that we can infallibly point out what is error and what is not? Those who think that they can do this, often give little evidence of understanding the nature of what they are doing. As a result of further study and also as a result of archaeology much of what formerly was regarded as error has been demonstrated to be no error at all. Adverse judgments against the Bible have had to be modified, not once or twice, but over and over again. There is no other document from antiquity which for accuracy can even begin to compare with the Bible. When therefore we meet difficulties in the Bible let us reserve judgment. If any explanation is not at hand, let us freely acknowledge that we do not know all things, that we do not know the solution. Rather than hastily to proclaim the presence of error is it not the part of wisdom to acknowledge our ignorance?

The Word of God is a pure Word. It is not a message marred by the annoyances of tiny faults and errors that had come to us from the mouth of Him Who is Truth itself. His Word is also a rich Word. It is varied and manifold indeed. The great need of the Church today is to hear that Word. The time that is devoted to tearing the Bible to pieces could far better be spent in seeking to understand it. Would that God would raise up in our day men who are qualified to study the Scriptures, men who first have bowed before Him in acknowledgment of their sins, who from His blessed Word have learned that through the work of Christ their sins have been forgiven and who, out of love for Him and His Word, would devote their lives to the study of those Holy Scriptures which cannot be broken.

Does It Matter How We Approach
the Bible?

". . . the history which Moses wrote by Divine inspiration . . . the Holy Spirit of prophecy taught through him."

JUSTIN MARTYR

"This, then, must be considered as a fixed principle, that, in order to enjoy the light of true religion, we ought to begin with the doctrine of heaven; and that no man can have the least knowledge of true and sound doctrine, without having been a disciple of the Scripture."

CALVIN

"But there has very generally prevailed a most pernicious error, that the Scriptures have only so much weight as is conceded to them by the suffrages of the Church; as though the eternal and inviolable truth of God depended on the arbitrary will of men."

CALVIN

8

Does It Matter How We Approach the Bible?

In our discussion hitherto we have approached the Bible as the Word of God and, consequently, as perfectly trustworthy in all that it says. Behind this approach lies the assumption that there is a God, even the one living and true Creator of heaven and earth. It is He in whose very hand is our life and breath, and to whom we owe our existence. Undergirding the entire argument, therefore, is the presupposition of Christian theism: God is, and God has spoken. He is not the god of modern science or philosophy but the blessed Creator of whom we have learned through the reading of Scripture.

That which the Bible makes so clear, however, namely, that God is the Creator of all things visible and invisible, is not congenial to modern thought. There is at the present much talk about God, but it is perfectly evident that the god of whom many speak is not the God of the Bible. If God is the Creator, it follows that man is a creature and, therefore, subject to God in his thought as well as in all else. And it is here that objections arise against the Biblical view of inspiration. In reality these objections are directed not only to the doctrine of inspiration but also to the high theism that undergirds this doctrine, and without which it could not exist.

It is claimed, then, in opposition to the position which we have been espousing, that even before we start we know how we shall end. The outcome is assured, the course which we are to follow has already been determined, and we have only to travel thereon. Because we begin with certain presuppositions, it is objected, the outcome for us is already sure and determined. Consequently, all historical research is, *ipso facto,* as it were, ruled out. The Bible is the Word of God. We need simply listen to it and thus obtain all the answers that we require. It is not incumbent upon us to engage in historical study of the Bible at all. All the great researches of the masters of the nineteenth century are unnecessary. All we must do is listen to the Bible itself, for the answer is known before we begin. Such, in effect, is one of the most serious of the charges which is brought against the method of approach to the Bible which we have been defending in these pages.

Before such a charge we need not fear. It is true enough that the outcome is known beforehand. If God, that is, the God of the Bible and not the god of modern thought, exists, and if God has spoken to us in words, and the Bible is that Word, it follows that what God has said is the truth. A friend, let us say, writes me a letter. In this letter he tells me that if I will follow the instructions which he lays down, I shall find a great treasure. If I believe that my friend is telling the truth, I shall follow the directions which he has given in his letter, and shall discover the treasure precisely where my friend said it would be. If I do this, I have acted upon certain presuppositions. I have assumed that my friend is alive and that he has written the letter, and that, furthermore, he has told me the truth. Perhaps, in thus believing these things, I have been somewhat naive; I have been just like a Bible-believing Christian who takes God at His Word. Naive or not, nevertheless, by acting in obedience to the directions of my friend, I have found the treasure which he has promised me.

The modern "critical" theologian, however, is unwilling to be so naive. He will not humble himself to the point of mere obedience. There are several things which he must first investigate. He berates me for knowing where I shall end even before I have started. He would rather employ a more "scientific" or "historical" method. Indeed, he is convinced that with respect to my friend's letter there must be "objective," "unbiased," "scientific," "historical" research. These are rather impressive words, and I watch eagerly to see what the modern theologian will do. It is clear that he does not believe that I have any such friend as I claim; nor does he think that the letter can be *bona fide*. Hence, he subjects the letter to a scrupulous examination. Finally, he publishes the results of his research. It is quite a learned piece of work; it has footnotes in several languages. There is, however, one thing that troubles me about all his learned and "unbiased" research; it has not brought the investigator to the treasure. With all his historical study, the investigator has not found the treasure nor has he come to know my friend. He has engaged in what I might well call an impoverished task and he has arrived at just those conclusions at which I suspected he would arrive.

Thus we come to what is central with respect to this present objection to Christian theism. It is perfectly true that if we begin with the assumption that God exists and that the Bible is His Word, we shall wish to be guided in all our study by what the Scripture says. It is equally true that if we reject this foundational presupposition of Christianity we shall arrive at results which are hostile to supernatural Christianity. If one begins with the presuppositions of unbelief, he will end with unbelief's conclusions. If at the start we have denied that the Bible is God's Word or if we have, whether consciously or not, modified the claims of the Scriptures, we shall come to a position which is consonant with our starting point. He who begins with the assumption that the words of the Scriptures contain error will never, if he is consistent, come to the point of view that the Scripture is the infallible Word of the one living and eternal God. He will rather conclude with a position that is consonant with his starting point. If one begins with man, he will end with man. All who study the Bible must be influenced by their foundational presuppositions. To charge that this is true only of those who approach Scripture believing it to be the infallible revelation of God is both unjust and untrue.

Does the position which we have been defending as a matter of fact preclude historical investigation? The answer is that it does no such thing. If anything, it encourages and makes such investigation possible. Scholarly research, however, must not run wild. It must not proceed upon the unfounded assumption that the mind of man can be the judge of all things. It must not entertain viewpoints and hypotheses which are not consonant with foundational principles of revealed Christianity. In his research one cannot employ non-Christian methods and expect to arrive at Christian conclusions. The genuine Christian investigator will endeavor in all of his research to act as a little child and to submit his own thinking to God's thoughts. The thoughts of God which have been revealed to man in the Bible will ever be the guide and norm for the one who in his investigation desires to glorify the Creator. A true Christian scientist will strive to think these revealed thoughts of God after Him.

A Christian student of Scripture should endeavor to use Christian or theistic methods of investigation; on the other hand, the one who denies true theism will follow methods which are consonant with a non-theistic viewpoint. And herein lies the difference. The question is not to be decided by the assertion that the great bulk of scholarly Biblical research has been carried on by those who, as far as one can judge from their writings, are not sympathetic to a consistent Christian-theistic position. That does not settle the issue. All investigators must of necessity employ methods of Biblical study that are consonant either with a true theistic position or else with one which is not truly theistic. Whether they have consciously adopted and embraced them or not, all investigators are guided by basic presuppositions.

Christian presuppositions do not preclude true scholarship and investigation. One need but think of some of the great Bible-believing commentators to experience scholarship at its best, for here is scholarship that is consecrated to the one true God. Rich and varied indeed are the fields of investigation that lie open to him who will approach them in the conviction that they are God's, that they will tell of Him, and that in them His glory will be discerned. We must therefore dismiss as false the charge that if one adopts the Biblical witness to itself, he is thereby precluded from engaging in true historical scholarship. Rather, other things being equal, he is the one that may most profitably devote himself to true, historical scholarship.

Another objection to the plenary view of inspiration is that it causes one to reason in a circle. You say that the Bible is the Word of God, it is objected. Very well, but you simply believe that upon the testimony of the Bible itself; the Bible claims that it is from God and it also tells you what you are to believe about God. The Bible tells you what you are to believe about God, and God tells you that the Bible is His Word; surely that is reasoning in a circle.

In reply we may answer that, in the nature of the case, if we are but creatures, and God is the Creator, this is the only way in which it is possible to reason. If God has actually created us, it follows that all we know we must receive from Him. He must tell us what we are to believe about anything. Apart from Him there is no other source to which we may go. God alone must be the fount of all our knowledge. If, therefore, He tells us, as He does in the work of the inward testimony of the Holy Spirit, that the Scriptures are His Word, we must obey His voice. On the other hand, because He has thus identified the Scriptures as His Word, we must in turn listen to them when they tell of Him. They point to Him and reveal what we are to believe concerning Him and what duty He has required of us. There is no other way. Any other way is a deception and will ultimately lead to the point where we shut God out of our thoughts. We need not be frightened by the charge that to accept the Scriptures as the infallible Word of God requires us to reason in a circle.

The Christian position demands one to be completely subject to God Himself. If God is the Creator, and man a creature, there is no way in which man can set himself up as a judge of what God has revealed. There is no independent standard which man can drag in by which he can pass judgment upon the "reasonableness" of God's revelation. Job expresses the truth when he says, "For *he* is not a man, as I *am, that* I should answer him, *and* we should come together in judgment. Neither is there any daysman betwixt us, *that* might lay his hand upon us both" (Job 9:32,33). "I cannot answer God," Job is saying in effect, "inasmuch as He is not a man like myself. If He were a man, I would be on an equality with Him and could then deal with Him as an equal. Such is not the case, however; He is God, and I am but man. Before Him I submit. He need not submit to me, but I must submit to Him. I am not His judge, but He is my judge. He is in the position of authority, and I in that of receptivity and obedience. Furthermore, there is no daysman between us, no umpire, who can judge us both and decide between us which is right and which is wrong. I cannot take my case to some third party, for there is no third party. I can go to God and to Him alone. He is the Creator, and I am a man, created by Him and subject to Him."

There are many who wish that there were a daysman between God and man. The followers of the "daysman" theology are legion indeed. If only there were some outside control or check to which we could submit the Scriptures for judgment! If only there were an umpire! According to many people there is an umpire. They do not agree with Job; they think that there actually is a daysman between man and God. This daysman goes by different names. He is known variously as the "common consciousness of mankind"; as "that which approves itself to reason"; as "the religious consciousness"; and as "Christ, the highest of all God's media of revelation." Even the blessed Name of Christ has been advanced as a daysman to which the teachings of the Scriptures and the Scriptures themselves must be subjected. Even Christ is set forth as the standard by which all Scripture must be judged. In modern times, particularly, Christ is advanced as the test that must be met by all Scripture. If the Scripture can pass the test of Christ, then, of course, we may recognize it as Divine. In reply, without going further into the matter, we would stress the fact that this Christ whom men are erecting as the daysman or standard by which the Scriptures are to be tested, is not the Divine Son of God, of whom we learn through the Scriptures themselves. He is some other Christ, one more palatable to modern thought.

The fact of the matter is that there is only one way in which we can legitimately study the Bible, and that is to approach it as those who have submitted their entire being to God, who have acknowledged Him as their Lord, and who come to His Word ready to harken to all that it has to say. The alternative is to erect a daysman between the Word of God and ourselves, by which the Word may be judged. Inasmuch, however, as man is the one to erect the daysman he is in fact no genuine daysman, but merely a creation of the human mind. Because the Bible is the very Word and revelation of God, any daysman which stands between it and man is in reality a daysman between God and man.

We are told that the view of approaching the Bible which we are defending in this book is old-fashioned and no longer tenable. Modern scholarship, it is asserted, has shown that this traditional (we would say, Biblical) way of coming to the Bible is no more possible. We must abandon such an old-fashioned approach to the Scriptures. If this claim of modern theology is correct then, of course, it follows that throughout the history of the Church men have been approaching the Bible in the wrong way. They have come to the Bible as to the authoritative Word of God and in the Bible they have found Jesus Christ the Savior. They were wrong, however; they should not have regarded the Bible as the final authority. With the insights and contributions of modern scholarship, we have now learned the correct approach to the Bible. There is, however, a question which at this point should be raised. If we must now approach the Bible in a way different from that which the Church has always used, how do we know that in the future the way which now seems acceptable to us will not then have been superseded by something more suitable to the men of that time? In the years ahead the approach to the Bible which present-day scholarship advocates may be entirely out of date. If it is then out of date, the scholars of that time will presumably have to discover a method of approach which will be more relevant to their day, more in keeping with their thoughts and attitudes. Should this be the case, then it would clearly follow that the benefit and blessing which in the past has seemed to come to mankind from the Bible, really was not derived from the Bible itself but rather from man's way of looking at the Bible at any given time. For nearly two thousand years the old approach to the Bible brought blessing. Today, we are told, this approach must go; it is not scientific. Today, a new approach is requisite. Very well, this new approach supposedly meets the needs of the present day. What, however, about the future? In the future, will not some other approach to the Bible be necessary? If such is the case, it is perfectly obvious that what brings help and blessing is not the Bible itself but the approach to the Bible which we find relevant for our own day. It is then not the Bible, but rather our way of looking at the Bible that is of importance; not the Bible, but what we bring to the Bible. Thus, in effect, the demand for a new approach to the Bible amounts to nothing other than a demand that we bring to the Bible what seems to us to be relevant to our time. This is subjectivism. He who rejects the Biblical view of Scripture, no matter how much it may be disguised, has set up the human mind as an arbiter to decide how the Bible is to be regarded.

One cannot but be struck by the apparent ease with which men seem willing to embrace the most recently propagated views as though they were the final truth. He, on the other hand, who has submitted to the teaching of the Scriptures may look at all things under the light of eternity. He has the voice of God speaking to Him, and by this voice of God may judge all men and movements. He, however, who has not submitted his thinking to the Word of God must depend upon the human mind as the ultimate authority. Consequently, he will probably accept what appears at the time to be relevant.

On the part of those who reject the absolute trustworthiness of the Bible we often meet with statements such as, "We are now prepared to admit." Or we encounter language such as, "Dr. X has showed us that such and such is the case." Who is this Dr. X? We discover that he is a young man who has written a brilliant doctoral dissertation. He has spoken the most recent word upon some given subject, and others seem ready to follow. If we do not build upon the impregnable rock of infallible Scripture we shall ever be at the mercy of the latest whims and fancies.

Human opinion is like the waves of the sea. One wave breaks upon the shore to be followed closely by another. To change the figure, we may speak of the climate of human thought. At times that climate is favorable to one viewpoint, at times to another. One climate of opinion follows another, and what one generation regards as the truth is heartily rejected by its successors. How often, just before a summer storm, we have noticed the deadly stillness of the air which hangs without motion. Sultry heat burns in the scorching sunshine. On the horizon black clouds begin to gather, heralds of a storm to come. The air commences to move, the wind blows and soon gains in strength. Before the onmarching clouds, gusts of wind blow and dispel the heat. Rain begins to fall, a few drops at first, but soon the downpour is strong and steady. The clouds hang overhead while the thunder peals and lightning flashes. In a short time the rain becomes lighter, and the blackness of the sky is broken. The thunder is at a distance, and the air cool. The storm is fading away, disappearing slowly. A blessing of water covers the once heated ground, and again the birds are singing. In only a few hours the climate has changed radically.

So it is with human thought which is not based upon the Bible. As the mind of man reacts to his environment he seeks to explain the meaning of his life. What appealed to one generation has been cast aside by another. What is today upon the throne of human reason will tomorrow be discarded for something more "reasonable," or possibly even by the conception that the irrational is to be preferred to the logical. Some seem to act as though it were most "reasonable" to espouse irrationality. The change in human opinion is particularly apparent with respect to the Bible. Toward the close of the last century human thought was greatly under the influence of the Darwinian theory of evolution. Mankind was said to be in an upward march, and the idea of a real fall into sin seemed absurd. Great strides in science and invention were being made; new discoveries were carried out. In the field of theology the ideas of Ritschl were widespread, and their practical effect made itself known in that phenomenon which is popularly called "modernism," a phenomenon which has wrought unbelievable harm to the well-being of the Church of Jesus Christ. In New Testament studies the influence of Adolph Harnack with his purely human Jesus was very prominent. The philosophy of Hegel undergirded certain views of the history of Israel. A veritable complex of ideas held sway. It was a climate of opinion which was hostile to supernatural redemptive Christianity and which proved to be one of the greatest foes of that religion.

With the Old Testament aspect of this climate of opinion we are at this moment particularly concerned. In Germany, through the activity of Julius Wellhausen, a certain view of the Old Testament had become very widespread. Wellhausen held very distinctive ideas concerning the nature of the Old Testament books and the time of their origin and composition. We may especially note his view of the growth of the first five books of the Bible, the Pentateuch. According to tradition, and according to the witness of the Bible itself, these five books were the work of Moses, Israel's great lawgiver. According to Wellhausen, however, such was not the case. Not only did Moses not write the Pentateuch, he maintained, but it was not even the work of one man. The earliest portions, he believed, came from two different and quite distinct documents, which in their origin were completely independent. The first major step in the compilation of the present Pentateuch was the formation of a work which was compiled from these two documents. At a later time the book of Deuteronomy came into existence, and after the exile, the so-called priestly portions were composed. Finally, the whole was edited, and our present Pentateuch was the result.

This view of the compilation of the first five books of the Bible went hand in hand with a particular theory of the growth of Israel's religious beliefs. Originally, it was asserted, Israel was permitted to erect altars and to worship wherever she wished. When the book of Deuteronomy was discovered in the temple in 622 B. C., however, a reform was instituted, a reform of such far-reaching proportions that from this time on only worship at the sanctuary in Jerusalem was to be considered legitimate. Later, as a result of growth and development, the pure monotheism of the latter portion of Isaiah came into existence as a part of Israel's faith.

Meager as this sketch is of the idea of development which Wellhausen imposed upon the religious history of Israel, it is nevertheless sufficient to make clear how far removed his theory was from the Biblical position that the Old Testament is a special revelation of God.

The views which Wellhausen advocated became very popular. In English-speaking countries they found a staunch advocate in William Robertson Smith, a Presbyterian clergyman who sought to accomplish the impossible task of reconciling the newer views of Wellhausen, which he himself essentially embraced, with the doctrine of inspiration stated in the first chapter of the Westminster Confession of Faith. What he attempted to do was, as we have said, impossible, and a trial for heresy resulted. Smith thought that those in the Church who were opposing him were "opponents of progressive Biblical science."[1] As a matter of fact, his opponents were no such thing; the views which Smith's opponents defended, views to which they had by solemn vow sworn allegiance at their ordination to the ministry, have more and more come to receive at least the tribute of lip service from many who in Smith's day would probably have gone along with him in his promulgation of Wellhausen's theories. The harm which accrued to the Church of Jesus Christ was not wrought by those who sought to be faithful to their ordination vows. It was rather brought about by the attempt to introduce into the Church theories which were in their very nature irreconcilable with the historic Protestant Reformed faith. As today we look back upon these once regnant ideas we see more clearly how incompatible they are with revealed religion. Had Dr. Smith been willing to listen to the infallible Word of God and so to the voice of the Holy Spirit speaking in the Scriptures, the Church might have been spared unnecessary harm.

1. William Robertson Smith, *The Old Testament in the Jewish Church,* 1883, p. v.

There is one point in particular in which it may be seen how utterly mistaken the views of Wellhausen are. It is not a minor or an obscure point but one of supreme importance. Wellhausen asserted that the Patriarchs were not historical characters. From the book of Genesis, he argued, we can learn nothing about the period in which Abraham, Isaac and Jacob lived. The reason for this was that Genesis did not come from the time of the Patriarchs, and Moses was not its author. Genesis, rather, consisted of several documents which had been later pieced together. Hence, it reflected the background of the period in which these documents had been written but it did not mirror the period of the Patriarchs. Consequently, concluded Wellhausen, Genesis is an unhistorical book. If we wish to learn something of the background of the patriarchal period, we shall not learn it from Genesis.[2]

Here was a flat denial of the historicity and truthfulness of the statements of Genesis concerning the Patriarchs. In the light of such flagrant denial of the truthfulness of a very precious portion of the Holy Scriptures, what were humble Christian people to do? Abraham, according to the Bible, was the father of the faithful. In the face of the most trying odds he believed the promises of God and was justified by faith. To the devout believer in Christ Abraham was a man whose life afforded much help. To one tempted to doubt God's promises he was a man who against hope believed in God. How blessed were the appeals which the Apostle Paul made to his life and example! And, furthermore, what about Jesus Christ Himself? He had spoken as though Abraham had been an historical character. "Before Abraham was, I am," He had said (John 8:58). Here, clearly, was a problem. What were humble Christians to do? Scholarship, which according to its own oft-repeated testimony was the latest and most objective, was asserting with that dogmatism which was a hallmark of Wellhausenism, that the Patriarchs were not historical characters, and that Genesis did not teach us anything about the background of the patriarchal period. On the other hand, there are the clear and simple statements of the Bible, setting forth Abraham as an historical character and, consequently, the background of his life as accurate.

---

2. J. Wellhausen, *Prolegomena zur Geschichte Israels,* Sechste Ausgabe, 1905, pp. 316ff.

There were two possible courses open. On the one hand, a person could follow the guidance of Wellhausen and other scholars, who were advocates of what William Robertson Smith called "progressive Biblical science." And, to be sure, there were many who did just this. There was, however, yet another way. It was to act the part of a trustful, humble Christian and to accept at face value the teaching of the Bible. This latter way has never been popular with the man who thinks that the unaided human mind is competent to pass judgment upon the Word of God. It is not popular with those to whom historic Christianity is something to be modified and adapted to every shifting wind of doctrine and conditioned to every changing climate of opinion. However, the Christian accepts the Bible as the Word of God. The Spirit of God has persuaded him of this fact, and he knows that the words of the Scriptures are words which have found their origin in God. Hence, the humble and devout Christian believer, whether he be scholarly or uneducated, no matter who the opponents of the Bible may be, will accept the words of the Bible as true.

At the same time it is not easy to go against the current. When all about us are proclaiming that there are serious errors in the Bible and are manifesting a low attitude toward the claims of the Scripture to itself, it is not an easy thing to take a stand for the Bible's complete trustworthiness. The earnest Christian believer is well aware of the difficulties in the Bible. He knows that Christianity is not an easy religion. He knows also that whatever difficulties there may be in the acceptance of the Bible as a fully trustworthy book, they are as nothing compared with the gigantic difficulties which must be faced — but which are rather generally ignored — by those who reject the testimony of Scripture to itself. The Christian believer would rather stand with Christ than against Him. Hence, when someone like Wellhausen declares that the book of Genesis does not present an accurate account of the patriarchal background, the believer will simply stay with his Bible and await the time until further information comes to light.

With respect to this particular point such information has finally come. As a Christian might expect, it supports what the Bible has to say and makes perfectly clear that in his assertions Wellhausen was utterly wrong. Reassuring and comforting indeed has the science of archaeology been to the believer in the Scriptures. Has then archaeology finally corroborated the Bible in its teaching that such a man as Abraham did after all live? No. As yet, Abraham has not appeared outside the Bible. What archaeology has done, however, is to make it clear that the background of the Patriarchs which is found in the book of Genesis is perfectly true to fact.

No sooner, it would seem, had Wellhausen come out with his broadside against the trustworthiness of Genesis, than the science of archaeology began its work. The first step was with the discovery in the winter of 1901-02 of the now famous Code of Hammurabi. On this rather remarkable code of laws there was mention of certain practices, which paralleled the action of Sarah in giving to Abraham her concubine Hagar. Excavation in the land of Palestine revealed the fact that during the patriarchal age the sedentary population of the land was to be found along the coastal plain, but that the hill country was more sparsely settled. This is precisely the condition of things that we find in the book of Genesis; for the most part the patriarchs wandered up and down the land in the hill country. Most of the cities mentioned in Genesis, namely, Bethel, Salem, Schechem, Gerar, Dothan, Beersheba, are now known to have been in existence during the days of the Patriarchs.

The results of archaeology make it clear that the Jordan valley was constantly occupied, and that Genesis is therefore correct when it mentions the cities of the plain. It is also corroborated in affirming the destruction of these cities, for about the beginning of the second millennium before Christ occupation of this district ceased. The documents from Ras Shamra show that writing was known to the inhabitants of the land at a very early time.

Perhaps the most important discovery, however, has to do with those interesting people known as the Horites. In Genesis 14:6 we read, "And the Horites in their mount Seir, unto El-paran, which is by the wilderness." Who were these Horites? There have been scholars who have asserted that there never was such a people. No one by that name was known. In the year 1925, however, excavations were undertaken at a place in Mesopotamia which bore the Turkish name, Yorgan Tepe (blanket mound). It appeared that this was an ancient city of the name Nuzi, which had been inhabited at a time contemporary with the Patriarchs. The people who once lived in this city were known as Hurrians, and it would seem that they are to be identified with the Horites of the Bible. They have proved to be a most interesting people. They did not write on paper, as we do, but rather on clay, and many clay tablets have remained to tell us about them.

The clay tablets which have been discovered in Nuzi are business documents, written in the form of a contract or agreement between two parties. Hence, they reveal many intimate details concerning the life of the early inhabitants of Nuzi. At the bottom of many of the tablets there is a list of the names of those who witnessed the drawing up of the contract. These names are largely Hurrian, and hence one may learn from these tablets quite a bit about this ancient Hurrian language.

In Nuzi it appears that one could not sell land. If, therefore, a person wished to obtain some land he could not do so by paying a purchase price. Another expedient for obtaining the land had to be devised. The person who desired the land could acquire it by having himself adopted by its owner. The owner would then will the land to him, and so, receiving the land by inheritance, he would become the lawful heir. In return for this he offered to his new parents what the tablets euphemistically call a "gift." The result was actually the same as if the land had been legitimately purchased. Consequently, many of the tablets which were unearthed at Nuzi are known as "adoption" tablets.

It will be seen how this practice could have been used to advantage by someone who was unscrupulous. One man, bearing the Hurrian name of Tehiptilla had himself adopted by quite a number of people. He must have become a rather rich person. When he saw that people could not keep up their land, or that they needed sheep, or that they were generally poor, he would have himself adopted by them and so obtain the possession of their property. Oftentimes the "gift" which he offered in exchange for what he inherited was surprisingly out of proportion with what he himself had acquired. Tehiptilla would manage to obtain quite a sizable piece of land, and in return would give a "gift" of possibly two or three sheep. He was an Hurrian forerunner of the modern racketeer.

Sometimes a person did not wish to dispose of his land, but rather wanted someone to care for him, to manage his estate, and after his death to see to it that he was given a decent burial. Hence, he would adopt a man to do these things for him, that man becoming his heir. In the light of this practice, we may understand the case of Abraham and Eleazar of Damascus. Abraham, in accordance with the custom of his times, had "adopted" Eleazar, and Eleazar was consequently the steward or manager of all that Abraham possessed. In return, Eleazar would become Abraham's heir, and it is precisely this to which the patriarch gives expression when he says, "Behold, to me thou hast given no heir, and lo, the Son of my house will inherit me" (Genesis 15:3, *author's translation*). According to the custom of the time, if, after the adoption contract had been entered into, a legitimate heir was born, that legitimate son would take precedence over the one who had been adopted. Hence, the Lord says unto Abraham, "This shall not be thine heir; but he that shall come forth out of thine own bowels shall be thine heir (Genesis 15:4).

It was also the practice of the time for a wife, if she was barren, to provide her husband with a concubine, just as Sarah did in giving Hagar to her husband. If the concubine should bear children, the legitimate wife could not then send her away. Sarah had violated this custom, which explains Abraham's concern over what she had done. With respect to the action of Esau in selling his birthright, we also learn that he acted in accordance with a custom of the day. One of the tablets which was found at Nuzi mentions a certain Tupkitilla who was the heir to a grove. For some reason he gave to his brother Kurpazah the rights of inheritance to this grove. In exchange he received only three sheep. How strikingly similar to the action of Esau!

A certain man by name of Tarmiya wished to marry, but his two brothers made objection. He brought a suit at law against them and won the case, inasmuch as he had received his father's blessing. It was an oral, not a written blessing; it was uttered by a dying father to his son, and also possessed legal validity. It strangely reminds of the blessing of Isaac. Perhaps one more illustration from Nuzi will be of interest. A man by the name of Nashwi had adopted a son Wullu and given his daughter to him. When Nashwi dies, Wullu is to be his heir. If, however, Nashwi should beget a son, then Wullu must share the fortune with that son, in other words, become a joint heir with him. Most important is the fact that the son will then receive the gods of Nashwi. It would seem that the one who possessed these household gods would have a position of headship in the family. In the light of this consideration the action of Rachel takes on new light. She had stolen the teraphim, which were the household gods, and evidently believed that as long as they were in her possession Jacob would be in a position of headship. Possession of the household gods, therefore, was of the utmost significance and importance. Lastly, we may note Jacob's action (Genesis 33:3) in bowing seven times to the ground as he approached his brother Esau. This indicated that Jacob wished to do great honor to Esau. On the Tell-El-Amarna tablets which date from about 1450 b. c.,[3] a king in writing to a superior would say that he bowed seven times. Hence, Jacob was performing an action whereby Esau would understand that Jacob came not as an enemy but as a servant. In the light of the Amarna documents, the action is seen to be one that was well understood at that period of history.

Ten years after the initial finds at Nuzi, more remarkable discoveries were made at the modern Tell el-Hariri in Mesopotamia, the ancient city of Mari. These texts from Mari are proving to be of immense importance for the study of the Biblical background. They substantiate very remarkably the claims of the Bible that the ancestors of Israel came from Haran. The entire period of the Patriarchs is consequently being better understood than was the case in Wellhausen's day. One can hardly overestimate the importance of the archaeological discoveries which have been made.

All of this makes it very clear that the background of the patriarchal narratives found in the book of Genesis is not at all the free creation of a later age. It was not made up out of the fancies of those who lived many hundred years later. It was rather a very accurate picture, and one that is in agreement with the documents from antiquity which have now come to light. Archaeology has made it clear that with respect to his attitude toward the background of the narratives of the Patriarchs, Wellhausen was just about as wrong as he could have been.

At the present time every competent and informed scholar must acknowledge that the background of Genesis is in agreement with the documents of antiquity. As a matter of fact, so far as the present writer knows, this is admitted. It is maintained, however, inasmuch as some scholars apparently do not wish

3. These tablets were discovered at Tell el-Amarna, about 200 miles south of Cairo, on the east bank of the Nile, in Egypt. The discovery was made in the winter of 1887-88 by a native Egyptian woman.

to acknowledge any more than they think they have to, that, whereas these discoveries do indeed substantiate the background of the patriarchal period given in Genesis, nevertheless they do not prove the historicity of the Patriarchs themselves. The background is accurate, it is acknowledged, but we cannot say that Abraham, Isaac, and Jacob themselves ever lived; their historicity has not been proved. Such is the assertion which some are making today. It is an assertion, frankly, which is not very impressive. Any competent investigator who reads some of the Nuzi tablets, for example, may say, and say correctly, that the background which they picture is accurate. He may acknowledge that the practice of adoption which figures so prominently in them is indeed true to fact. If, however, this investigator were to deny the existence of people like Tehiptilla and some of the others who appear frequently in these texts, we should think it strange. Why then do such investigators refuse to acknowledge the historicity of the Patriarchs? To say the least, it is a most inconsistent procedure! For our part, we believe that such denial is based upon a certain theory of the origin and composition of the early books of the Bible. We are not, as a result, impressed by the assertion of those who now deny the historicity of the Patriarchs. Wellhausen in his day had far more excuse.

In defense of Wellhausen it is now said that we must not be too hard on him. He did not have the discoveries of Nuzi and Mari to show him how accurate the background of Genesis actually is. He was, we are told, a child of his age, and we must not therefore be too severe with him. True enough, he did not have the information which Nuzi and Mari in particular have brought to light. He did have something, however, that was far more to the point than are these discoveries. He had the written revelation of God, and that revelation stated very plainly that the Patriarchs were historical characters, and it pictured them as living in a definite social and cultural milieu. If Wellhausen had listened to the voice of the Spirit of God speaking in the Scriptures, he would not have made the tremendous blunder which he did make. Wellhausen had no business to set up his own ideas in opposition to revealed truth, for it was precisely that which he did. The whole elaborate structure which he erected is one not supported by evidence, but is the product of unaided human thought. Wellhausen flew in the face of express statements of revealed truth, and as a result it was to be expected that in many respects his theories would be abandoned even by those who share his basic antagonism toward the infallibility of Holy Scripture. Meanwhile, the plain Christian man can find great consolation as he sees the results of excavation support, as — when properly interpreted — they always will, the Bible.

Instructive indeed is this example of Wellhausen, for it makes very clear the manner in which we are not to approach the Bible, and as we learn how we are not to come to Scripture we may understand more clearly how we may and should approach thereto. If the Bible is the Word of God we certainly may not approach it believing that we are capable of subjecting it to the test of our own unaided reason. If we think that we can employ theories and hypotheses which conflict with the express statements of the Bible, we deceive only ourselves, and the reason why we deceive ourselves is that we are thus setting up the human mind above God. Our great objection to the entire reconstruction of Israel's history which was advanced by Wellhausen and others is not so much that we differ with individual details here and there. That is a comparatively minor matter. Our basic disagreement is that this reconstruction is at variance with express statements of the Bible. If the picture of Israel which Wellhausen gives is correct, then that which God has given in inspired words is incorrect. At basis, therefore, the Wellhausen scheme is anti-theistic in nature. It conflicts with the revelation of God and hence must be abandoned. It is only to be expected that, as further discovery is made and as time progresses, more and more the entire scheme which at one time was so popular will be once and for all time abandoned. Climates of opinion do change. When the present writer studied Hebrew in the university the instructor constantly presented the tenets of Wellhausen. Today, the climate of opinion is quite different. Some of the modern Scandinavian scholars, who in their basic assumptions are as far removed from historical Christianity as was Wellhausen, place more severe strictures upon Wellhausen than do Bible-believing scholars.[4]

We are not, therefore, to come to the Bible in the belief that

---

4. It should be apparent to the careful reader that we are not expressing a judgment upon the question whether Wellhausen was himself a Christian. That is a matter upon which no man can speak. Only God knows those that are His and only He can judge the hearts. What we are concerned with are the views which Wellhausen has presented in writing, and these views are not consonant with Christian theism.

we can subject it to certain tests of our own devising. Nor, in our study, may we advance theories which conflict with what the Bible itself says. How then must we approach the Bible? There is only one way; it is the way of humility. We are coming unto the message which the Creator of heaven and earth has given. Ours must be the receptive attitude. We are to pattern all our thought upon what God has said. We shall never understand the Bible aright until we accept it for what it claims to be, the infallible Word of the ever-living and true God. It is to be received by us simply because it is the Word of God. Our thoughts must be captive to its Divine thoughts. Thus, and thus alone, will we think after Him God's revealed thoughts.

Such an approach of course involves right thinking about God. We must know Him whom to know aright is life eternal. "He that cometh to God must believe that he is, and *that* he is a rewarder of them that diligently seek him" (Hebrews 11:6b). Our theism will not be worthy of the name unless we believe that God is. And yet, we are not to believe in the existence of any god whatsoever; we must believe that the true God exists, the God of Scripture, the Triune God. We must believe that He is, or we shall never come to Him. More than that, we must believe that He is a rewarder of them that diligently seek Him. If we believe this of Him, it is clear that we already know Him. If we believe this of Him, we shall come, repenting of our sins, trembling before His holy law, embracing His gracious promises in Jesus Christ, and fleeing for refuge to Him who rewards them that diligently seek Him.

To know Him aright involves a ready acceptance of His Word. In the very words of Scripture we hear the voice of the Father in Heaven. They are His words, and because we love Him we shall wish to harken to them. To submit all our thinking unto the Scriptures thus makes us a captive to God; yet, strangely enough, in this captivity we are of all men the most free. We cannot turn from the Scriptures, we cannot listen with approval to theories which seek to account for the Bible as a purely human book and which, in effect, deny its divinity. All such theories are barren and desolate indeed. Beginning with man, they also end with man. Wellhausen did that, but so also do the more modern theologians who, as much as Wellhausen, reject the express statements of the Scriptures. What we have been trying to say in this chapter has been so much more capably stated in the noble Westminster Confession of Faith: "The authority of the Holy Scripture, for which it ought to be believed, and obeyed, dependeth not upon the testimony of any man, or Church; but wholly upon God (who is truth itself) the author thereof: and therefore, it is to be received, because it is the Word of God." Would that God would open the eyes of men, that they might see the Word of God in all its beauty and perfection, in all its harmony and purity. Then, in humble confession of the sin of judging the Scriptures, men might cry out as they contemplate the Bible's incomparable majesty, "Thy Word is Truth."

Some Modern Views of the Bible (I)

"In the words of the Scripture is the Lord."

ATHANASIUS

" . . . believing that the divine foreknowledge, which supplies superhuman wisdom to the race of man by the Scriptures, has placed, so to speak, the seeds of saving truth in each letter. . . . "

ORIGEN

"All the God-breathed Scriptures make known God the Son of God."

THE SYNOD OF ANTIOCH

9

Some Modern Views of the Bible (I)

In the year 1924 there appeared a book by Harry Emerson Fosdick under the title *The Modern Use of the Bible.* It was rather a pretentious designation. Was there at that time only one use of the Bible which could be labeled "modern" and had Dr. Fosdick set forth that one use? Because of the popularity of the author, the book was widely received, and indeed seemed to speak for many people. One thing about it was its vigorous rejection of the traditional view of the Bible, which it merely dismissed as "verbal dictation." It was clear that the time-honored Biblical view of inspiration had no place in Dr. Fosdick's thinking.

Widespread as was the book's reception, nevertheless, upon the part of those who were concerned to do justice to what the Bible itself had to say as to its own nature, it met with vigorous opposition. From the pen of J. Gresham Machen, for example, appeared a critique that was nothing short of devastating.[1] Dr. Machen went right to the heart of the matter, and brought to light the easy-going evolutionary view of history and the nondoctrinal attitude toward Christianity which the work espoused.

What can be said today about the conception of the Bible which Dr. Fosdick presented? No doubt there would be widespread agreement with the author's rejection of the traditional or Biblical view of inspiration. As was the case when Fosdick's book appeared, so also today there is a widespread agreement that one cannot believe in the infallibility of God's Word. It is also to be feared that today there is much misrepresentation of the doctrine of Scriptural infallibility.

At the same time, because of present emphases upon the "theological" study of Scripture, it is probably not amiss to say that the "modernism" which in large measure characterized Fosdick's book, is out of date. This does not mean that the

1. "The Princeton Theological Review," Vol. xxiii, 1925, pp. 66-81.

devisive phenomenon known as "modernism" is dead. Such is not at all the case. Even today, long after its basic tenets have been exploded, the destructive, barren viewpoint which went under the name of "modernism" is still with us. To many people, however, the view which Dr. Fosdick labeled "modern" is no longer regarded as such. What then can today be labeled the "modern" use of the Bible?

Perhaps we cannot rightly speak of a modern view of the Bible as though there were just one widely prevailing attitude. It would indeed be difficult to set forth any one particular conception of Scripture as that which secures the greatest number of adherents. There are extant many ways of considering the Bible, and they have this in common that they are unalterably opposed to the Scriptural explanation of itself. When it comes to a positive substitute for the Scriptural position, however, differences of opinion begin to emerge. We cannot therefore speak today of any one particular attitude as *the* modern view of the Bible, for there are many attitudes. They have much in common, however, and for that reason it is not too difficult to obtain a general idea of what is now being offered as a substitute for the Biblical position.

Differing as modern views do in particulars they are essentially one in this respect, that they are founded upon modern ideas of God and man. We cannot really understand modern thought as it comes to expression in the field of theology unless we first realize that much that is offered for our consumption today is founded upon and has its roots in the philosophy of Immanuel Kant. The modern movement, despite disclaimers to the contrary, is really sceptical in nature, and goes back to the element of scepticism found in Kant himself.

Beyond "Criticism"

There is rather general recognition today of the fact that the results of nineteenth-century "criticism" in themselves were somewhat barren. Great gains, we are told, were made but, despite these gains, the process of "criticism" in itself left unsatisfactory results. Such a conclusion is not at all surprising, inasmuch as there is, after all, something more to the study of the Bible than the identification of the supposed documents of which it is compiled. During the nineteenth century a vast amount of time and energy was expended in the attempt to discover the documents of which the Old Testament books, for example were thought to have been composed.

The present writer remembers with great interest a novel which he read during his student days in Leipzig. Its name is now forgotten, as well as that of its author. It was the story of a rector in the Church of England who believed it was his duty in the Sunday sermon to point out the identity of the various documents which in his opinion composed the Scripture upon which he was speaking. He made it clear to his people just where document "J" began and where it ended, wherein "J" differed from "E" and so on. It was all very learned and quite in keeping with the scholarship of the time. Learned as it was, however, and scholarly as it was, the people began to lag in their church attendance. After a time most of them were not coming at all, and soon on Sabbath mornings the church was empty. Documentary analysis will not feed the souls of men.

This fact is apparently being realized today, for we hear much about the need of going beyond mere "criticism" itself. It is, of course, true that everyone who deals with such questions as the origin, nature and date of composition of the Biblical books is engaging in critical study. There is, however, a difference. There is a right and a wrong way to engage in such study. The right way involves the willingness of the investigator to subject his own mind to the teachings of Scripture, to follow Scripture wherever it leads. The other way, however, is quite different. It involves no acceptance of the statements of Scripture. Rather, it assumes that the investigator may submit these statements to his own judgment. He may decide whether they are trustworthy or not. One method demands that the Scriptures be followed in all that they teach. The other simply assumes that the Scriptures must be submitted to the judgment of the investigator as though they were on a par with any other writing. It is this latter kind of investigation which, when applied to the study of the date, composition, nature and origin of the Old Testament books, is what has popularly come to be known as "higher criticism." It has, in the judgment of the present writer, been responsible for incalculable harm to the well-being of the Church of Jesus Christ. To say this is in no sense to cast reflection upon the intentions or the character of those who have engaged in this type of criticism. It is simply a fact, however, that one cannot set the human mind up as a judge of Scripture. To do so is to destroy Scripture. The results must always be disastrous.

That they are disastrous has been recognized right along by Bible-believing Christian scholars. Those, however, who have engaged in "criticism" are themselves now recognizing that in their studies something has been lacking. They sincerely believe that the method of study which they have engaged in and which has been carried on during the nineteenth century has been productive of great gains. It has not, they acknowledge, been in itself sufficient, for it has in fact neglected the actual message of the Bible. But before we turn to consider what that message of the Bible is we must first ask, What are the gains which "critical" scholars believe have been made as a result of the "critical" investigation of the Bible during the past century?

There was a time when the first five books of the Bible were generally regarded as the work of Moses. We have now come to see, so it is claimed, that this is not the case. The "critical" study of the nineteenth century has made it clear that the first five books of the Bible, the Pentateuch, are not at all the work of one man. Rather, as we have them in our Bibles, they are a compilation of several originally independent documents. These documents, over the long years of Israel's history, have been pieced together by editors and redactors, with the result that the Pentateuch, in its present form, came into being. Thus, for example, there are said to be two accounts of creation, and two accounts of the flood. There is also said to be discernible a difference of outlook in various parts of the Pentateuch. Likewise, we now know that the book of Isaiah is not the work of one man, but that, at least beginning with the fortieth chapter, we have the writing of one who lived long after Isaiah's time. Daniel likewise did not come from the period of the Babylonian exile but in its present form is a work of the second century before Christ.

Alan Richardson sums it up thus:

It cannot be too strongly urged that our appreciation of the meaning and value of the Bible will be vastly strengthened in proportion as we come to understand, by the aid of all the light which scholarship can throw on the matter, more of the life and times of the men who wrote the various Scriptural books, their motives and experiences. To know, for instance, how St. Luke Collected the materials of his Gospel from earlier sources, including St. Mark, or why there are two accounts of the Creation or the Flood in Genesis, will help us considerably in our efforts to appreciate the meaning of what we read. To know that as we pass on to the fortieth chapter of the Book of Isaiah we are moving a century and a half forward from the period of chapters one to thirty-nine will obviously make a considerable difference to our understanding. And moreover, these things are not in doubt; they are not hypothetical reconstructions or tentative suggestions, but truths as assured as anything ever can be in the sphere of literary research.[2]

In this last sentence we come head on against the dogmatism that characterizes so much of "critical" scholarship. For our part we do not regard these "gains" of criticism as gains at all. We believe that these positions which the "critics" regard as gains are wrong, and the principal reason why we believe them to be wrong is that they conflict with the plain testimony of the Bible itself. Richardson says that these things are not in doubt. It is, however, only to those who refuse to accept the testimony of the Bible to itself, that they are not in doubt. Many competent scholars, scholars who wish to submit their thinking to the infallible revelation of God, have vigorously challenged these conclusions of "criticism." This, however, in passing. Our purpose now is to point out that the same type of critical scholar who in the nineteenth century would have paid little attention to a theological message of the Bible is now very much concerned to pay attention to such a message and in so doing is also very eager to preserve what he believes to be the gains of critical method. We have indicated our disagreement with these alleged gains merely to make it clear where we stand on the question.

These gains, we are being told, must not be allowed to go by the board. We want no return to the old-fashioned way of looking at the Bible, the way, for example, which is being defended in the present book. The gains of criticism must be preserved. In themselves, however, these gains are not sufficient. There is a theological message of the Bible which must not be neglected. Let us listen to William Neil who has written an attractive book on the subject:

> We are now more prepared to admit that it may have been possible that, in addition to the general revelation of His nature, will and purpose given by God to men in many ways

2. Alan Richardson, *Preface to Bible-Study,* London, 1943, pp. 28-29.

and in many different epochs, He chose to communicate a special revelation of Himself in a particular way and at a particular time, and that the Old and New Testaments do not consist of theories about God, but record a series of events which must be taken into account if we are to form any true picture of man's role in the universe.[3]

For our part we read this quotation with sadness of heart. We do not for an instant believe that it represents a return to the historic Christian faith. The sentiment which these words present is to us evidence of a tragic condition in the religious world. If the above words are taken at face value they would seem to teach that modern scholars are now prepared to admit that there may have been a special revelation and that the Scriptures record the events in which this revelation was manifested. It might, to be sure, be mentioned in passing that since her founding the Church has been proclaiming constantly that God has revealed Himself in a special way, and the Church has based this message squarely upon the Bible. If modern scholars had been willing to listen to the Bible they would have known all along that God had revealed Himself in a special way.

What then has caused some modern scholars to acknowledge finally that there may have been a special revelation? Is there new evidence to support that fact? Of course there is not. The heavens right along have been declaring the glory of God, and the infallible Word, which God Himself has given us in words so clear, that he who refuses to heed them is without excuse, proclaimed that God has given to man a special revelation. No, there is no new evidence upon the basis of which men may now see that there is a special revelation. Why, then, do some theologians say that they are willing to admit the possibility of such a revelation? For one thing, we may say by way of reply, it has indeed become apparent to many thinking people of the day that, in themselves, the scientific studies of the last century were somewhat barren and sterile. The Protestant Church, it is now being acknowledged, has passed through a rather gloomy and somber period. That men are beginning to recognize the inadequacy of mere critical study, such as that which was engaged in by the critics of the nineteenth century, is probably a cause for rejoicing. There are, however, some questions that naturally come to mind. If this period of critical study was so barren,

3. William Neil, *The Rediscovery of the Bible,* London, 1954, p. 40.

what profit did it bring to those who engaged in it? We today, it is said, realize the need for a theological interpretation of Scripture. What, however, about those who did not have this realization? Of what benefit was the Bible to them? If only today we are prepared to admit that there may have been a special revelation of God, may it not be in order to ask whether that special revelation can be of genuine aid to us? What about the years before our day, when men were not prepared to admit that there might have been a special revelation? Of what benefit to them was this special revelation? It is difficult to escape the thought that the "special revelation," the existence of which modern theologians are prepared to admit, is something rather unreal. Certainly they are not now prepared to admit that the Triune God has intervened in human history and has spoken to men in words. It is not special revelation in the old-fashioned orthodox sense, the existence of which modern men are now willing to admit.

If the critical study of the nineteenth century were really as theologically bankrupt as is today maintained, we may well ask why this discovery was not earlier made? Why did not men learn much earlier that the methods of study in which they were engaged could only produce a gloomy period in Protestant history? If they had listened to the Bible they would have realized that they were on the wrong track. This, however, they would not do, any more than modern men will listen to the Bible. What was it then which caused the dissatisfaction with the critical methods of last century?

It is, for one thing, apparent today that the liberalism which was an outgrowth of the nineteenth-century world and life view was itself entirely too shallow. The penetrating thought of Kierkegaard and Dostoevski's incisive analyses of human life have made themselves felt. Coupled with this is the tragedy of two world wars. Inasmuch, then, as it does not do justice to the facts of human experience, the older liberalism is more and more considered outmoded. In its place there must be something that will meet the needs of the human soul. The entire climate of opinion, therefore, has shifted, and the emphases which one hears at the present time are quite different from those of thirty years ago.

There is much talk today about a rediscovery of the Bible. To the Bible-believing Christian this kind of language is almost meaningless. The Bible-believing Christian was not aware that the Bible had been lost and needed to be rediscovered. It may be that the critical study of the nineteenth and the early part of the present century have indeed covered the Bible with a blanket of obscurity; it may be that leaders in high places in the Protestant churches have been too "advanced" to take the Scriptures seriously; it may be that the faith of many has been shaken through the willingness of some of the clergy to compromise with the "assured results of modern criticism." Despite all that, however, despite all the efforts to make of the Bible something that it is not, there still are those who love that Bible as the infallible Word of the living God.

Is the Bible actually being rediscovered? While critics have been busily engaged in pointing out what they have regarded as flaws and errors, while they have been occupied in submitting the holy Word of Truth to the authority and judgment of the human mind, there have been humble believers whose hearts have been blessed by the words of this holy Book. When temptation has come, its words of admonition have been to them a warning; in the face of the severities of life, its promises have given courage and hope; in the presence of death, its blessed truths have brought consolation. For them the Bible has never been a lost Book. It has always been present, ready at any moment to be read and cherished. Who can tell of the blessing that has come to believing hearts because in time of need this blessed Book was on hand?

Now, however, we are told that the Bible is being rediscovered. What, however, is this Bible which is being rediscovered? Is it the holy Word of Truth, or it is a Bible reconstructed according to the latest findings of critical scholarship? To ask that question is to answer it. A close examination makes it clear that the Bible which some critical scholars are interested in today is not the Bible we have always known. It is, in fact, something quite different. What is this Bible which the modern theologian is rediscovering?

One thing that stands out immediately is that the Bible which is being rediscovered is the Bible of "criticism," and not of historic Christianity. This is to be expected, inasmuch as it is impossible for men to hold the principles of higher criticism, as it has been practiced by those who reject the infallibility of Scripture, and at the same time arrive at the position of evangelical Christianity.

A man may practice the principles of criticism or he may be a believer in evangelical Christianity. One thing, however, is clear: if he is consistent, he cannot possibly espouse both. Either he will practice the principles of "criticism" or else he will follow a Christian method of study. If he follows the principles of "criticism," these principles will not lead him to evangelical Christianity. If he is an ardent believer in evangelical Christianity, he will not want to follow the principles of "criticism." Consequently, we must note well that the modern scholar who is unwilling to abandon the principles which characterized so much of the Bible study during the nineteenth century cannot and does not arrive at the position of historic orthodox Christianity. The orthodox terminology which is so frequently employed today by modern theologians means something quite different from that which the humble Bible believer would expect it to mean. The Bible which modern scholarship is presenting to us is quite different from that infallible Word to which the Christian has been accustomed to turn to hear the voice of God.

The Bible and Proof Texts

On all sides one hears it asserted that we must not use the Bible as a book of proof texts. To use the Bible in such a way is, we are told, to betray a profound misunderstanding of its nature. It is not a storehouse of proof texts where, when occasion arises, we may find a verse to support our ideas. Modern theologians seem unable to speak with sufficient scorn of this practice. Of all the sins of evangelical Christians, this is apparently regarded as one of the worst.

One thing, however, may be said about this practice. It was employed by none other than our Lord Himself. Jesus Christ used the method of appeal to proof texts which is so much decried today. When the evil one came to tempt Him, our Lord said, "It is written, Man shall not live by bread alone, but by every word that proceedeth out of the mouth of God" (Matthew 4:4). If the modern theologians are correct, Jesus Christ should not have done this. He showed by His appeal to a proof text that He had an improper understanding of the nature of the Bible. He must have thought that the Bible was actually a body of truth to which one could appeal at will. Very obviously Jesus Christ did not have the advantage of a knowledge of the modern use of the Bible. Our Lord simply regarded the Bible as in itself an authoritative revelation to which He might turn in support of His teaching.

Christ set a blessed precedent. He appealed to the words of the Old Testament Scriptures and so did the Apostles. In this practice they have been followed throughout the ages by those who have sought to be obedient to them. Luther and Calvin were constantly appealing to the Bible for support of their teachings. If the Reformers had not used the Bible in precisely the manner which the modern theologian says is the wrong way to use it, there never would have been a Reformation.

More than that, it is most interesting to note that those who are strong in their protests against using the Bible as a book of proof texts are themselves guilty of doing just this thing. In support of their teaching they also appeal to the Bible, and that constantly, for support of what they are saying. It is, of course, difficult to see how they can refrain from so doing, for the simple reason that the moment one appeals to the Bible for support, he is, whether he likes it or not, using the Bible as a book of proof texts. If one will examine the indices in the writings of modern theologians, he will make the discovery that, despite their protestations against the practice, they themselves use the Bible as a book of proof texts and do so constantly. If the Bible is not to be employed for proof texts, it follows that we have no right to make any kind of an appeal to it, for the moment that we appeal to the Bible for anything, that very moment are we engaged in using it as a book of proof texts. It is impossible to avoid using Scripture in this sense, nor should we seek to avoid so using it unless we wish to give it up altogether.[4]

IS THE BIBLE A COMPLETED REVELATION?

The objection which some raise against using the Bible as a book of proof texts arises from the view that the Bible is not a permanent statement or revelation of the truth. At this

---

4. It goes without saying that an indiscriminate usage of proof texts is unwarranted. We are not to read our own ideas into the Bible and then appeal to the Bible for support of those ideas. In any appeal to Scripture its organic character and the progressive nature of revelation must always be kept in mind. Nevertheless, to turn to Scripture for support is not only legitimate, it is essential. How else can one use Scripture?

point modern thought makes a sharp break with the historic Christian view of the Bible. That historic Christian view finds a remarkable expression, for example, in the Westminster Confession of Faith (VI a): "The whole counsel of God concerning all things necessary for His own glory, man's salvation, faith and life, is either expressly set down in Scripture, or by good and necessary consequence may be deduced from Scripture . . . ." This conception of the Bible, however, is regarded by many modern theologians as being static, and consequently they reject it. Otto A. Piper, for example, who a few years ago wrote a most engaging presentation of some aspects of the newer view of the Bible, has said that the greatest obstacle to his own understanding of the Bible was that he believed the Bible to be "a collection of theological doctrine plus a record of historical events."[5]

We can indeed admire the candor of Dr. Piper in speaking as he has. What he is condemning, however, as having been an obstacle to his understanding of the Bible, is the very thing which the Westminster Confession so forcefully asserts. According to the Confession and the traditional Christian position, the Bible is indeed a collection of theological doctrines. True enough, these doctrines are not stated therein in systematic form, but they are there nevertheless. "The whole counsel of God concerning all things necessary for His own glory, man's salvation, faith and life," all these things, and they are certainly theological doctrines, the very things which were a hindrance to Dr. Piper's understanding of the Bible. "All these things," the Confession declares, are to be found in the Bible.

In depreciating the Scriptures as a source book of doctrine, Dr. Piper, although he is one of the most gifted expounders of his position, is by no means alone. Let us listen again to Alan Richardson:

> . . . they [i.e., Christians] do not think of the Bible as a message which God wrote several centuries ago and which remains unalterably the same for all time, finished, perfect, static. They think rather of God still speaking through the Bible to men. Thus, the Bible is not the record of a dead revelation, but the living medium of a present revelation.[6]

5. Otto A. Piper, "The Theme of the Bible" in *The Christian Century*, March 13, 1946, p. 334.
6. *Op. cit.*, p. 21.

With this statement we cannot possibly agree. The Bible *is* a message which God wrote several centuries ago; it is precisely that and, since it is the truth of God, does not change. It is a revelation that is finished and perfect. Is it, however, static? As this word is used, it is used in a derogatory sense. Is the connotation of the word, however, always derogatory? If by "static" we merely mean that the truth of the Bible does not change, then, of course, the Bible is a static revelation. There are times, however, when one may indeed be thankful that some things are static. The writer remembers an occasion when he was travelling high in the Colorado Rockies. Far ahead the road crossed a deep canyon on a bridge which seemed to be swaying in mid-air. No visible support for the bridge could be seen. Beneath the bridge, the chasm yawned, dropping deep down to the floor of the valley far below. As one approached the bridge, he soon realized that his earlier impressions were groundless; the bridge was, after all, solid and firm. The bridge, fortunately, was completely static, and since it was a static bridge, one could drive across it in perfect safety. If, therefore, when it is said that the Bible is static, we merely mean that the Bible does not change, by all means let us not be afraid to assert that the Bible is static. The Bible is true, and the truth of the Bible is not something that grows and changes. Despite whatever derogatory words may be employed to describe the historic, orthodox view of the Bible, we must insist that the truth of the Bible does not change with every wind of doctrine.

When Richardson speaks of a dead revelation, we must again ask what is meant. It does not follow that a revelation given once for all is thereby dead. It is perfectly true that God today does not speak to mankind as He did in Biblical times. The Bible is indeed the record of those wondrous revelations which God once gave to the sinful race. It is, of course, far more than a mere record of those revelations; it is itself a revelation. It is, however, a record of revelations which God gave once and for all in history. "God", we read in that matchless first verse of the epistle to the Hebrews, "who at sundry times and in divers manners spoke in time past unto the fathers by the prophets, hath in these last days spoken unto us by *his* Son." When these grand words were written the speaking of God was an accomplished historical fact. Does it, however, follow therefrom that the revelation which He gave is a dead revelation?

What, one may ask, is a dead revelation? If, by this unfortunate term, Dr. Richardson simply means that the revelation is completed, a *fait accompli*, we have no objection, for this is precisely the case; the revelation is actually completed. The Word which God has spoken, however, is no dead, lifeless thing. Rather, that Word which God has once for all spoken is "quick, and powerful, and sharper than any twoedged sword, piercing even to the dividing asunder of soul and spirit, and of the joints and marrow, and *is* a discerner of the thoughts and intents of the heart" (Hebrews 4:12). It is this so-called "dead" revelation which has pointed out to many a sinner the heinousness of his sin and has revealed to him the gracious saving work of Jesus Christ upon the cross. If that is a dead revelation, so be it. As a matter of fact, there is not, nor can there be, such a thing as a dead revelation. All that God has spoken to us is "spirit" and "life." Well may the Christian rejoice that God has dealt so lovingly with him as to give him a sure foundation upon which he may rest his soul. Well may the Christian sing from the heart:

> "How firm a foundation, ye saints of the Lord,
> Is laid for your faith in His excellent Word.
> What more can He say than to you He hath said,
> To you who for refuge to Jesus have fled?"

This excellent Word, given once for all to mankind, is the very breath of life to those whose consciences have been awakened by the Spirit of God to the guilt of their sins. Instead of speaking of a static word and a dead revelation, one might far more accurately refer to the Scriptures as God's excellent Word.

The Bible, we are told today, is not a body of infallible doctrine, nor does it contain a system of doctrine. Thus, Professor G. Ernest Wright remarks:

> Yet, for the most part, the second presupposition mentioned above is still accepted. That is to the effect that theology is propositional dogmatics, the systematic presentation of abstract propositions or beliefs about God, man and salvation. The churches retain and encourage this conception in their liturgy and creeds. For example, every elder, deacon, commissioned church worker and minister in the Presbyterian Church of the U.S.A. is required to affirm when he or she is ordained that the confession of faith of that church contains "the system of doctrine taught in the Holy Scriptures." But does the Bible

contain a *system* of doctrine? Certainly none of its writers was primarily concerned with the presentation of such a scheme. Consequently, we must say that static, propositional systems are those which the church itself erects by inference from the Biblical writings. The systems are very good and very important, but we cannot define the Bible by means of them. No system of propositions can deal adequately with the inner dynamics of Biblical faith.[7]

All of this is stated as over against the positive position which Dr. Wright wishes to expound, namely, that in the Bible God is presented to us, not by means of statements and propositions but as a God who acts.

These words of Dr. Wright are by no means isolated phenomena. His little work, however, is distinguished for clarity of expression and may be regarded as a first-rate presentation of one aspect of the modern position. In response we would of course assert that the Bible is not a treatise upon theology. For that matter, we have never heard of any Bible believers who maintained that it was. True enough, there are modern writers who insist that we must not regard the Bible as a treatise on theology, but we have never heard of anyone who ever did so regard the Bible. The Bible is not a theological treatise, but it does not therefore follow that the content upon which the discipline of systematic theology builds is not found in the Bible.

From beginning to end this life-giving Book which we call the Bible is filled with doctrine. The doctrine is not arranged in systematic fashion; but the doctrine is there. "I *am* the Lord thy God, which have brought thee out of the land of Egypt, out of the house of bondage" (Exodus 20:1). That is doctrine, doctrine profound and rich. "The Hebrew knowledge of God," says Alan Richardson, "was founded upon historical events, not upon metaphysical ideas and arguments."[8] To speak thus, however, is to obscure the question. Historical events are of no significance to man unless they are interpreted in words. And when God performed mighty acts of deliverance He accompanied those acts with words of explanation. He told Israel who He was. "Hear, O Israel: the Lord our God *is* one Lord" (Deuteronomy 6:4).

7. G. Ernest Wright, *God Who Acts,* London, 1954, p. 35, 36.
8. *Op. cit.,* p. 46.

That is doctrine; that is propositional dogmatics; that is a metaphysical statement; and it is upon the basis of statements such as these that Israel received her knowledge of God.

When Moses drew near to the burning bush (and since modern theologians are so concerned with God's great act of deliverance from Egypt we shall appeal to that section of the Bible), God gave to Moses some rather straightforward "static," "dead" revelation which consisted in propositional dogmatics and metaphysical statements. Hear these wondrous words of life: "I *am* the God of thy father, the God of Abraham, the God of Isaac, and the God of Jacob" (Exodus 3:6a). And again, "I have surely seen the affliction of my people which *are* in Egypt, and have heard their cry by reason of their taskmasters; for I know their sorrows; and I am come down to deliver them out of the hand of the Egyptians, and to bring them up out of that land unto a good land and a large, unto a land flowing with milk and honey . . . " (Exodus 3:7, 8a). The Lord further said, "I AM THAT I AM: And he said, Thus shalt thou say unto the children of Israel, I AM hath sent me unto you" (Exodus 3:14). This language simply bristles with statements about God. They tell us who God is, what kind of a God He is, and what His relation is to Israel. They are statements which are filled with doctrine. They are the very thing which some modern theologians seem to think is not found in the Bible. This denial that God has revealed Himself in theological propositions has become so widespread that even some evangelicals are also guilty of employing similar language. Thus in an interesting article which appeared in the *Evangelical Quarterly* (Vol. 26, p. 216) Professor H. L. Ellison writes:

> But we must never forget that while God could have inspired a manual of theology, He did not. He could have made Himself known in a series of theological propositions, but He used instead the experiences of men. This is partly because experience must always be fuller and richer than its verbal expression, even when guided in its being written down by the Holy Spirit.

Thought-provoking words these are and worthy of careful consideration. Perhaps it will be well to begin with the statement, ". . . experience must always be fuller than its verbal expression, even when guided in its being written down by the Holy Spirit." It would seem that these words contain the heart of much that is said today by way of depreciation of a verbal revelation. It is, of course, true that we receive more information about an event or situation from being present on the spot than we do from hearing or reading an account at a later time. There is not the slightest doubt in the world, nor has any Bible believer, as far as the present writer is aware, ever denied the fact, that if we had been present we would have known far more about Moses' encounter with Pharaoh, to take but one example, than we can learn from reading the account in the words of the Bible. Had we been there on the scene we would have seen the king in all his rich regalia, we would have understood the setting, with the palace, the Nile, the palm trees, and all the rest. We would have seen the expressions upon Pharaoh's face, the anger in his countenance, the terror with which he was overcome when the hand of God acted. We would have beheld the demeanor of Moses and Aaron; these, and many other points we would have known. Inasmuch as we are today dependent upon a written account, we cannot have the knowledge which would have been ours had we been present in ancient Egypt. In this sense, without a doubt, the experience is fuller than a written record, even an infallible record, of that experience. All of this may freely be granted.

As a matter of actual fact, however, we today are dependent upon a written record. We cannot go back and somehow become unseen spectators at the court of Pharaoh when Moses and Aaron came before him. No doubt it would have been a most wonderful thing to experience, could we have been present and have heard the ambassadors of God proclaim the powerful deeds of their Lord. Wonderful as it might have been, however, it is something that cannot be ours. We are, whether we like it or not, shut up to a written record — thank God that it is an infallible record — of what God wrought in the land of Egypt. Since we are thus restricted to a written record it would be a most grievous error to suppose that somehow we have been defrauded of things which we should know. It is a written record which God in His goodness has seen fit to give us, but it is a remarkably full and complete record. It does not, however, cater to our whims and curiosity. Rather, it tells us everything that we need to know. Wise indeed are those beautiful words of the Westminster Confession of Faith: "The whole counsel of God concerning all things necessary for His own glory, man's salvation, faith and life, is either expressly set down in Scripture, or by good and necessary consequence may be deduced from Scripture . . . ." It is not necessary for us to know the expression upon the countenance of the angry Pharaoh, nor the color of the Egyptian sky, nor the heat of the day. Interesting these things might have been; interesting, but not at all necessary. All that is necessary for our salvation God has graciously caused to be recorded in His Word. The Bible is not a novel, written for entertainment. It is the life-giving Word of the God of Truth, wherein men and women, wearied with the toil of life, may find the blessed announcement of that which God has done once for all for the salvation of sinners. Rich and full are the words of the Bible, and they tell us all that the Lord wished us to know. Far from depreciating a word-revelation, we should the rather ever give thanks to God that He has permitted us to have so full and complete an expression of His holy will.

Since experiences are fuller than written words, must it therefore follow that God made Himself known to mankind in experiences rather than in a series of theological propositions? To assert this is to establish a disjunction that is utterly unwarranted. It is, of course, true that God in Biblical times did reveal Himself in wondrous deeds. That point has been insisted upon by Bible-believing scholars throughout the history of the Church. That men should speak today of God revealing Himself in His acts is nothing new. In the wondrous deliverance recorded in Exodus, for example, God most certainly did reveal Himself and His working. About that there is no doubt whatever. And we would not only acknowledge the fact, we would lay great stress upon it. The miracles in connection with the bondage in Egypt and the Exodus, for example, are revelatory of the power and glory of God. Truly, these miracles revealed God and His ways.

At the same time, revelatory as are the wondrous acts of God, they cannot properly be interpreted by men without an accompanying explanation given in words. When Isaiah had his vision of the holy God in the temple, the Lord, through His servant the seraph, performed a symbolical act. The seraph, with a live coal in his hand flew to Isaiah and touched the coal upon his lips. What was the meaning of that act? Was it to punish Isaiah, who, recognizing his own uncleanness, had heard beings with pure lips praise God? Was it to assure Isaiah of pardon and forgiveness? The fact is that Isaiah would not

have known the meaning of the act, he would not have understood
its significance, no matter how rich the experience might have
been, unless the act was accompanied by words. Hence, the
seraph said: "Lo, this hath touched thy lips; and thine iniquity
is taken away, and thy sin purged" (Isaiah 6:7b). Not merely
is a word-revelation an important accompaniment of a revelation
of God in acts; it is indispensable.

One of the great acts of God whereby He manifested His
sovereignty over the armies of this earth was the destruction of
the hosts of the Assyrian Sennacherib. The Bible relates, "And
it came to pass that night, that the angel of the LORD went out,
and smote in the camp of the Assyrians an hundred fourscore and
five thousand: and when they arose early in the morning, behold,
they *were* all dead corpses" (2 Kings 19:35). In those words
the Bible gives an explanation of that which transpired. For
us today and for the Israelite of old to whom God also gave
an explanation in words, there is an interpretation of this tragic
event. The Assyrian army died, and the ultimate reason why
it died was that the God of Israel had sent His angel to bring
about its destruction. At the time of His people's peril, God intervened for their deliverance. To the Assyrian, however, there was
no such interpretation. He could not have rightly interpreted this
event, for the simple matter that, revelatory as the event was,
nevertheless, since there was no revelation in words accompanying
it, the event could not properly be interpreted nor understood by
the Assyrians. The Assyrians knew that a great calamity had
occurred; they did not, however, know nor understand its
true meaning.

The reason why the Assyrians could not correctly interpret
this one particular revelation, and the reason why mankind itself
cannot properly interpret the wondrous acts of God is that man
is a sinner. The eyes of his understanding are darkened so
that he does not interpret as he should. It is because of man's
sin that God has given a revelation in words. Without this
revelation in words therefore, mankind, just as were the Assyrians,
is left in ignorance. The gift of a word-revelation is but an
evidence of the goodness and wisdom of God. Instead of depreciating such a revelation in words, we should offer our humble
thanks to Almighty God that He has so condescended to help
our weakness and our sinful estate as to give such a clear and

full explanation of those wondrous saving acts which He has performed.

It might also be pointed out that the Egyptians, and even the Israelites, could not rightly have discovered the significance of the events of the Exodus had there been no accompanying revelation or explanation in words. The very events of the Exodus, about which modern theologians delight to speak, would be bereft of all their richness were it not for the accompanying revelation that God graciously gave to His people in words. Not through experiences or acts alone did the Lord God reveal Himself, but also, and we may thank God that it is so, in words. Even the revelation of these words, we may note in passing, was an act of God, and the reception of these words upon the part of a man an experience; in fact, one would think, one of the richest and most blessed experiences that could come to a man.

It is not true, therefore, that God did not reveal Himself in a series of theological propositions or that He did not inspire a manual of theology. No one will dispute the fact that the Bible is not written in the style of Melanchthon's *Loci Communes,* the *Systematic Theology* of Charles Hodge, or the *Institutiones* of Francis Turretin. That the Bible is not written in the form of a textbook of systematic theology is true. It does not follow, however, that there are no theological propositions in the Bible and that the Bible is not a manual of theology. The Bible is simply teeming with theological propositions. Here are a few of them selected at random:

1. "I *am* the Almighty God; walk before me, and be thou perfect. And I will make my covenant between me and thee, and will multiply thee exceedingly" (Genesis 17:1b, 2).

2. "And God saw every thing that he had made, and, behold, *it was* very good" (Genesis 1:31).

3. "And the LORD passed by before him, and proclaimed, the LORD, The LORD God, merciful and gracious, longsuffering, and abundant in goodness and truth" (Exodus 34:6).

4. "My servant Moses *is* not so, who *is* faithful in all mine house. With him will I speak mouth to mouth, even apparently, and not in dark speeches; and the similitude of the LORD shall he behold . . . " (Numbers 12:7, 8a).

5. "Blessed *is he whose* transgression *is* forgiven, *whose* sin *is* covered" (Psalm 32:1).

6. "The LORD *is* my shepherd; I shall not want" (Psalm 23:1).

7. "The earth *is* the LORD'S, and the fullness thereof; the world, and they that dwell therein" (Psalm 24:1).

8. "God *is* a Spirit: and they that worship him must worship *him* in spirit and in truth" (John 4:24).

9. "For had ye believed Moses, ye would have believed me: for he wrote of me" (John 5:46).

10. "I am the resurrection, and the life: he that believeth in me, though he were dead, yet shall he live" (John 11:25).

It is, of course, undeniable that the above statements are not systematically formulated propositions. They are, however, statements of the truth; they are the indispensable material from which systematically formulated propositions must be constructed. To state the matter in a slightly different manner: they are statements of that which is true and is to be believed. In this sense they are indeed theological propositions, and the Bible, inasmuch as it states the truth which we are to believe about God and the duty which God demands of us, most surely is a manual of theology. Consequently it is not justifiable to erect a separation between theological propositions on the one hand, and the experiences of men on the other, as though they were mutually exclusive media of revelation. God did make Himself known through mighty acts, but He also gave an explanation of those acts. This explanation was in words, words which are instructive and which explain the meaning of the acts of power in which God displayed Himself.

It is sometimes said that the Bible does not teach dogmatics, but rather God's dealings with mankind. This disjunction, we believe, is a most dangerous one. How can one possibly know about God's dealings with mankind unless he also knows something of that despised subject "dogmatics"? The moment we discuss the question, "Who is God?" we are discussing dogmatics. The moment we ask, "What did God do?" we are considering dogmatics. The moment we learn that God has dealt with mankind, we are studying dogmatics. The attempt of modern writers to divorce the two as though it were somehow possible to consider the Bible as a Book treating of God's dealings with mankind without at the same time giving consideration to dogmatics is misleading in the extreme. The tragedy of the present day is that good Christian people are being deceived by this kind of reasoning.

Is the Bible the Word of God?

We have spoken earlier of a tendency to depreciate the written words of the Bible. These written words of the Bible, we are told, are not themselves the actual Word of God. Rather, that Word is to be distinguished from the words of the Bible. Professor Piper holds that the truth of God is contained in the Bible, but that Jesus showed that the Jews were mistaken in identifying the Bible as the Word of God.[9] But the Lord Jesus Christ never showed the Jews of His time that they were mistaken in identifying the Bible with the Word of God; both Jesus Christ and the Jews were one in identifying the Bible as the Word of God. What concerns us now, however, is the separation which Professor Piper makes between the Word of God and the Bible itself. It is freely admitted today that God speaks to us through the Bible but, we are told, it is not the actual printed page before us which is His Word. His Word, rather, is the message which reaches us through the Scriptures. Behind the human words of the Bible there is a divine message, but we make a great mistake, it is said, if we think that the message of God, His glorious Gospel, is tied to this or that verse of the Bible in particular. As Helmuth Schreiner has put it, "The Holy Scripture is the Word of God, concealed and veiled in the word of men."[10]

Emil Brunner has illustrated the relationship which he thinks exists by means of a comparison with the phonograph record and the music which it conveys.[11] We hear the voice of the singer but we also hear the scratching of the record. This may be compared with the words of the Bible through which the Word of God comes. The Word of God, then, is conveyed by human words, the human words of the Bible, and to them it is related, Brunner asserts, as reality to its sign and framework. The words of the Bible, therefore, are not themselves the Word of God. They are, rather, simply a framework or sign by means of which this Word of God is conveyed to the hearer.

Karl Barth has been most outspoken in his refusal to identify in the traditional Christian sense the Bible with the actual Word of God.

9. Otto A. Piper, *God in History*, 1939, p. 147.
10. Helmuth Schreiner, *Ist die Bibel Gottes Wort?* 1953, p. 50.
11. Emil Brunner, *Our Faith*, 1936, p. 10.

> If God has not been ashamed to speak through the Scriptures with its fallible human words, with its historical and scientific blunders, its theological contradictions, with the uncertainty of its transmission and above all with its Jewish character, but rather accepted it in all its fallibility to make it serve Him, we ought not to be ashamed of it when with all its fallibility it wants anew to be to us a witness; it would be self-will and disobedience to wish to seek in the Bible for infallible elements.[12]

The Bible is not then as such the Word of God, nor does it become such until it is accepted by the believer. There is a sense therefore in which Barth does speak of the Bible as the Word of God. It is the Word of God, however, only in so far as God speaks through it. Dr. Cornelius Van Til has well summed up this position:

> When we say that the Bible *is* the Word of God, we express our faith in an act of God's redemption of man in the present. The Bible becomes the Word of God in this event and it is with respect to its being in this becoming that the little word *is*, in the sentence that the Bible is the Word of God, refers.[13]

Certainly it is our duty and the duty of everyone who loves the Lord of Glory and is not ashamed of Him and His words to protest with all vigor against this unbiblical separation between the Bible and the Word of God. How different is this modern view from that, for example, of Calvin! Calvin would have reacted with all his being against this false idea that the Bible and the Word of God are not to be identified. Hear him as he says:

> But since we are not favoured with daily oracles from heaven, and since it is only in the Scriptures that the Lord hath been pleased to preserve his truth in perpetual remembrance, it obtains the same complete credit and authority with believers, when they are satisfied of its divine origin, as if they heard the very words pronounced by God himself.[14]

With this thought of Calvin Luther is in perfect agreement:

---

12. Kard Barth, *Kirchliche Dogmatik*, I, 2, p. 590 (translated by Cornelius Van Til, *The New Modernism*, 1946, p. 286).

13. *Has Karl Barth Become Orthodox?* 1954, p. 140. Barth's original statement may be found in his *Kirchliche Dogmatik*, I, 1, p. 113.

14. John Calvin, *Institutes of the Christian Religion* (translated by John Allen), 1930, Book I, Chapter 7, p. 75.

"It cannot be otherwise," he says, "for the Scriptures are divine; in them God speaks and they are His Word."[15]

A sympathetic study of the beliefs of the Reformers can only produce the conclusion that these men considered the actual words of the Bible to be the words of God Himself. They were as far removed from the idea that the Word of God is not to be equated with the words of the Bible as is the modern adherent of the infallibility of Scripture.

There is, we believe, a valid criticism which may be made of the position which we are now considering. If the Word of God is not to be identified with or equated with the words of the Bible, we may well ask, Who is to identify this Word of God? How are we to know this Word when we meet it? It is brought to us in connection with the words of the Bible and yet it is not itself to be equated with those words. What then is this Word, and how shall we know it when we meet it? In answer to these questions we are told that when we read the Bible, the truth of God, or the Word of God, finds us. It may be, however, that a certain passage of Scripture actually does not inspire us. We turn therefore to something else, and suddenly our souls are inspired. The Truth has met us. Another person, however, turns to the passage of the Bible which we have not found inspiring. To him this passage becomes meaningful. Here the Word of God has found him. In reading one passage of Scripture, one man is inspired; the Word of God has found him. In reading the same passage, another person is not found of the Word at all. Is not this subjectivism? Is not, in the last analysis, man himself the judge of that which is and that which is not the Word of God? It is very difficult to escape the conclusion that after all the Word of God amounts to nothing more than that which happens to inspire one upon a particular occasion. Surely this is subjectivism of a blatant kind. What is this Word of God? We cannot point to it and say, "There it is; these verses of the Bible have inspired us; they are the Word of God." To do that would be to fall into the very position which the adherents of the modern

15. Translations in M. Reu, *Luther and the Scriptures,* 1944, p. 17.

view condemn as unwarranted. It would be to equate the Word of God with particular words or verses of the Bible. That, we are told, we must not do. What then actually is this Word of God? One can only conclude that it is something very nebulous. To pin it down is something that is beyond our power.

Thus we come to a further criticism. This distinction which some modern theologians are making between the Word of God and the words of the Bible is an impossible one. That it is an impossible distinction is shown by the fact that its most ardent protagonists themselves constantly act as though the distinction did not exist. Those who are most vociferous in defense of the position that the Word of God and the words of the Bible are not to be equated, themselves in actual practice refuse to make the distinction. They constantly appeal to the *words* of the Bible as though those words were authoritative. Indeed, since the distinction which they profess is an impossible one, they cannot do otherwise. If it were a valid distinction, they should have nothing to do with the words of the Bible. Those words, according to them, are not the Word of God. They are nothing more than human words. Hence, there should be no appeal to them as to an authority. Inasmuch as, according to the modern view, they are shot through with human error and are not in themselves the Word of God, they should not be set up as an authority for settling any religious matters. Yet, what do we find? We find that the protagonists of the modern view do just this. In reality, they should never appeal to the words of the Bible. If they appeal to anything, they should limit their appeal to the nebulous "Word" of God. This, of course, they do not do. They do not do it because they cannot do it. They appeal to the words of the Bible which they claim are nothing more than human words. In thus appealing they are tacitly acknowledging that these words of the Bible are authoritative. Else, why appeal to them? Not only are they, by their appeal to the words of the Bible, tacitly acknowledging the authority of these words, they are doing something far more — they are tacitly acknowledging that these words possess a divine authority. That such is the case will, upon a little reflection, become clear. If it be acknowledged that God has spoken, and that there is a Word of God, I must harken to that Word of God if I wish to learn what I am to believe about God and what He requires of me. If I am to know what He has spoken, I must harken to His Word. Where, then, am I to find this Word? I say that it is not to be identified with the words of the Bible. Well and good, if that is the case, then I have no right to appeal to the words of the Bible for information about God. The moment I appeal to the words of the Bible to tell me what I am to believe about God and to learn from them what is right and what is wrong, in that very moment I am, whether I wish it or not, giving tacit acknowledgement to the fact that I do actually regard those words as divinely authoritative. Otherwise, if such were not the case, why should I bother to appeal to the words of the Bible? Modern scholars appeal to the Bible all the time. They proclaim loudly that we must not employ the Bible as a book of proof texts, but they themselves so employ it constantly. All that they have to say about God is supported by appeals to the Bible. One need but examine the large indices to the writings of Karl Barth, for example, who vigorously disclaims any belief in verbal inspiration, to make the discovery that in his actual procedure he acts as do the staunchest advocates of verbal inspiration. The disjunction between the Word of God and the Words of the Bible is one that is impossible to make.

Whatever else may be said about it, this disjunction is not one which the Reformers made. To them the very words of the Bible were the words of God. Nor were they ashamed to acknowledge this fact. A vigorous proclamation of this position of the Reformers is the greatest need of the hour. The challenges of the day and the present ravages of sin cannot be met by ecclesiastical machinery and programs of man's devising. There is, however, one thing, and only one thing, that will meet the deep need of men's souls. It is not the word of man, but the Word of Him who is Truth itself. Where is that Word to be found? There is only one place where it may be found. The pride of man would seek for it elsewhere. Those, however, whose hearts have been renewed by the Spirit of God know that there is, after all, only one place where the voice of God may be heard telling man what he is to believe and how he is to act. That Word is found in a Book that is by many rejected. When, however, the men of our day are willing once more to open the pages of that Book and to listen to the voice of the living God, then blessing will come. Not in some esoteric or elusive sense is the Word of God connected with the Bible.

Rather, the very words of Scripture are the words of God, breathed forth to tell us what His will is. The greatest need of the day is for a return to the Bible, a return which will involve a hearty acceptance of the message that is found in its life-giving words. Then will the clouds of doubt and despair be dispelled, the long dark night of sin will be swept away, and the path to the heavenly city will lead through rich pastures where the flowers of blessing will spring up and the free sun of God's grace will shine.

Some Modern Views of the Bible (II)

"I think you will agree with me that it is a sad thing to see words like these die like this. And I hope you will determine that, God helping you, you will not let them die thus, if any care of your part can preserve them in life and vigor. But the dying of the words is not the saddest thing which we see here. The saddest thing is the dying out of the hearts of men of the things for which the words stand." BENJAMIN B. WARFIELD

"The Jesus of the New Testament has at least one advantage over the Jesus of modern reconstruction — He is real. He is not a manufactured figure suitable as a point of support for ethical maxims, but a genuine Person whom a man can love. Men have loved Him through all the Christian centuries. And the strange thing is that despite all the efforts to remove Him from the pages of history, there are those who love Him still."

J. GRESHAM MACHEN

10

Some Modern Views of the Bible (II)

In the preceding chapter we have given some consideration to the position that the Word of God and the words of the Bible are not to be identified. We cannot maintain, it is today affirmed, that the speaking of God was all in the past, and that it is now concluded. To maintain that it was, we are told, would be to hold to a static view of revelation. Hence, in order to avoid embracing a static view of revelation, men make a distinction between the Word of God and the actual words of Scripture. In practice, we have sought to point out, this distinction breaks down. As a matter of actual fact, those who are most insistent to make the distinction appeal themselves to the very words of the Bible for support of the things which they say about God.

If, however, we do justice to the position which is now under consideration, we must go a step further. The words of the Bible, we are told, do not become the Word of God, unless God so wills it. The Bible evinces itself as the Word of God in that it convinces me. As Otto A. Piper has so aptly stated this position: "In other words, the Bible is the Word of God because and when God uses it as a means of grace to make me believe in his saving purpose."[1] The authority of the Bible is not to be found in its very words as they stand written; that is a static (a favorite word of the neo-orthodox) view of revelation; the Bible, rather, is authoritative because through it God speaks His Word to His people. By means of the Bible God addresses His personal message to those who follow Him.

Therefore, on this view, the inspiration of the Bible does not reside in the fact that it is God-breathed Scripture, and that its human writers, as they wrote, were borne of the Holy Spirit. The human words of the Bible may, on the contrary, very

1. Piper, "How I Study my Bible," in *The Christian Century,* Vol. LXIII, No. 10, March 6, 1946, p. 301.

likely even contain error and imperfection. The inspiration of
the Bible is really not to be sought in the Bible at all but,
rather, in the person who responds to its message. According
to the modern view, inspiration is in reality to be equated with
the response which I make to the message of God. It has been
well stated by Alan Richardson:

> In the proper Christian sense of the term, the meaning of the
> inspiration of Scripture for me is that I recognize that God's
> message has been sent into the world with my name and address
> on it. The authority of the Bible means for me that God's
> message claims me, my obedience and faith; I must listen to
> what God says and hasten to direct my life in accordance with
> His will.[2]

On this position inspiration amounts to the recognition of what
is true for me personally. To receive the truth of God, therefore, one must be inspired. Biblical truth, we are told, is
personal truth.

It will be well to grasp the significance of these statements.
The authority of the Bible, upon the position which we are
now considering, resides in the fact that in a specific crisis
the Word of God is borne home to a particular man. It is
the decision of God whereby the witness of the Bible is brought
home to us in power that gives to the Bible its authority. Unless,
through the divine decision and choice of God, I personally am
challenged by the Word of God, the Bible is not the Word of
God for me. Unless there is a personal response to the truth
the Bible does not become the Word of God to me. The Bible
is a message addressed to me personally.

Now it is perfectly obvious that upon this view the authority
of the Bible is not conceived as residing in itself. The historic
Christian position, as we have sought to make clear, is that the
Bible is inherently the Word of God. Inasmuch as it was
breathed from the very mouth of God Himself, it is truly His
Word. The human writers who penned its words were holy men
from God and they spoke as they were under the superintendence
and supervision of the Holy Spirit. We may speak of them
as being subjected to an influence of the Spirit, to His oversight,
direction, and sovereign control. The very words of the Bible,

2. *Op. cit.*, pp. 36, 37.

therefore, are of absolute authority for they are themselves the Word, the message of God.

Very different from the Christian position, however, is the one which we are now engaged in considering. According to this modern view the authority of the Bible does not at all reside in itself; it resides rather in the fact that when the truth of the Bible meets me in a Divine-human encounter, then, in that particular case, the Bible becomes the Word of God for me. It will be a great gain indeed if we can at least make it clear that this modern position is not to be identified with that of historic Christianity. Historic Christianity, inasmuch as it is founded upon the Bible, teaches that the Bible is itself the authoritative Word of God. The Bible is authoritative, therefore, whether there is any Divine-human encounter or not. The Bible is authoritative whether or not its message is borne home to me in compelling power. It is authoritative whether I believe it or not; whether I believe in Jesus Christ or not. The Bible, according to the Christian position, is authoritative in itself; its authority resides in the fact that it is the Word of God.

Have we not, however, been too harsh toward the modern view? Have we ourselves not made too sharp the disjunction between the Word of God and the human words of the Bible? Is it not true even upon the modern view that the Bible can have no authority apart from the human words which bear witness to the Divine Word? Is not then a certain amount of objective authority to be found after all in the Bible, and is not the charge of subjectivism thereby rendered invalid? If these questions should be raised in opposition to what we have said, we should reply that, even though the modern position does speak of the uniqueness of the Bible, and does assert that its human words must bear record to the Divine Word, it nevertheless follows that these human words are not of themselves accepted as authoritative. The authority of the Bible, if the position which we are now considering is correct, simply does not reside antecedently in the Bible itself. Say what one will, he cannot escape the fact that subjectivism is involved. The authority of the Bible, if the modern view be correct, despite the unique origin of the Bible and the fact that its human words witness to the Word of God, resides not at all in the Bible itself. The authority of the Bible resides in the one who receives its message.

A superficial criticism of this position would be that it confuses inspiration with the inward testimony of the Holy Spirit. It is perfectly true that the message of the Bible does not become of profit to a man until the Holy Spirit, who is the Third Person of the Trinity, by an act of sovereign grace opens the eyes of that man's understanding so that he sees the Bible as indeed the Word of God. Those who have been most zealous to defend the doctrine of the plenary and verbal inspiration of the Bible have also been desirous of giving proper emphasis to the work of the Spirit of God. Calvin, it is well to remember, has become known as the theologian of the Holy Spirit. And the designation is perfectly just and appropriate, for Calvin was eager to give a proportionately Scriptural emphasis to the various teachings of the Bible. Calvin, and others like him, who have insisted strongly upon the absolute authority of the Bible, have also been insistent upon a proper recognition of the work of the Spirit of God. The Bible, we would insist, is the Word of God whether a man believes it to be so or not. And it is the Word of God to that particular man whether he believes it to be so or not. If he does believe it, well and good, he shall then enjoy the blessings of its heavenly message. If he does not believe it, it is still the Word of God to him, and it will rise up in the last day to condemn him. Wholly apart from any one particular individual's reaction to the Bible, the Bible is the Word of God. At the same time, it is of course true that, unless he believes the message of the Bible to be true, no man enjoys the spiritual blessings of the Bible's message. The sinner remains in his sins until the Spirit of God applies to his heart the blessings which the Lord Jesus, by His death, has obtained. The sinner in his sins and trespasses is spiritually dead, and needs to be made alive. It is the Spirit who makes him alive. He raises him to newness of life, giving to him a second birth, a birth from above, a resurrection from the dead. The newly awakened soul sees Jesus Christ as his Redeemer and embraces Jesus Christ in living faith. And he furthermore regards the Bible as the Holy Word of God. He does this because the Spirit has borne witness by and with the Word to his own spirit that the Bible is the Word of God. This supernatural work is that which has been designated the internal testimony of the Spirit. It is a witness-bearing to the soul that the Bible is the Word of God. In the newly awakened soul a conviction is formed that the Scriptures are Divine.

We are, of course, far from saying that a well-formulated doctrine of Scripture is thus given to the believer. Such is not the case. A well-formulated doctrine of Scripture can come only upon the basis of careful study of Scripture itself. But it is a fact that the believer, through the testimony of the Spirit, is convinced that the Bible is the Word of God. We are also far from saying that this is all that is to be understood by the work of the Spirit's bearing witness by and with the Word to the believer. It is, however, this particular emphasis with which we are now concerned. Our purpose is not to give a fully developed statement of the doctrine of the internal testimony of the Holy Spirit. What we are now concerned to point out and make clear is that, apart from the fact of the Spirit's applying to the individual soul the blessings which have been obtained for him through the saving work of Christ, no man can properly understand the Bible. And one of these blessings which the Spirit brings is the conviction that the Scriptures are Divine.

Is the modern view simply confusing terms? Is it merely insisting upon the necessity of a belief in the work of the Spirit? Is it doing nothing more than emphasizing the importance of the doctrine of the internal testimony of the Holy Spirit? If such were the case, our disagreement with it would not be serious. We would indeed even then maintain that in employing such a word as "inspiration" to designate the internal testimony of the Spirit, advocates of this particular view were guilty of introducing confusion into the discussion. Such, however, we believe, is not the case. The advocates of the position which we are now considering are not merely guilty of confusing matters by an inappropriate usage of theological terms. We could wish that that were all that were involved. The issue, however, is far more serious than that.

Those who maintain that the human words of the Bible are nothing more than the cradle in which the Word of God is to be found are perfectly willing to employ the methods of negative Biblical criticism. This criticism presupposes that the investigator may subject the words of the Bible to his own unaided mind and may pass a judgment upon them. An illustration of this type of criticism will be in place. The New Testament teaches very clearly that the prophet Isaiah was the author of the entire book which bears his name. This is seen in the fact that the

New Testament quotes from all parts of the prophecy and ascribes them to the man Isaiah. The Christian believes that the New Testament is the infallible Word of God and hence he simply accepts this clear testimony. Not so the critic. He thinks that he can subject the prophecy of Isaiah to tests which he regards as legitimate and, then, upon the basis of his own investigations, declare whether or not the prophecy is the work of Isaiah. He disregards the evidence of the New Testament and proceeds to assert, in effect, that the witness of the New Testament is incorrect and that, as a matter of fact, the prophecy is not in its entirety from the great eighth-century prophet. Thus he sets his own judgments over against the express declarations of the Word of God, the Bible. In doing this, he is, of course, placing his mind above the written revelation of God. He is spurning the clear testimony of God and placing as an authority above it the human mind. Those who make a distinction between the words of Scripture and the "Word" of God regard such criticism as legitimate. They ride roughshod over the statements of the Bible whenever they think that those statements are not in accord with the facts. Thus, apparently, one may hold to the most radical forms of modern criticism and yet maintain that such criticism has reference only to the human words of the Bible, and does not affect the Divine message.

At this point a question may be raised. The human words of the Bible, we are told, are a witness to the Word of God. They are not themselves to be identified with that Word, and, inasmuch as this is the case, "criticism," apparently even in radical forms, is, as we have just stated, regarded as perfectly legitimate. That this is the case is seen by the fact that many, if not all, of those who make this distinction between the Word of God and the words of the Bible, themselves practice such criticism. This criticism, however, often conflicts with the express statements of the Bible. It maintains that these statements cannot always be accepted. In other words, if such criticism is legitimate, it has shown rather clearly that the human words of the Bible do not offer an accurate and trustworthy witness to themselves. They assert, among other things, that Isaiah wrote the entire prophecy that bears his name; "criticism," on the other hand, tells us that this is wrong. They assert that there was an historical resurrection of Jesus Christ on the third day; "criticism," tells us that this is wrong. They assert that there was a Garden of Eden and an historical fall; "criticism" tells us that this is wrong. If, therefore, these human words of the Bible do not even succeed in being a trustworthy witness to themselves, how can we be sure that they are a trustworthy witness to the "Word" of God which is supposed to come somehow through them? All that we know of this nebulous "Word" of God, we know from the human *words* of the Bible. Let us make no mistake upon that point. Say what they will, the adherents of neo-orthodoxy, whatever be the particular brand espoused, have received all the knowledge that they possess about God, the Trinity, the Person of Christ, the Holy Spirit, the Resurrection, the Word of God, from the *words* of the Bible. May it not be, however, inasmuch as these *words* are not even trustworthy witnesses to themselves, that they are also not trustworthy as a witness or pointer to the "Word" of God? The question, we think, is worthy of the most serious consideration.

Our criticism of the thesis that the human words of the Bible are not to be identified with the Word of God, but rather are mere witnesses to that "Word" has up to this point been of a more or less surface character. Valid and legitimate as are the criticisms which have so far been advanced, they do not, nevertheless, go to the heart of the matter.

We may indeed point out inconsistencies and incongruities in the view which is now under discussion (and these inconsistencies are of so great and serious a nature that they make clear that this view is false), but we do not actually get to the heart of things until we first realize that much of modern theological thought is, whether consciously or not, based upon the philosophical thought of Kant.

To discover this fact one need not be a specialist in philosophy. That such is the case will become apparent even to the one who reads but little in modern philosophy. Kant made a distinction between what he called the phenomenal and the noumenal, and it is this distinction which has exerted tremendous influence upon modern thought.

The phenomenal is that realm which we know through our senses, and *phenomena* themselves, according to Kant, are objects which we may possibly experience. That which does not belong to the phenomenal realm cannot be an object of our experience. Objects are alone presented to us within the limits of that which we may know through the senses. Unless what we conceive with the mind corresponds to some object which we know in this phenomenal realm, we simply cannot demonstrate the reality of what we are conceiving.

Kant has stated the matter forcefully as follows:

It follows incontestably, that the pure conceptions of the understanding are incapable of the *transcendental,* and must always be of *empirical* use alone, and that the principles of the pure understanding relate only to the general conditions of a possible experience, to objects of the senses, and never to things in general, apart from the mode in which we intuit them.[3]

What, however, about those things which are not the objects of our senses? These Kant calls unintelligible existences or noumena. Their possibility, he says, is beyond the sphere of the phenomenal and indeed is quite incomprehensible. For us the noumenal is a void. We do not possess either an intuition or even the conception of a possible intuition by means of which objects beyond the phenomenal realm can be given to us. At best, he maintains, the concept of the noumenal has a negative use in that it restrains our sensuous intuition within the bounds of phenomena. That which belongs to the noumenal, inasmuch as it has no definite object which corresponds to it, cannot possess objective validity. It is not a particular *intelligible* object for our understanding; it is an unknown something. Can our understanding and reason then be applied to that which belongs to the noumenal world? This question Kant answers with a strong negative.

It is as though we lived on an island in the midst of the sea. Upon this island we are kings. We may study and investigate and think about the island to our heart's content. As we study our island, however, we learn to know things which are really only the appearance, not the things in themselves.

Surrounding the island is the limitless sea; yet we cannot approach this sea, for over it hangs a dense fog, and whenever we seek to enter it a blackness that is darker than night descends upon us, and keeps us upon the island where we belong. And yet, somehow, in this nebulous realm things exist as they are in themselves. About this realm, however, we can know nothing.

It is not our purpose to endeavor to make a more detailed

3. *The Critique of Pure Reason,* translated by J. M. D. Meikeljohn (Everyman's Library), p. 184.

analysis of Kant's distinction. What has been stated is sufficient to make clear how radically removed this position is from historic Christianity. According to the Bible all things, whether they are visible or not, were brought into existence by a creative act of God. Christianity teaches that, inasmuch as it was created by God, we may truly know the phenomenal realm. "The heavens declare the glory of God, and the firmament maketh known His handiwork" (Psalm 19:1, *translation by the author*). This world which we know through our senses is God's world.

What, however, about that which we do not know through the senses? Is the noumenal actually enshrouded with blackness? This question Christianity answers with a negative. We may indeed know God, for He has revealed Himself unto us. We may know about life beyond the grave, the resurrection of Christ, heaven, and many other things, for God has told us about them. God, according to Christianity, controls the phenomenal realm, and He also controls the noumenal. He permits man to know just as much as He desires man to know about these realms, for they are His and He is their Creator.

Very different, however, is Kant's understanding of the phenomenal and the noumenal. He does not regard God as the true Creator of all, for in effect he makes man the master of all. Man cannot know about the noumenal, he says. What then shall we say, for example, concerning the miracles of Jesus Christ? Obviously the miracles, on Kant's position, belong not to the phenomenal, for there is no definite object which corresponds to them, but rather to the noumenal. They are, therefore, beyond us; they do not possess objective validity; they are an unknown something. We might go on and thus discuss every doctrine of the Christian faith; if Kant is correct, they are all removed from the sphere of history; they cannot possess objective validity.

It is this Kantian distinction between the phenomenal and noumenal realm which undergirds much of modern theological thought. Consequently, insofar as modern thought is in harmony with its Kantian foundation, it is diametrically opposed to supernatural Christianity. This is true, despite the constant usage of orthodox terminology. It does scant justice to the facts to assert that those who make the divorce between the human words of the Bible and the "Word" of God are not sound in their doctrine of Scripture but otherwise are proclaiming

the historic Christian faith. Superficial indeed is such a judgment; superficial, and far removed from the truth. For, insofar
as modern theologians embrace the Kantian distinction which we
are now considering, they are not merely unsound at this or that
point, but they are unsound right down the line and are guilty
of maintaining a point of view which is hostile to revealed
Christianity. A few examples will make clear this particular
point. Modern theologians speak much about the resurrection
of the Lord. Is not this commendable? Does not the believer
also assert the importance of the resurrection? If, then, modern
theologians have much to say about the resurrection, is not this
a good sign? When we read, for example, that the resurrection
shattered history, should not we be thrilled at such a "return to
orthodoxy?" For our part, however, we are not thrilled at
all by this language. It is perfectly true that at the present
time there is much being said and written about the resurrection.
What, however, is meant by the term? If modern writers mean
that on the third day the body of the Lord Jesus miraculously
rose from the dead, we shall indeed rejoice. Is this, then, what
they have in mind? We fear not. To believe in a historical
resurrection, as it is taught in Scripture, involves belief in the
intrusion of the supernatural into human history. It involves
belief that the Sovereign God did indeed intervene and by
means of a miracle did bring again to life the Lord Jesus.
Such, however, is not at all what modern theologians wish us
to believe. The resurrection for which they are contending is,
we fear, part of that "Word" of God which they would distinguish
from the words of the Bible. Did the resurrection shatter
history? To this question we reply, it did no such thing. The
resurrection of the Lord took place in history; it was itself an
historical event of the utmost importance. There was a tomb
outside the wall of Jerusalem situated at a particular spot.
Furthermore, at a definite moment in history the Lord Jesus,
having risen from the dead, emerged from that tomb. If the
resurrection in any sense belongs to the noumenal realm of
Kant, or to any realm other than that of human history, there
simply was no resurrection.

In the fifty-third chapter of Isaiah, to take another example,
we meet the Messiah under the designation "Servant of the
Lord." Who is this Servant of the Lord? To this question
the Bible-believing Christian has a ready answer. He says

that the Servant is none other than Jesus Christ, and that Isaiah prophesied in this chapter of Christ. In support of this interpretation he makes appeal to the New Testament. If he accepts at face value the words of the New Testament he learns that the Servant is Jesus Christ. It is an example of predictive prophecy, and upon the basis of the testimony of the words of Scripture, the Christian who would be true to the Bible believes that the Lord Jesus fulfilled this particular prophecy of Isaiah.

It goes without saying that this view is not acceptable to modern thought. Consequently, it is said by some that in the realm of faith we may indeed believe that Jesus Christ is the Servant of the Lord. In the realm of scientific study, however, we must subject this prophecy to close scrutiny and study it as scholars. If we do that we, of course, arrive at a conclusion quite different. In the realm of scholarly study we may come to the conclusion (although in this realm this conclusion was not always reached) that the Servant is a prophetic remodelling of an old myth. What then is this realm of faith in which we may believe that Jesus is the Servant? It is, we believe, the "Word" (in the modern sense) of God, and we think that it is not essentially different from that which Kant designated the noumenal. To say that in the realm of faith Jesus is the Servant, but that in the empirical realm of everyday life He is not the Servant, is simply to say that He is not the Servant at all.

The disjunction which we are now considering has been stated with unusual clarity by President John Mackay of Princeton Theological Seminary. He says:

> Moreover, being a book about redemption, the Bible is authoritative only in its own particular sphere. As a document with a history, it is to be studied and investigated with the most rigorous historical and scientific criteria.[4]

We may be grateful to Dr. Mackay for thus stating the case so pointedly. Has Dr. Mackay, however, really said anything that is essentially different from the position of Kant? When we speak of the Bible as a document with a history, are we not in effect positing Kant's phenomenal realm? And is there an essential difference between Dr. Mackay's sphere of redemption and Kant's noumenal? One thing is surely true. If this

4. John A. Mackay, "Protestantism" in *Presbyterian Life,* Vol. 8, No. 25, December 24, 1955, p. 18.

divorce between the "sphere" of redemption and the Bible as a document with a history is legitimate, historic Christianity is done for; we are yet in our sins. Do the atonement and the resurrection belong to the "sphere" of redemption? Are they to be removed from the realm of history where we as Christians, seeking to think God's revealed thoughts after Him, may study what the Scriptures say concerning them? If they are to be removed from the historical realm and placed in some "sphere" of redemption we can only look forward, of all men the most miserable, to utter despair, as the eternal darkness settles down upon us. Thank God, however, that this distinction is not a valid one. Thank God that here upon this earth on a certain day of our calendar and at a particular place in Palestine the Lord Jesus bore our guilt upon the Cross and on the third day by a mighty miracle rose from the dead. Thank God for giving us His Word, which is authoritative in every sphere of which it speaks, and which has told us of the wondrous thing that God did in the giving of His only begotten Son.

One of the clearest and most cogent presentations of the modern viewpoint with respect to this particular problem of the disjunction between the sphere of what Dr. Mackay calls redemption and the realm of history has been given by one of the greatest of American archaeologists, Dr. William F. Albright. Says Dr. Albright:

> In other words, the historian cannot control the details of Jesus' birth and resurrection and thus has no right to pass judgment on their historicity. On the other hand the historian is qualified to estimate the historical significance of the pattern and its vital importance for the nascent Christian movement as embodied in the person of its Master. Since, accordingly, there can be no complete factual judgment and since the historian cannot settle questions which are outside of his jurisdiction, the decision must be left to the Church and to the individual believer, who are historically warranted in accepting the whole of the messianic framework of the Gospels or in regarding it as partly true literally and as partly true spiritually — which is far more important in the region of the spirit with which the Christian faith must primarily deal. The historian, *qua* historian, must stop at the threshold, unable to enter the shrine of the Christian mysteria without removing

his shoes, conscious that there are realms where history and nature are inadequate, and where God reigns over them in eternal majesty.[5]

Does the virgin birth, however, lie beyond the jurisdiction of the historian? Does it belong in a realm or region where history is inadequate? In answer to these questions the historic Christian Church in her great creeds has answered with a mighty negative. In following the Bible the Church has maintained that Jesus Christ was born of the virgin Mary for the reason that God has said He was so born. Each Lord's Day, in the worship service of the Church countless Christians repeat the words of the Apostles' Creed, "I believe . . . in Jesus Christ His only Son, our Lord; who was conceived by the Holy Ghost, born of the Virgin Mary . . . ." What is the basis upon which Christians believe such a thing concerning the Lord? It is simply that God has revealed to them the fact that Christ was indeed, as a matter of historical fact, born of the virgin Mary. The virgin birth, in other words, is an historical fact. It took place here upon this earth at a definite point in time and in history. And if there is any book in the Bible which lays its emphasis upon historical details, it is the beautiful third Gospel in which one account of the virgin birth is given. One is almost tempted to think that this particular Gospel was written with modern critical theory in view.

If the virgin birth belongs to some region where history and nature are inadequate, we must then acknowledge that there never was a virgin birth. If the virgin birth is not historical, there was no virgin birth. We, however, as Christian historians, accept the testimony of the first and third Gospels, believing that they are part of the infallible Word of God. When they speak upon matters of redemption, they are trustworthy and we believe them; when they speak upon matters of historical detail, they are likewise trustworthy, and we also believe them. The Bible knows nothing about any region or realm which, in distinction from the historical, is to be labeled faith, or redemption, or supra-temporal, or supra-historical, or *Urgeschichte,* or a realm where history and nature are inadequate. To put the matter baldly, it would seem that these are but new names for the old area of myth and legend. If the virgin birth belongs to this

5. William F. Albright, *From the Stone Age to Christianity,* 1940, pp. 307-308.

realm where history and nature are inadequate, there was no virgin birth. If the resurrection also belongs to this region, there was no resurrection, and the body of our blessed Lord still lies in some unknown tomb in Palestine.

We are told that critical study of the Bible can shed much light upon the human words of the Bible, but that it does not affect the sphere of redemption. That sphere, it is asserted, is beyond the reach of the critical historian. Criticism cannot affect the "abiding" message of the Bible; it cannot touch the sphere of redemption. Here, it would surely seem, is the old philosophy of Kant making its appearance under the guise of a form of modern theology. In opposition to this it cannot be emphasized with sufficient force that Christianity is an historical religion. It is based squarely upon certain things that God did in history. The eternal Son of God became man, being conceived in the womb of a particular virgin who lived in the first century of our era in the land of Palestine. Of her He was born, and He lived and taught and wrought mighty miracles. Then, having been betrayed and arrested, He was unjustly condemned to die upon the cross. In so dying, He offered a sacrifice to satisfy the justice of God and to reconcile God to us. On the third day, a definite day upon the calendar, He came to life from the dead, and came forth from the tomb. These wondrous acts which have procured our redemption were not wrought in some nebulous realm or region about which we know nothing. They took place here upon this earth at definite times and places. Remove the historical basis from Christianity and there is no Christianity. Place the great truths of Christianity in some region of "redemption," and divorce this region from the historical, and we are yet in our sins. Can there be a religion that is filled with greater despair than is this modern religion which makes a separation, yea, a divorce between the sphere of redemption and the sphere of the historical? If this new religion is true, we are yet under the curse of the law, and we can look forward only to everlasting punishment in hell. But life has been filled with hope because of the wondrous sacrifice that Christ wrought when He was crucified on a green hill, far away, outside the city wall.

If the view which is now under consideration is correct, what, we may well ask, is actually the function of the Bible? The answer to this question is ready at hand. The Bible, we are told, is the record of revelation, the witness to the Word of God. It is of course true, we would reply, that the Bible is a record of revelation. It tells us of the revelation which God made in times past to His people. The Bible is indeed a record of revelation. More than that, it is an accurate record of revelation. Inasmuch as it is God-breathed, it is an infallible record of revelation. When we read the Bible, we are not deceived. We know exactly what God spoke in former times, for the Bible is a perfectly trustworthy record of revelation.

To say that the Bible is a record of revelation and to stop at that point, however, is not to do full justice to the Bible. The Bible is indeed a record of revelation, but, inasmuch as it is the God-breathed Word, it is more than that. The Bible is also itself revelation. The words of the Bible find their origin in God. He is their Author, and for this reason, these very words are revelatory of Him. They are themselves revelation. We cannot, therefore, as Christians, be content with the modern position which merely asserts that the Bible is a witness to revelation. Our difference, however, with this position is not merely that it declares that the Bible is the witness or pointer to revelations which God has given in times past. That is not, in fact, the heart of the view which is espoused today. If that were the main emphasis, the difference between the Christian view of the Bible and this modern one would not be so great. It is being asserted, however, that the Bible is the witness to revelation, and the revelation to which it points or witnesses is the nebulous realm of "redemption" or the "Word" of which we have already spoken. The "Word" of God, it is stated, is cradled in the words of the Bible. These latter point to the former. How different this is from the Christian position! How different from the teaching of the Bible itself! It cannot be sufficiently emphasized that the Bible is itself the Word of God; it is itself revelatory. The Scriptures, we are compelled to assert, are themselves the very revelation of the God of Truth. They are not mere pointers to the truth, they are themselves the truth.

THE BIBLE AS HOLY HISTORY

In line with the idea that the truth of the Bible is personal truth there has been considerable emphasis in recent times upon a view of Biblical history which is variously designated as holy or sacred history. History, we are told, consists of events that are remembered. Some events are not of sufficient importance to be remembered; they do not have sufficient meaning therefore. Hence, in Biblical history we have to do both with events which occurred and also in addition to that with the meaning which these events had for a number of human beings.

The events of Biblical history are, therefore, events which are laden with meaning, and their meaning is found in the meeting of man with God. Holy history, therefore, is that part of history in which the Holy Spirit takes a direct part. The historical events are recorded for the reason that in them a special working of God takes place and these recorded events are part of a plan of God. There is, then, a plan to holy history; it is the history of God's dealings with mankind.

What may be said about this method of conceiving history? In the first place, it should be noted that those who speak of sacred or holy history are also perfectly willing to embrace the methods and results of a criticism which is hostile to the Bible's witness to itself. It is when one realizes this fact that he begins to ask what, in fact, is intended by the terms "holy" or "sacred" history. There is of course no question but that the events of the Bible are unique events. We may very legitimately speak of the uniqueness of those things which God wrought in history for the salvation of sinners. We are saved from our sins, not by the exploits of Alexander the Great, but by the death of Jesus Christ upon the cross. For the believer, the latter event is rich with meaning that is lacking in the former. The Christian is naturally more interested in those events in history by means of which his redemption was obtained.

When all this is granted, however, we must insist that the events of Biblical history took place in history. They were, in other words, historical events. As such, they are related to all other events of history. Since the sovereign God in His providence upholds all things, we may be assured that all events of history are related. The matter has been accurately stated — accurately, because it is in agreement with the teaching of the Bible — by the Westminster Confession of Faith:

> God the great Creator of all things doth uphold, direct, dispose, and govern all creatures, actions, and things, from the

greatest even to the least, by His most wise and holy providence, according to His infallible fore-knowledge, and the free and immutable counsel of His own will, to the praise of the glory of His wisdom, power, justice, goodness and mercy.[6]

All things that occur, according to the Confession's statement, are ordained of God. They occur because He has decreed that they should occur. All are parts of His over-all plan. All are parts of His one all-embracing eternal purpose and decree. Inasmuch as this is the case, all events of history in the very nature of the case, are related. With the words of Pascal, we may well agree, "If the nose of Cleopatra had been shorter, the whole face of the earth would have been changed."[7]

The events of Biblical history are parts of this eternal purpose of God. As such they occur in the realm of history. They cannot be removed or separated from their historical context and background. Our salvation was wrought by the Lord of Glory when He died upon the cross and rose again from the dead. It must be remembered, however, that He was nailed to the cross by Roman soldiers at a particular place outside the city of Jerusalem, on a certain day of the calendar year and at a particular time of that day. The country in which He died was at that time subject to the Roman Empire, and the one who allowed Him to be crucified was a minor Roman official by the name of Pontius Pilate.

The encounters of God with men did not take place upon a cloud or in a vacuum. They took place upon this very earth, in time and in history. To modern men this fact may seem unimportant, to the Bible it is supremely important. Certainly one of the great "encounters" of man and God was that between the Lord and John the Baptist. We might easily be tempted to say that the matter of concern here is simply the fact that the holy God met with the Baptist. Such, however, is not the manner in which the Bible presents the encounter. Hear what the evangelist says: "Now in the fifteenth year of the reign of Tiberius Caesar, Pontius Pilate being Governor of Judaea, and Herod being tetrarch of Galilee, and his brother Philip tetrarch of Ituraea and of the region of Trachonitis, and Lysanias the

6. The Westminster Confession, V: I.
7. Pensées, 8:29.

tetrarch of Abilene, Annas and Caiaphas being the high priests, the word of God came unto John the son of Zacharias in the wilderness" (Luke 3:1,2).

Why this stress upon historical detail? What difference does it make who was upon the throne of Rome at the time? How can these historical details be of any possible benefit to our spiritual life? Questions such as these, however, are based upon a misunderstanding of the nature of Christianity. It makes all the difference in the world who was upon the throne of Rome. It makes all the difference in the world where the "encounter" between God and John the Baptist took place. Luke is most concerned to give us the necessary details which form the proper background of the revelation of God to John, for this revelation took place in history. At a definite point of time and at a certain place upon the face of this earth, God met with John the Baptist. Remove this historical background from Christianity, and you remove Christianity itself, for Christianity is a religion which is founded squarely upon that which was done once for all in history.

We may well be thankful to God that Luke, the inspired penman, stated so carefully and painstakingly the historical background in which the wondrous revelation of God took place. How assuring are these details! Luke has not left us with the impression that this "encounter" was something vague and nebulous. On the contrary, he wished to assure his readers that it took place under certain very definite conditions, and it is the mention of these conditions which assures us that we are reading the account of something historical and not simply a "cunningly devised fable." Luke may not have been a very good writer of "holy" history, inasmuch as he was too concerned about historical details. As a writer of true history, however, he was superb. His very words make upon one the impression that the things which he relates actually occurred here upon this earth. We turn from the Gospel of Luke with the very definite conviction that, having read his words, we have also known the certainty of those things which it seemed good to him to write.

Christianity, therefore, is rooted and grounded in history. At the same time it is true, as we noted above, that there is indeed a uniqueness about Biblical history. This uniqueness has been expressed in the words of the Westminster Confession as follows:

> As the providence of God doth, in general reach to all creatures, so, after a most special manner, it taketh care of His Church, and disposeth all things to the good thereof.[8]

Jesus Christ is, without controversy, the center of history. There is a *Before Christ* and an *In the year of our Lord.* The distinction is perfectly legitimate. There is a certain sense in which all things may be said to subserve the purpose of God in salvation. And surely, despite what evil men and nations may do, all things are for the good of the redeemed. In the words of comfort which are dear to the Christian heart God has given us a true philosophy of history, "And we know that all things work together for good to them that love God, to them who are the called according to *his* purpose" (Romans 8:28). To say this, however, is, we believe, to say something quite different from that which is intended by the modern proponents of "holy" history.

When we read the writings of these men we receive the distinct impression that the great "encounters" between man and God were not necessarily historical events. When we hear it said that the Flood was a great act of God's judgment, we are tempted to ask the question, "Could a person have drowned in that flood?" The answer, we fear, must all too often be negative. Not only could one not have drowned in the flood, one could not even have wet his feet. And the reason for this is simply that this flood belongs to the sphere of "holy" history, or redemption, or call it what one will. To put it in simple terms, there never was upon this earth a flood such as that of which the Bible records. The flood, in other words, was not historical. To say that this great "encounter" took place in some other realm is simply to remove it from the pages of history. Either there was a flood upon this earth, as the Bible records, or else there was no flood.

What shall we say about the fall of man? Surely the events of the early chapters of Genesis were "encounters" between man and God. Are these events then historical? Was there a Garden of Eden, an Adam and an Eve? Was the fall, in other words,

8. The Westminster Confession of Faith, V:VII.

something that occurred upon this earth? In answer to questions such as these we are sometimes told that the events of the early chapters of Genesis took place in prehistory. They are events in the spiritual world, and are to be regarded as myths. By this word myth we are not to understand a legend or fable, but simply

> . . . a story by which the events in the spiritual world are described in terms of earthly occurrences, or earthly events are shown in relation to their spiritual roots.[9]

If we understand this definition aright, it means that the events of the first three chapters of Genesis did not take place upon this earth. They took place in some other realm, the "spiritual world," and they are told in story form in terms of earthly occurrences. They are told as though they did occur upon this earth, yet, as a matter of fact, they did not take place upon this earth, but rather, in the "spiritual" world. Here again, it appears, is the hand of Kant. Here again is the distinction between this historical world which we know and some region beyond, the nebulous realm into which we are to place the great verities of Christianity.

At present, however, we wish to do something else than point out the underlying philosophical basis upon which the above interpretation of the early chapters of Genesis seems to rest. At present we wish simply to ask the question, Who is to tell where the limits of myth begin and where they end? What is the standard or measure by means of which we may identify in the Bible that which is myth and that which is history? If the distinction between this earth and the "spiritual world" is correct, this question, we should think, is rather important. It would surely be a grave fault to relegate to the realm of the "spiritual world" or the realm of "redemption" that which actually belongs to this present world of history. We should probably not have much company, for example, if we insisted that the account of Sennacherib's invasion of Palestine belonged to the realm of the "spiritual world," and the reason, we fear, why we would not have much company in maintaining this position is simply that Sennacherib himself has left an account of his exploits. But is that a sufficient reason? Apparently, when there is some outside check, we are in the realm of history.

9. Otto A. Piper, *God in History*, Macmillan, New York, 1939, p. 61.

Such a check, however, is not always present. Who then is to say where the realm of the "spiritual world" begins and where it ends? If the events of prehistory, the events of the early chapters of Genesis, let us say, belong to the "spiritual world," where does the resurrection of Jesus Christ belong? May it not be, after all, that here also we are dealing with a myth? May it not be that the resurrection did not actually take place here upon this earth in history but rather is simply an event of the "spiritual world?" If such is the case, it follows, of course, that there is no resurrection. The Apostle spoke truly when he said. "And if Christ be not risen, then *is* our preaching vain, and your faith *is* also vain" (1 Corinthians 15:14). If the resurrection belongs to the realm of the "spiritual world" or, for that matter, to any other than the historical realm, it simply follows that Jesus Christ did not rise from the dead. It would have been possible on that third day to visit the tomb and to make the sad discovery that it was not empty. The dead body of the Lord still remained there. If, therefore, the resurrection is anything other than an historical one, there is no resurrection. If there is no historical resurrection, there is no Christianity, and we are yet under the terrible curse of the law of God.

Who then is to judge where myth begins and where it ends? What portions of the Bible are myth and what are history? To this question no clear-cut answer is given. We cannot escape the conviction that the proponents of the modern forms of "holy history" are actually guilty of using the term "holy" or "sacred" history as a synonym for the realm of "redemption," the noumenal realm of Kant. To state the matter in a slightly different way, it is difficult to avoid the conclusion that the great "encounters" between man and God, "encounters" in which a Divine activity is seen, are after all not encounters in history but rather in some other sphere. The great saving events of Biblical history, we fear, are thus actually removed from the sphere of history. If this is the case, these great events of Biblical history are not historical, and if they are not historical, they simply did not take place.

There is another point that must be stressed. We are told that these great events and encounters are those in which a Divine activity was seen. Such, we suppose we may safely say, was the exodus from Egypt. Now the question that keeps arising is this. Was this deliverance from Egypt merely an event in which the historians of Israel saw a mighty Divine activity, or was there, as a matter of actual historical fact, a special Divine activity in the exodus? Did God, in other words, actually lead the people forth from the land of Egypt, as the Bible states, or rather, did the Israelitish historians simply think that in this event they saw the Divine hand at work? The proponents of "holy" history are not always as clear about this matter as they might be. At any rate, we must insist upon one thing. The great saving events of the Bible were not recorded in the Bible merely because the writers happened to infer therefrom the presence of a Divine activity in them. If that had actually been the case, how could we ever have known whether or not there actually had been such a Divine activity in them? How could we have known whether these writers of the Bible might not have omitted some very important events; how do we know that those which they chose to record were actually such as manifested a Divine activity? Might not these writers of the Bible have been greatly mistaken?

Thank God, however, that the Bible does not merely record events in which, according to the mere inferences of the Biblical writers, there was a Divine activity. Such is not the Christian position. The Christian position is not that the writers of the Bible merely recorded those mighty events in which they thought there was manifest a Divine activity. The Christian position, rather, is that, as a matter of historical fact, God, the Triune God, was actually working in the mighty events of redemption, and that He, in His sovereign and inscrutable wisdom, revealed to the writers of the Scripture just those events which they were to record, those and no more. Modern "holy history" may assert that the writers of the Bible inferred in these events a Divine activity at work and so recorded them in the Scriptures. Christianity, on the other hand, teaches that God Himself did work in history in a saving way, and that He told the inspired penmen of Scripture what they were to record. The attitude which some modern proponents of "holy" history take toward the recording of these great saving events and the attitude of historical Christianity are mutually exclusive.

The writers of the Bible, we are sometimes told, were not concerned about the truth of the stories which they recorded. Their first question was not, "Is it true?" but rather, "What does it mean?", "What is its point?" Hence, we of the twentieth century with our literal-minded attitude are said to be more likely to insist upon a literal interpretation of the Bible than were its authors. This charge fits in well with the whole congeries of modern attitudes which we have been considering. It is a very interesting claim, and, surely, if it were true, we should do well to examine again our own attitude toward Scripture. There is, however, one rather important point that must be mentioned in connection with this claim that the Hebrews were not interested in whether or not a story was true but were merely interested in what it meant. It is that this claim is not in accord with the facts.

Let us examine again the much-disputed early chapters of Genesis. Did the human author of those chapters believe that he was recounting something that was true? If he were simply relating something the truthfulness of which did not at all concern him, we may well ask why he took such pains to make it appear to his readers that he was recounting historical fact. Why, for example, did he bother to tell his readers the names of the rivers which flowed from the Garden of Eden? Might not some unsophisticated reader, who did not have the advantage of the idea that the writer was not interested in the truth of what he was recording, simply come to the conclusion that the writer, by mentioning the rivers of the garden, was trying to locate the garden? Why, too, did he speak of the gold of the land of Havilah as being good, and why did he note the fact that there, in the land of Havilah, there was also bdellium and the onyx stone? What was the point of mentioning such things unless it were that the writer wished his readers to know where the garden actually was situated? It would seem that the writer of Genesis was indeed interested in the truthfulness of that which he recounted. This fact is further illustrated in the manner in which he relates the tragic consequences that resulted from the disobedience recorded in the third chapter.

When we turn to the New Testament we find that the Apostle Paul was quite interested in the truthfulness of this particular narrative of the fall. Paul contrasts the work of Adam with that of Christ. He furthermore does this in such a way as to make it clear that he believed in the accuracy of what was recorded about Adam. The very work of Christ, according to Paul, depends upon the truthfulness of what is stated concerning Adam. If what is stated concerning Adam is not true, we have every reason also for denying the truthfulness of what is said concerning Christ. Paul, it would seem, was very much concerned about the truthfulness of the Genesis account of the fall. A careful study of the Bible will make it clear that this modern assertion that the Hebrews were not interested in the truthfulness of a story has no foundation whatever in fact.

One may perhaps be pardoned for asking in passing the question why a nation or people would be interested in the meaning of something which they did not believe to be true. One can understand that a person would be interested in the meaning of what he believed to be true, but it is difficult to discover why anyone would have any particular concern over something which he believed was not true. And it is simply too much to be asked to believe that the writers of the Bible were not interested in the truth of what they were recording, but merely in its meaning. Such a view must be dismissed as frivolous. The writers of Scripture were not writing for entertainment; they were recording what they believed to be the Word of God. If they had had no concern for the truthfulness of what they were writing, they would not have written the Bible.

With the various modern views of the Bible the true Christian can have nothing to do. Underlying these modern views there is apparent the influence of Kant. The Bible, as an historical document, is simply a witness, we are told, to the "Word" of God. This "Word" of God, however, is something very foreign to us. It is not that Word of truth which the Triune God has Himself revealed to man in words; it is something beyond that. Very different is the position of historic Christianity. According to historic Christianty, and so, according to the Bible, the Triune God did actually speak to human beings. He conveyed to them the truth in a form in which they could receive it. He spoke to them in words and they, His creatures, created in His image, could receive and understand those words. Christianity is thus diametrically opposed to modern thought. Christianity is a revelation of the one living and true God. The Bible is not merely a witness to some nebulous "Word" of God; the Bible itself is the Word of God. It is not only a pointer to revelation; it is revelation. Pray God that the men of our day may once more realize this fact.   Then will sinners heed the thunderings of Sinai and look unto Him who is their Redeemer.   Then will they truly pray, "Thy word *is* a lamp unto my feet, and a light unto my path" (Psalm 119:105).

The Bible and Salvation

"And that from a child thou hast known the holy scriptures, which are able to make thee wise unto salvation through faith which is in Christ Jesus."

2 TIMOTHY 3:15

11

The Bible and Salvation

In the words which have come to be known as His high-priestly prayer, our Lord said, "Sanctify them through thy truth: thy word is truth" (John 17:17). It was an utterance filled with loving concern for the disciples from whom He would soon be taken. They were to remain in a world of evil, and that they might serve effectively as His witnesses, they must be sanctified. It is to God the Holy Father that Christ prays and, in view of the fact that the disciples are to be kept through the Name of the Father, He prays that they may partake of holiness. This work of holiness or sanctification is to be accomplished in the truth or through the truth.

There then follows the remarkable statement, "Thy word is truth." At first blush it might seem that Christ is speaking of Himself, for He is indeed the Word of God and He is the Truth. Upon second glance, however, it is apparent that this is not what Christ had in mind, for He identifies the Word of God as something distinct from Himself. He had already stated (verse 6) that He had manifested the Name of God to the disciples, and they had kept God's Word. It was this revelation concerning the Name of God which Christ called the Word of God. Again, in verse 14, the Lord says that He has given to the disciples God's Word. He declares that He gave the words which God had given unto Him (verse 8). It would then seem evident that our Lord, in speaking of the Word of God, had in mind something other than Himself. There is, however, a further consideration which makes it clear that Christ in the present verse of the prayer was not identifying Himself as the Word of God. It must never be forgotten that Christ lived His earthly life in the very atmosphere of the Old Testament Scriptures, and even in the present statement concerning the Word of God He seems to be reflecting upon the Old Testament. In Psalm 119:142, we read, ". . . and thy law *is* the

267

truth." And again in the same Psalm (verse 160) it is stated, "Thy word *is* true *from* the beginning." Furthermore, in 2 Samuel 7:28 we find the words, "And now, O Lord GOD, thou *art* that God, and thy words be true, and thou hast promised this goodness unto thy servant." It would appear, then, that in His prayer, our Lord was giving expression to the thought of the Old Testament, and most likely was actually basing the form of His expression upon the longest of the Psalms. This makes it clear that in His prayer He was not alluding to Himself when He mentioned the Word of God.

Our Lord does not say, "Thy word is the truth." He remarks rather, "Thy word is truth." Earlier in the Gospel of John He had indeed identified Himself as the truth (14:6). "I am . . . the truth," were His words. In the present passage, however, when He is not speaking of Himself, but of the Word of God, He characterizes that Word as true. Christ is Himself the Truth, and when He speaks of Himself, there is need for Him to employ the definite article. In the prayer, however, He merely intends to characterize the Word of God as truth. "The Word of God," we may paraphrase, "is true; it speaks the truth; the message which it offers is a true message. It is the truth." It is most necessary that Christ make this clear, for He will not always be with His disciples. The time will come, when He will be taken from them and they will be constrained to depend upon His Word. That Word, however, is dependable; it is truth. The Word of which He speaks is the message of God; it is information which God has communicated to the world; it is that which God has spoken. The Word of God, which Jesus Christ Himself has spoken, is truth.

Christ does not say that this Word is a witness to the truth. He does not affirm that it is a pointer thereto or a record of revelation. Rather, it is this Word itself, the message which has come from God and which Christ has given to the disciples, that is truth, and this truth is given to men for a practical purpose. That which is the Word of God, therefore, is truth, and by means thereof men may be sanctified.

When our Lord uttered this unusual prayer He seems to have used the phrase "thy word" in a broad sense. We incline to the belief that He simply wished to express the thought that the message of God was truth. Whatever God had spoken was truth, and, inasmuch as God had spoken it, could be nothing else. It is, to be sure, a startling thought. God, who is infinite in wisdom and knowledge, has nevertheless revealed His truth to man in human words, words which man's finite mind cannot fully comprehend, but which man can understand. What then is the Word of God? For us today the Word of God is that which He has spoken. It is, we believe, the Bible in its entirety, and this Word is truth. Because it was all breathed out of God, the Bible is truth. God is the Author of every word thereof and, hence, we may rightly speak of it as truth.

However, must we as orthodox Christians insist upon the full truthfulness of the Bible? Is it incumbent upon us to maintain the infallibility of Scripture? Cannot we meet the challenges of modern thought with a Scripture that is partially human and partially fallible? Some true believers in Jesus Christ, embarrassed by the presence of serious difficulties in the Bible, seem ready to toy with the idea of thought-inspiration, as though it were somehow possible for thoughts, apart from the words in which those thoughts are expressed, to be inspired. The volume of literature which represents modern views of the Bible is making its weight felt, and before this oppressing load some evangelicals are ready to retreat. Shall we not, they ask in effect, give up the old-fashioned doctrine of Scripture? Let us no longer speak of "verbal" inspiration; let us rather use the word "plenary." Or, let us simply speak of a "dynamic" inspiration. To admit the presence of a few minor errors here and there, it is said, will not impair our evangelical witness.

With those who speak thus we do indeed have sympathy, for we, too, are often troubled by the difficulties in the Bible, and we also feel the strength of some of the arguments which are advanced against God's Word. Despite this fact, we cannot agree with those who wish to dispense with the idea of Biblical infallibility. The whole purpose of the present book has been to stress the fact that if we do dispense with the doctrine of Biblical infallibility, then, slowly but surely, we shall lose all the other doctrines of Christianity. If God has erred in even one utterance, how do we know that He has not erred in more than one? If in so-called minor points, He has inspired error, can we be sure that He has not done so in "more important" matters? That is the issue which is at stake. We as orthodox Christians are not called upon to explain every difficulty in the Bible. We are the rather called upon to study that Bible constantly, to expound it and, when necessary, to rise to its defense.

In the face of the tremendous force of modern thought, the worst thing that the believer in Christ can do is to throw overboard the Bible. With this Bible, rather, he must challenge modern thought. In Christ's Name, he must command men to repent of their sin, and to receive in saving faith Him who died on the cross and rose again. He must command men to trust in Christ, for the reason that God Himself commands it. He must be able to back his preaching with a "thus saith the Lord." Unless he can present the claims of the Bible as absolutely trustworthy, he cannot preach the Gospel with any effectiveness whatever. Those who think that they can continue to preach the Gospel and yet reject its infallibility will soon find that what they are preaching is not the Gospel, but rather a message which is congenial to modern unbelief.

The Bible is indeed indispensable, for without it we could not know the will of God. One of the Reformed catechisms asks the pertinent question, "Whence do you know your misery?" The answer which it gives is very simple, but also very penetrating. It merely says, "Out of the law of God."[1] According to this catechism one would not know how great his misery was, were it not for the law of God. The Bible, of course, teaches the same thing: "for by the law *is* the knowledge of sin" (Romans 3: 20). This law to which the Bible refers is something that was once for all written down. It is there in the Bible, accessible at all times to those who desire to consult it.

This law which is found in the Bible is not a record of some "revelation"; it is not a pointer to the "Word" of God. It is a revelation of God, and, inasmuch as it is a revelation of God, it convicts men of sin. It is a law that is abiding and unchangeable, for it was given to man by God Himself. It is the reading of the words in which this law of God is couched that convinces men of their sin and misery. Were it not for this law written down, man would not and could not realize the true nature of his condition. In the allegory, Bunyan has illustrated the matter well. Christian lived in the City of Destruction until he began to read the words of a certain Book, and then, as a result of

1. The Heidelberg Catechism, Question No. 3.

his reading, he cried, "What shall I do?" All seemed well until Christian began to read a Book. The reading of that Book brought about a realization upon his part that he was a sinner.

Despite all that is said today to the contrary, were it not for the Bible we would not know what Christianity is. It is true that garbled traditions might have been handed down, but we could then never be sure whether we were believing the truth. The matter has been admirably stated in the first paragraph of the Westminster Confession, a paragraph which is worthy of most careful thought and consideration:

> Although the light of nature, and the works of creation and providence do so far manifest the goodness, wisdom, and power of God, as to leave men unexcusable; yet are they not sufficient to give that knowledge of God, and of His will, which is necessary unto salvation. Therefore it pleased the Lord, at sundry times, and in divers manners, to reveal Himself, and to declare that His will unto His Church; and afterwards, for the better preserving and propagating of the truth, and for the more sure establishment and comfort of the Church against the corruption of the flesh, and the malice of Satan and of the world, to commit the same wholly unto writing; which maketh the Holy Scripture to be most necessary; those former ways of God's revealing His will unto His people being now ceased.

The Holy Scripture is indeed "most necessary" and only with the Holy Scripture has the truth been better preserved and propagated. How has it been with those of us who have come to confess Christ as our Saviour? We learned the true nature of our sin from reading the Bible. The words of Scripture brought home to us the dreadful fact that we had sinned against the law of a holy God. Furthermore, those very words of the Bible told about that God. It was the Bible which told us that we were transgressors of God's law, and which brought before us the fact that, because of our sin, we could await only eternal punishment.

It was also the words of the Bible which told of the love of God in Jesus Christ. How precious to the believing heart are those promises of salvation! From childhood many a believer has known words of life such as, "For God so loved the world, that he gave his only begotten Son, that whosoever believeth in him should not perish, but have everlasting life" (John 3:16). Trusting these words, believing them to be true, he has placed his confidence in Jesus Christ as his Redeemer. One who through the Holy Spirit has placed his trust in Christ cannot take seriously the attempts which are today being made to discover the Word of God apart from the words of the Bible. In the words of Scripture is to be found the only message of hope and life.

The majority of professing Christendom does not take seriously the Word of God. He, however, who has fled to Christ for refuge from the accusing finger of God's law must take that Word seriously. It may be a very unpopular thing today to base one's life upon such an authority as the Bible. But if it is unpopular, it surely is a very blessed thing. To know that the words of Scripture are not merely the words of men, but that in them a Divine authority resides, is indeed strengthening to one's faith. On every hand are change and decay. The wisdom of man fails, his science and philosophy almost daily become out of date, and the whirling stream of time rushes on, bathing the shores of his life with the results of the latest discoveries, the newest knowledge. Where are we to stand? To what may we cleave? As a lamp unto our feet and a light unto our path stands this Book. And we Christians, knowing full well the scorn of the world and of the modern church, can only declare — if we, too, are not to be caught in the swirling eddies of today's human thought —: "Thy word have I hid in mine heart, that I might not sin against thee" (Psalm 119:11).

A return to the Bible is the greatest need of the day. Unless the Church turns to this authoritative Word of the sovereign God as — let us say it boldly — an external authority; unless the Church is willing to hear the Word of God in the one place where that Word may be heard, she will soon cease to be the Church of the living God. When, however, in humble submission to the gracious, loving Word of her glorious King, she bows to His will, she may courageously challenge all opponents. Far and wide, with majestic boldness, she may proclaim the truth: I am not ashamed of the Gospel, for it was given me of Him who is the same, yesterday, today, and forever. He tells me that this Book is His, and this Book tells me about Him. Come, then, ye wise of this world, ye doubters, ye disputers of the age. Come with your whisperings of doubt, your mockeries of uncertainty. I take my stand upon the solid, unchanging rock of His eternal truth, and in the everlasting Name of Him who brought into being the fair fields of earth and the blue heaven above, I command you,

> Hear Him, ye deaf, His praise, ye dumb,
> Your loosened tongues employ.
> Ye blind, behold your Saviour come
> And leap, ye lame, for joy.

The Christian must live in the midst of a world which is hostile to supernatural redemptive Christianity and to the theism upon which Christianity is founded. He must be a prophet, a witness to the truth. The great majority of those whom he meets are unconcerned with his message. They are held fast in the grip of indifference, and they live from day to day with little or no reflection upon the great issues of life. Believing that they are rich and increased with goods, they are in fact poor and miserable and dying. There are those, however, who realize that they are dissatisfied. The world and its philosophy have lost their glamor. The religion of humanitarian works does not satisfy the deep needs of the heart. Outwardly all may go well, but inwardly, because of sin, there is a vast question mark. Is man, after all, the measure of all things? What, if — bold thought that it is — there is a God who will by no means clear the guilty? What, if some day man must stand before Him in judgment? Oh! that man might hear the truth from an omniscient authority! Weary of trying to solve life's problems, some would ask, "Is there any word from the Lord?"

To all such, Christianity comes with its message of life and hope. To proclaim that message is the most beautiful task upon earth today. To be a witness to truth — an ambassador for the King — is the Christian's position in this life. "How beautiful upon the mountains are the feet of him that bringeth good tidings, that publisheth peace; that bringeth good tidings of good, that publisheth salvation; that saith unto Zion, Thy God reigneth!" (Isaiah, 52:7).

Thy God reigneth, and He has given to us good tidings! Such is the message which we have been seeking to present in this book. Thy God reigneth. He is upon the throne; and He alone is King. He has spoken, and His Word is truth. Behind lies the long night of our sin, the dark realm in which we created gods in our own image and constructed philosophies according to our likeness. Ahead is Emmanuel's land. The way is straight and the day clear, for "the entrance of thy words giveth light."

Appendix

Appendix

THE WESTMINSTER CONFESSION OF FAITH

CHAPTER I

OF THE HOLY SCRIPTURE

I. Although the light of nature, and the works of creation and providence do so far manifest the goodness, wisdom, and power of God, as to leave men unexcusable;[1] yet are they not sufficient to give that knowledge of God, and His will, which is necessary unto salvation.[2] Therefore it pleased the Lord, at sundry times, and in divers manners, to reveal Himself, and to declare that His will unto His Church;[3] and afterwards, for the better preserving and propagating of the truth, and for the more sure establishment and comfort of the Church against the corruption of the flesh, and the malice of Satan and of the world, to commit the same wholly unto writing:[4] which maketh the Holy Scripture to be most necessary;[5] those former ways of God's revealing His will unto His people being now ceased.[6]

II. Under the name of Holy Scripture, or the Word of God written, are now contained all the books of the Old and New Testament, which are these:

OF THE OLD TESTAMENT

Genesis	Judges	I. Chronicles
Exodus	Ruth	II. Chronicles
Leviticus	I. Samuel	Ezra
Numbers	II. Samuel	Nehemiah
Deuteronomy	I. Kings	Esther
Joshua	II. Kings	Job

1. Rom. 2:14, 15; Rom. 1:17, 20; Ps. 19:1-4; see Rom. 1:32; 2:1.
2. John 17:3; I Cor. 1:21; I Cor. 2:13, 14.
3. Heb. 1:1, 2.
4. Luke 1:3, 4; Rom. 15:4; Matt. 4:4, 7, 10; Isa. 8:20.
5. II Tim. 3:15; II Pet. 2:19.
6. John 20:31; I Cor. 14:37; I John 5:13; I Cor. 10:11; Heb. 1:1, 2; 2:2-4.

Psalms	Ezekiel	Micah
Proverbs	Daniel	Nahum
Ecclesiastes	Hosea	Habakkuk
The Song of Songs	Joel	Zephaniah
Isaiah	Amos	Haggai
Jeremiah	Obadiah	Zechariah
Lamentations	Jonah	Malachi

OF THE NEW TESTMENT:

The Gospels	Galatians	The Epistle of
according to	Ephesians	James
Matthew	Philippians	The first and second
Mark	Colossians	Epistles of
Luke	Thessalonians I.	Peter
John	Thessalonians II.	The first, second,
The Acts of	To Timothy I.	and third Epistles
the Apostles	To Timothy II.	of John
Paul's Epistles	To Titus	The Epistle of
to the Romans	To Philemon	Jude
Corinthians I.	The Epistle to	The Revelation
Corinthians II.	the Hebrews	of John.

All which are given by inspiration of God to be the rule of faith and life.[7]

III. The books commonly called Apocrypha, not being of divine inspiration, are no part of the canon of the Scripture, and therefore are of no authority in the Church of God, nor to be any otherwise approved, or made use of, than other human writings.[8]

IV. The authority of the Holy Scripture, for which it ought to be believed, and obeyed, dependeth not upon the testimony of any man, or Church; but wholly upon God (who is truth itself) the author thereof: and therefore it is to be received, because it is the Word of God.[9]

V. We may be moved and induced by the testimony of the Church to an high and reverent esteem of the Holy Scripture.[10] And the heavenliness of the matter, the efficacy of the doctrine, the majesty of the style, the consent of all the parts, the scope of

---

7. Luke 16:29, 31; Luke 24:27, 44; II Tim. 3:15, 16; John 5:46, 47.
8. Rev. 22:18, 19; Rom. 3:2; II Pet. 1:21.
9. II Pet. 1:19, 20; II Tim. 3:16; I John 5:9; I Thess. 2:13; Rev. 1:1, 2.
10. I Tim. 3:15.

the whole (which is, to give all glory to God), the full discovery it makes of the only way of man's salvation, the many other incomparable excellencies, and the entire perfection thereof, are arguments whereby it doth abundantly evidence itself to be the Word of God: yet notwithstanding, our full persuasion and assurance of the infallible truth and divine authority thereof, is from the inward work of the Holy Spirit bearing witness by and with the Word in our hearts.[11]

VI. The whole counsel of God concerning all things necessary for His own glory, man's salvation, faith and life, is either expressly set down in Scripture, or by good and necessary consequence may be deduced from Scripture: unto which nothing at any time is to be added, whether by new revelations of the Spirit, or traditions of men.[12] Nevertheless, we acknowledge the inward illumination of the Spirit of God to be necessary for the saving understanding of such things as are revealed in the Word[13] and that there are some circumstances concerning the worship of God, and government of the Church, common to human actions and societies, which are to be ordered by the light of nature, and Christian prudence, according to the general rules of the Word, which are always to be observed.[14]

VII. All things in Scripture are not alike plain in themselves, nor alike clear unto all:[15] yet those things which are necessary to be known, believed, and observed for salvation, are so clearly propounded, and opened in some place of Scripture or other, that not only the learned, but the unlearned, in a due use of the ordinary means, may attain unto a sufficient understanding of them.[16]

VIII. The Old Testament in Hebrew (which was the native language of the people of God of old), and the New Testament in Greek (which, at the time of the writing of it, was most generally known to the nations), being immediately inspired by God, and, by His singular care and providence, kept pure in

11. I Cor. 2:9, 10; Heb. 4:12; John 10:35; Isa. 55:11; see Rom. 11:36; Ps. 19:7-11; see II Tim. 3:15. I Cor. 2:4, 5; I Thess. 1:5; I John 2:20, 27; see Isa. 59:21.
12. II Tim. 3:16-17; Gal. 1:8, 9; II Thess. 2:2.
13. John 6:45; I Cor. 2:12, 14, 15; Eph. 1:18; see II Cor. 4:6.
14. I Cor. 11:13, 14; I Cor. 14:26, 40.
15. II Pet. 3:16.
16. Ps. 119:105, 130; Deut. 29:29; Deut. 30:10-14; Acts 17:11.

all ages, are therefore authentical;[17] so as, in all controversies of religion, the Church is finally to appeal unto them.[18] But, because these original tongues are not known to all the people of God, who have right unto, and interest in the Scriptures, and are commanded, in the fear of God, to read and search them,[19] therefore they are to be translated into the vulgar language of every nation unto which they come, [20] that, the Word of God dwelling plentifully in all, they may worship Him in an acceptable manner,[21] and, through patience and comfort of the Scriptures, may have hope.[22]

XI. The infallible rule of interpretation of Scripture is the Scripture itself: and therefore, when there is a question about the true and full sense of any Scripture (which is not manifold, but one), it must be searched and known by other places that speak more clearly.[23]

X. The supreme Judge by which all controversies of religion are to be determined, and all decrees of councils, opinions of ancient writers, doctrines of men, and private spirits, are to be examined, and in whose sentence, we are to rest, can be no other but the Holy Spirit speaking in the Scripture.[24]

17. Matt. 5:18; Ps. 119:89.
18. Isa. 8:20; Matt. 15:3, 6; Acts 15:15; see Luke 16:31.
19. John 5:39; Acts 17:11; Rev. 1:3; see II Tim. 3:14, 15.
20. Matt. 28:19, 20; I Cor. 14:6; Mark 15:34.
21. Col. 3:16; see Exod. 20:4-6; Matt. 15:7-9.
22. Rom. 15:4.
23. Acts 15:15; John 5:46; see II Pet. 1:20, 21.
24. Matt. 22:29, 31; Acts 28:25; see I John 4:1-6.

Indexes

INDEX OF NAMES AND SUBJECTS

Albright, Wm. F., 250, 251
American Protestant Church, 39
Apostles' Creed, 251
Athanasius, 14
Auburn Affirmation, 50-53
Autographa,
  alone inspired, 55, 56
  importance of, 85-89

Baba Bathra, 14, 173
Bannerman, 137
Barth, K., 232
Battle between supernaturalism and
  naturalism, 14, 32, 79, 170
Bertheau, 126
Best, Nolan R., 134
Bible: importance of, 30-31
  alleged errors in, 165-185
  a completed revelation, 220ff.
  evidence of divinity, 33
  English Revised Version, 19
  Holy History, 253-263
  Human side of, 26, 65ff.
  King James Version, 18, 19, 57,
    129, 156
  infallibility of, 50
  the Word of God, 231ff.
Brahams, J., 22
Briggs, Charles A., 100, 102
Bruce, A. B., 127-129
Brunner, E., 231

Calvin, J., 65-67, 93, 107, 232, 233
Celsus, 98
Christianity, historical basis of, 101
Christ's view of Scripture, 47-49

Darwin, Charles, 16
Deity of Christ, 1, 14
Demand for a new doctrine of in-
  spiration, 15, 16
Dewar, 168
Dictation, 65ff.
Difficulties in Christianity, 59, 60
Doctrine of inspiration must be
  taught in Bible, 17, 18, 28, 30
Dostoevski, 217
Egypt, length of bondage in, 179ff.

Ellison, H. L., 225
Evans, L. J., 129, 132, 176, 180
Evolution, 29

Fallibility and human nature, 72-78
Fosdick, H. E., 211
Fundamental Christianity, 53

Gaussen, 137
General Assembly of Presbyterian
  Church, U.S.A., 1923, 50

Hammurabi, Code of, 201
Harnack, Adolf, 197
Hartmann, Anton F., 60
Hegel, 16, 197
Heidelberg Catechism, 270
Henry, Matthew, 133
Hexapla, 98
Higher criticism, 29
Hodge, A. A., 96, 144, 145
Hodge, Charles, 58, 96, 137, 229
Holy History, 253-263
Homer, 90
Horites, 201
Human writers not always infall-
  ible, 80
Human writers not sinless, 68
Hurrians, 201, 202

Iliad, 90
Inerrancy, 143-161
Infallibility, 50
  extent of, 100-104
Inspiration,
  Biblical evidence for, 45ff.
  definition of, 27
  illogical, 78
  objections to Biblical doctrine,
    72-73
  organs of, 44, 45
  plenary, 48ff.
  purpose of, 41, 42, 54
  providence and inspiration, 69, 70
  static?, 14, 15
Inward testimony of Holy Spirit,
  34, 35

Issue before the Church 13ff., 28, 31, 32

Jeremiah, 42
Justin Martyr, 98

Kant, Immanuel, 212, 245, 246, 262
Kierkegaard, 217
Koran, doctrine of inspiration, 114, 115, 119

Lee, 137
Literal interpretation, 137-139
Luther, Martin, 93-95, 99, 107, 233

Machen, J. Gresham, 116, 117, 137, 211
Mackay, John, 249; 250
Mari, 204
Mechanical dictation, 26, 65, 66
Melachanton, Philip, 229
Mystery in the Christian faith, 71

Near-Eastern letters, 43
Neil, William, 104, 216
Neo-orthodoxy, 29
Nicene Creed, 29, 56
Nuzi, 201, 202, 205

Odyssey, 90,
Origen, 98
Orr, James, 143

Parallel passages, 119-126
Parallel passages in the Gospels, 127-137
Patton, Francis L., 53-55
Piper, Otto A., 221, 231, 239, 258
Proof texts, 219, 220
Protestant misuse of Bible, alleged, 104-109
Protestant scholastics, 94-96

Providence and inspiration, 69, 70
Ras Shamra, 201
Reformation, 16
Reformation monument, 109
Relation between Genesis 1 and 2, 122
Reu, M., 99, 233
Revelation, 41, 42
Richardson, Alan, 214, 221, 222, 224, 240
Ritschl, A., 197

Schreiner, H., 231
Shelton, 168
Smith, H. P., 114, 115, 119
Smith, Wm. R., 198, 220
Stephen's speech, 175-183

Tell el-Amarna, 204
Tell el-Hariri, 204
Textual criticism, 57, 58
Thenius, 126
Theodidaktos, 20
Theopneustos, 20, 21
Toy, C. H., 175
Trinity, 59, 71, 124
Turretin, F., 67, 95, 137, 152, 229

Van Til, C., 171, 232
Virgin Birth, 92

Warfield, B. B., 19, 96, 115, 137
Wellhausen, J., 197-198, 199, 200, 204, 205, 206, 207
Westminster Confession, 50, 56, 198, 208, 221, 226, 254, 255, 257, 271
Wright, G. E., 223, 224
Writing, known in Moses' day, 60, 61

Yorgan Tepe, 201

INDEX OF SCRIPTURE

GENESIS
Genesis 1   167-169, 171, 101-103
1:31   229
2:4a   122
6:9   122
11:26   176, 178
11:32   176-178
12:4   176, 178
14:6   201
15:3   203
15:4   203
15:13   180
17:1b, 2   229
17:17   178
22:18   46
28:3-20   183
33:8   204
33:19   183

EXODUS
3:6a   225
3:7, 8a   225
3:14   225
4:15   42
7:1   42
12:40   180, 181
12:40ff.   182
19:1   182
20:1   224
34:6   229

NUMBERS
12:7, 8a   29

DEUTERONOMY
6:4   224
18:18   41

I SAMUEL
21:1-6   183
22:17   184
22:20   184

II SAMUEL
7:28   268
11:15   81

I KINGS
14:15   183
15:14   59, 123

II KINGS
19:35   228

II CHRONICLES
14:5   59, 123, 125, 126
15:17   123, 125, 126
17:6   126

JOB
9:32, 33   193

PSALMS
12:6   40
19:1   247
23:1   230
24:1   230
32:1   229
82:6   26ff.
90:2   171
119   116
119:11   272
119:105   263
119:142   267
119:160   268

ISAIAH
2:1-4   119
5:3   43
6:7b   228
6:9, 10   157-161
7:14   145, 146
40:3   151
45:21   156
52:7   273
53:5   93

JEREMIAH
1:9   42
1:17   42
12:15   155
18   173, 174
18:11   174
23:5   174
32:6-8   174

285

33:9	183
35:15	174

DANIEL

4:35b	74

AMOS

9	156

MICAH

4:1-3	119

ZECHARIAH

1:14	174
3:8	174
11:13	172

MALACHI

3:1	150

MATTHEW

1:21	145-149
1:22	68
4:4	48, 219
5:3	134
5:17, 18	48
8:28	133
10:1ff.	135
11:1ff.	135
13:14, 15	158, 159
16:14	173
19:6	166
19:16	130
19:17	128ff.
20:29ff.	132
22:32	68
22:43	47, 67
24:6	108
26:54	52
26:56	52
27:9	172-175

MARK

1:1-3	150-153
2:23-25	135
2:26	183
3:14:19	135
4:11, 12	159
10:17	130
10:46	132
12:26	68
12:36	67
14:27	51
14:49	52

LUKE

Luke 1	117
3:1, 2	256
6:1-12	135
6:13-16	135
6:20	134
8:10	159
18:18	130
18:35	133
20:42	67
24:44	173

JOHN

3:16	271
4:24	230
5:39	48
5:45, 46	48
5:46	230
8:50	199
10:31	113
10:35	26-27
11:25, 26	75
11:25	230
12:31	53
12:40	159-161
14:6	268
14:26	44
17:17	267

THE ACTS

4	46
6:10	175
7:2	179
7:4	179
7:16	183
7:54	176
15:14-18	153-157
28:25	46
28:25, 26a	68
28:26, 27	159

ROMANS

1:2	45
3:2	45
3:20	270
9:17	46
15:4	115

I CORINTHIANS

2:13	66
15:14	259

II CORINTHIANS

5:21	93

GALATIANS
3:8   46
3:17   180

EPHESIANS
6:12   13

I THESSALONIANS
1:13   44
2:13b   55

II TIMOTHY
3:16   18-23, 40, 88

HEBREWS
4:12   223
11:6b   207

II PETER
1:21   23-26, 70